The Unbalanced Economy

The Unbalanced Economy

A Policy Appraisal

Ciaran Driver
Professor of Economics, Department of Finance and Management, SOAS, University of London, UK

and

Paul Temple
Reader in Economics, University of Surrey, UK

First published in 2012
Published in paperback 2014 by
PALGRAVE MACMILLAN

Palgrave Macmillan in the UK is an imprint of Macmillan Publishers Limited, registered in England, company number 785998, of Houndmills, Basingstoke, Hampshire RG21 6XS.

Palgrave Macmillan in the US is a division of St Martin's Press LLC, 175 Fifth Avenue, New York, NY 10010.

Palgrave Macmillan is the global academic imprint of the above companies and has companies and representatives throughout the world.

Palgrave® and Macmillan® are registered trademarks in the United States, the United Kingdom, Europe and other countries

ISBN 978–0–230–28031–1   hardback
ISBN 978–1–137–46828–4   paperback

This book is printed on paper suitable for recycling and made from fully managed and sustained forest sources. Logging, pulping and manufacturing processes are expected to conform to the environmental regulations of the country of origin.

A catalogue record for this book is available from the British Library.

A catalog record for this book is available from the Library of Congress.

Typeset by MPS Limited, Chennai, India.

Transferred to Digital Printing in 2014

Contents

List of Tables and Figures

Tables

Figures

Preface

This book provides a context for debating the course of the British economy and for discussing which fresh policy measures are needed to propel growth. It will appeal to those with an interest in understanding the trajectory of the economy from the inception of market-led policies in 1979 to the current state of financial distress and seeming policy impasse. It is a book written by economists but not, we hope, just for economists: the big economic policy choices that face us are essentially political. Given the extent of disagreement about how the economy actually works in practice, there can only be risky choices that are made with an eye to which class or group will bear the brunt if things go wrong. As Gamble (2009) recently noted, we are entering the third generalized crisis of capitalism of the last hundred years, 'they arise politically, they are constructed politically and they are resolved politically' (p.10).[1]

In our view, the biggest policy wager in recent decades has been that a more market-friendly regime – aimed in particular at restoring profitability by bearing down on organized labour – would by itself raise productivity growth and general prosperity. Although much was wrong with pre-1980s Britain, we show in this book that such optimism in markets was misplaced. More worryingly, the policy direction, once chosen, became difficult to reverse, as the market based agenda became the default for policy initiatives. Beginning with the first Labour administration of 1997 there was some acceptance that more proactive policies were needed to coordinate economic activity, but for the most part these lacked substance. Instead, for a variety of reasons, policymakers chose the 'double-up' option and pursued a course of continuous liberalization under the twin beliefs that global capital markets were necessarily benign and that states possessed very little leverage over them in any case.

The book argues that the market based approach was unbalanced leading to the unbalanced economy to which our title refers. We want to restore coherence to economic policy so that the great problems of jobs, incomes and wealth distribution between citizens are addressed.

---

[1] Gamble, A. (2009) *The Spectre at the Feast: Capitalist crisis and the politics of recession*, Palgrave Macmillan.

It has become commonplace to call for a 'rebalancing' that means something else – including a switch from public to private provision and from consumption to savings. Neither of these ideas of rebalancing feature strongly in our account because they conflate means (budget cuts and more savings) with ends (sound finance and strong investment). We do however address other imbalances that have a direct bearing on jobs, such as the sectoral composition of output – which, as we argue in Chapter 8, requires new institutions for industrial strategy and coordination – and the neglect of capital investment and R&D which has impeded growth. Our emphasis on these twin concerns of manufacturing and investment does not stem from any mercantilist notion, but is based on the argument in Chapter 4 that a sector's policy importance should be inferred from the extent of the frictions and failures of actual markets. We have all too little to say about the important issue of regional disparities which is too large a subject to be easily addressed in a general text such as this. However some of these inequalities would be ameliorated were the allocation of resources to shift back toward investment and manufacturing.

This book is not in any sense against markets, an institution that has often brought both progress and liberty. But any serious economist is as aware of the deficiencies of markets as much as their benefits. Our objection is rather to what might be called the *market as metaphor* where market affirmation is used to convey a political intention that the interests of capital will be privileged over those of labour. It was in this spirit that much of both labour market reform and the liberalization of capital markets were conceived, sometimes in the belief that greater profitability would necessarily lead to more innovation and investment. The process of liberalization was inherently dangerous because the market as metaphor naturally led to a generally held belief in efficient markets, including the ideas that asset bubbles could not and should not be constrained, that credit expansion was warranted by the demand for it and that ownership of companies did not greatly matter to how they were run. Much of the market rhetoric failed to notice that there were deep implications for economic institutions; and in particular for that of the modern industrial enterprise.

In the months after the financial crisis some of the big hitters of the old era were for a while contrite. The Chairman of the US Federal Reserve, for whom New Labour arranged a knighthood, expressed doubts about his earlier free market beliefs while the previous enthusiast for shareholder value, General Electric's Jack Welch now called it the 'dumbest idea'. Others recanted from excess liberalization saying that too much faith was put in financial markets and that income inequality had got out of hand. It seems that some things happened that we didn't much like in the days before the financial crash. But the damage inflicted by that event was as much associated with the real economy as with banks and finance. The same ideas of markets as both omniscient and efficient have allowed a hollowing out of the real economy and a lack of coherence in the domestic industrial structure. 'Industrial policy in Britain since 1979 has been minimal at best', wrote Kitson and Michie in 1997.[2] It is no less true today. The market as metaphor came to paralyze decision-making to the point where, in the UK at least, policy advisers could only set out the issues, while lacking the policy levers to resolve them. Paradoxically perhaps, it is now often top industrialists and employers' organizations that are backing a strategic interventionist policy and supply chain planning to reinvigorate corporate Britain.

The great financial crash of 2007 was international in scope but its effects are in large measure due to the domestic policy stance taken in the decades leading up to the crash. Among the policies that contributed were of course an over-reliance on a lightly regulated banking and shadow banking sector that drove the asset bubbles; the corresponding excessive private debt and a neglect of capital investment and of sectors where sunk costs meant that market solutions were inadequate. There was also a lack of attention to the interplay between income disparities and sustainable growth; a failure to build a sense of fairness with an equitable tax system; and a reluctance to implement far-reaching reform of company law that would align the interest of companies with those of its stakeholders and permit better decision-making. The book traces the policy debates by relating them to the economic theories that shaped or supported the market-oriented agenda in the UK. We have tried to present these economic ideas as simply and transparently as possible. Where we have added technical detail we hope to have done so in a way that complements the textual discussion in a manner that allows it to be skimmed by the general reader who is more interested in the flow of the argument. In particular parts of Chapter 2 outline the 'NAIRU model' that we see as underpinning the heavy emphasis on labour market reform so evident in the UK. It discusses the historical emergence of these ideas and inevitably has to engage with the relevant economic theory. Chapter 3, while also addressing economic concepts

---

[2] Kitson, M. and J. Michie 'Does Manufacturing Matter?', *International Journal of the Economics of Business*, (1997) 4(1), 71–95.

such as the balance of payments, is on the whole less technical. A central argument of the book is that capital investment is not well supported by market signals and we make that point at length in Chapter 4, with a discussion of the economics of investment and decision-making.

While the book contains some formal content, the writing style is intended to be direct and may at times seem to verge on the polemical. However much of what we say in these pages has been contained in previous, more technical accounts, which are referenced throughout for the interested reader. Our practice has been to omit many of the caveats and doubts that any academic feels in the hope that readers themselves will weigh the merits of the arguments. While the approach is a critical one, it reflects our belief that orthodoxy has not served the country well in recent decades.

We are grateful to those who provided forums for us to test out these ideas in debate during their long inception period, including presentations at The French Economic Association 2009, The Wharton School Conference on Corporate Governance 2010, The Centre for Corporate Governance, University of Birmingham 2010, The European Network on the Economics of the Firm 2011 and presentations at the Royal Economic Society, the Australian National University and the University of London. Paul would like to acknowledge members of the innovation policy community for providing inspiration including in particular Peter Swann and Ray Lambert. Thanks also to our colleagues at SOAS and the School of Economics at Surrey, who inadvertently or otherwise stimulated our thoughts. The forbearance of our families certainly needs acknowledgement. Especial thanks are due to Monika Temple who read and commented on the entire manuscript. The mistakes are of course all our own.

Our target audience is wide. We hope that the book will be used in advanced undergraduate and postgraduate courses in economics, politics and the social sciences generally. We hope also that it will appeal to decision-makers and the informed public who desire an overview of events and theories of the past few decades. Those who have lived through them should find much to recognize while those who have not will, we trust, be able to see a pattern in the drift of events that we chart. The analysis, of course, is just the beginning; the point, as ever, is to bring about change.

Preface to the Paperback Edition

The financial crisis that began in 2007/8 forced a rethink of the UK's 'unbalanced economy', whose origins and nature are examined in this book. Investment, exports and manufacturing were the new mantra. But even before our hardback edition was in print, Britain had already experienced a false dawn recovery in 2010 in which indicators such as investment intentions rose sharply only to fall back again within a year. At the time of writing this new preface (mid-2014), total economic output is just above the pre-crisis peak but there is little sign of the promised rebalancing. This is the slowest recovery on record, surprising on the downside year by year and sluggish also by international comparisons, which Figure 1 vividly illustrates. Given what has transpired, we believe that our book illuminates not only the trends up to the crisis, but the aftermath as well.

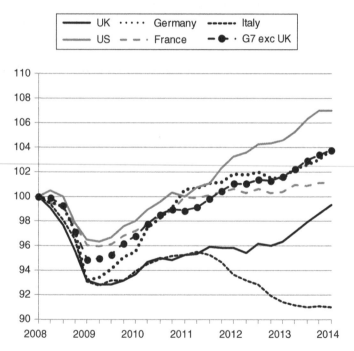

Figure 1 Volumes of GDP at market prices (2008q1=100)
Source: Derived from OECD Quarterly National Accounts (OECD Stat.Extracts accessed 28/05/14).

The incoming government of 2010 expected the bulk of the recovery to come from the 'sustainable' sources of business investment and net exports, thus rebalancing the economy in what was termed – in the first budget – the 'march of the makers'. The source of the expansion since then has nevertheless been very different, with domestic consumption contributing almost three-quarters of the long-awaited growth that set in from 2013. In typical British fashion, this growth was also propelled by public support for the housing market. Rebalancing is off the agenda for the moment, although officials must hope that it happens eventually, as it is clearly not sustainable for savings rates to fall while incomes stagnate. The present conjuncture is only possible at all because, with stagnant real wages, household income is nevertheless reflecting private sector re-employment of excess labour. Success on this front has prompted a reorientation of rhetoric away from rebalancing towards the 'fight' for 'full employment', pledged by the Chancellor in 2014. It would, however, be foolish to substitute the provision of poor-quality, low-paid, precarious and part-time jobs or self-employment for the larger project of rebalancing the economy onto a sustainable path. The former route has been facilitated by the 'flexible' labour market policies whose origins are analysed in Chapter 2 and which Andrew Haldane of the Bank of England has recently suggested could actually *undermine* economic performance: '...inequality may have a direct bearing on the fragility of the financial system...lower income inequality delivers faster and more durable growth.' (Haldane 2014, p.5). One result of a fixation with flexible labour markets is a fall-off in productivity growth. International comparisons show that GDP for each hour of work in the UK in 2012 was still 2 per cent below its level in 2008. For the G7 (excluding the UK) it was 4% higher. The result has been that the lead of the rest of the G7 over the UK in terms of GDP per hour widened considerably to 21 per cent between 2008 and 2012. Moreover, the latest domestic data show no rise on 2012 levels during the 2013 recovery. This is no surprise given that the major prerequisite of productivity growth is capital spending and that has severely disappointed expectations.

Many commentators seem to believe that capital spending will pick up automatically as confidence builds. However, as surveyed in our book to almost comic effect, this triumph of optimism over experience is nothing new. Typically, in the UK, investment spending occurs far too late in the cycle and quite possibly in assets distorted by price bubbles. It would in any event take many years of above normal investment for the capital stock to make up for the shortfall engendered by the crisis and by decades of a comparatively low rate of investment. The Office for Budget Responsibility reports that the level of real investment business spending at the end of 2013 was 20 per cent below its pre-crisis peak so that on current trends it will not be until 2016 at least that *investment* recovers to previous levels. Recalling that investment is the rate of change of the capital stock it would require investment to take a much bigger share and grow much stronger than its historical rate for many years to make up the loss in the capital stock incurred since the financial crisis. The scale of the issue has recently been emphasized by the McKinsey Global Institute (2012) which pointed to lower rates of investment *in every one* of the eight economic sectors reported compared to its 'peers' in Europe (the EU top 15) in 2011 and adding up to a huge overall deficit in capital stock per worker.

There are also question marks over the UK's export performance which has responded only weakly to the large devaluation at the start of the crisis. Bank of England rate-setter Martin Weale (2013) has suggested some theoretical reasons for a delayed response. However, as late as the first half of 2014, CBI data (Confederation of British Industry) show that firms with export order books below normal outnumber those above normal by a ratio of 3:2. While current accounts are hard to predict far into the future, and especially so in the present climate, there must be a concern that macroeconomic policy will be constrained by poor capability in the export sector for years to come (Rowthorn and Coutts 2013).

As we argue in the book, exports, innovation and the manufacturing sector are closely linked given that manufacturing accounts for the bulk of exports and research and development (R&D) activity. The recent government sponsored *Future of Manufacturing* project (Foresight 2013) has underscored how central manufacturing is for the performance of the whole economy, acting as an important hub for learning and productivity advance elsewhere. Yet, there is little evidence of any serious structural shift to the manufacturing sector and the 'march of the makers' is not so much halted as yet to begin, for reasons explored in our own contribution to the project (Driver and Temple 2013). Manufacturing remains almost 8 per cent below its pre-crisis output peak.

Why has it proved so hard to implement sensible policies to rebalance the economy when policymakers of all stripes agree it to be necessary? Of course global economic conditions have created headwinds but there seem also to be systematic constraints that relate to the framework in which policy is made. Our book points to the fact that the UK is an outlier in recent decades in its commitment to market liberalism and the idea that the market works best without much steer from government. As demonstrated in our Chapter 7, the role of liberal corporate governance is key to understanding many of the cultural and institutional tendencies that bias the UK towards a low-investment, low-productivity economy. One perennial concern over UK boardroom agendas is short-termism. Since the financial crash, we have had several contributions on this from the Bank of England, Lords Myners and Cox in separate contributions and a review of financial intermediation from John Kay (the Kay Report). More recently still, in their respective contributions to the *Future of Manufacturing*, Alan Hughes and Simon Deakin (2013) point to the distorting effect of UK corporate governance arrangements on company objectives. Hughes, for example, identifies the inefficiency of buying and selling whole companies in the name of shareholder value, arguing that the 'excessive preoccupation with takeovers rather than organic investment makes the market for corporate control a hindrance rather than a help to improving UK economic performance" (p73). Given the dominance of shareholder value, it is no surprise that UK firms remain focused on costs rather than organic growth. The top items elevated to boardroom discussion in recent years according to Ernst and Young (2014) are cost-reduction, cash-dividend payments, share buybacks and strategic divestment. Less than half of the companies surveyed saw growth as their main focus.

In short, little has happened since the publication of the hardback edition to shake our belief in the importance of analysing the unbalanced economy. The problems of the British economy are deep-seated and the solutions must emerge, not from any quick fix, but from a reconsideration of the role of the corporation and of the contribution of the financial sector in a modern economy.

References

Deakin, S. (2013) Evidence Paper 5 < https://www.gov.uk/government/collec tions/future-of-manufacturing#project-report> accessed June 05. 2014.

Driver, C. and Temple, P. (2013) Evidence Paper 8 <https://www.gov.uk/govern ment/collections/future-of-manufacturing#project-report> accessed June 05, 2014.

Foresight (2013) The Future of Manufacturing: a new era of opportunity and challenge for the UK – summary report, Department of Business Innovation and Skills <https://www.gov.uk/government/publications/future-of-manu facturing/future-of-manufacturing-a-new-era-of-opportunity-and-challenge-forthe-uk-summary-report> accessed June 09. 2014.

Haldane, A. (2014) Unfair Shares, <http://www.bankofengland.co.uk/publica
tions/Pages/speeches/2014/732.aspx> accessed June 08.2014.

Hughes, A. (2013) Evidence Paper 16 <https://www.gov.uk/government/collec
tions/future-of-manufacturing#project-report> accessed June 05. 2014.

Ernst & Young (2014) UK *capital confidence barometer*, April <http://www.
ey.com/GL/en/Services/Transactions/EY-capital-confidence-barometer-april-
2014-october-2014> accessed June 05. 2014.

McKinsey Global Institute (2012) Investing in Growth: Europe's Next Challenge,
McKinsey and Co. <http://www.mckinsey.com/insights/europe/investing in
growth> accessed June 05. 2014.

Rowthorn R and Coutts K (2013) Evidence Paper 30 at https://www.gov.uk/
government/collections/future-of-manufacturing#project-report accessed June
05, 2014.

Weale, M (2013) The Balance of Payments. http://www.bankofengland.co.uk/
publications/Documents/speeches/2013/speech635.pdf accessed June 05, 2014.

About the Book

In this book, Driver and Temple examine how the simple faith of economists and policymakers in free-markets and financialization masqueraded as an economic theory justifying the neglect of investment in capital, skills and technology. The authors write that their book is not in any sense against markets, an institution that has often brought both progress and liberty. Their objection is rather to what might be called the market as metaphor where market affirmation is used to convey a political intention that the interests of capital will be privileged over those of labour. The authors conclude that radical reforms are needed both at the level of the company, through changes in corporate governance, and at the level of industry, by giving institutional form to a system of social partnership for a fair and high performance economy.

About the Authors

Ciaran Driver is Professor of Economics in the Department of Finance and Management, SOAS, University of London, UK. His research interests are capital investment and corporate governance. Recent publications include *Research Policy,* the *Cambridge Journal of Economics, Oxford Economic Papers, JEBO, JBES, IJIO* and the *Journal of Macroeconomics.* He has held visiting posts at the Australian National University, been attached to several global business schools and has advised UK and Irish public bodies on capital investment policies.

Paul Temple is a Reader in Economics at the University of Surrey, UK, with research interests in the economics of innovation, investment, and international trade. He has edited various books including *Britain's Economic Performance* and has published widely in economics journals including the *Cambridge Journal of Economics,* the *International Journal of Industrial Organization* and the *Journal of Business and Economic Statistics.* Previous appointments have been at the Centre for Business Strategy, and the National Economic Development Office (NEDO).

1
Economic Performance in the Market Era

1.1 Introduction

The fallout from the worst economic crisis within living memory has commanded unprecedented attention from economists and others attempting to understand and contain it through a mixture of global and domestic action. In this book we approach the crisis not as a single event but as part of a process whose roots reside in longer-term tendencies that have developed in previous historical periods. To make the study manageable we investigate the issues largely from the perspective of the British economy, which we believe to be representative, indeed an exemplar, of similar liberal market economies. Britain is now one of the most market friendly economies in the world following several decades of a reform programme that began in 1979 with the election of a Conservative government, and which has continued to underpin that of subsequent governments, including that of New Labour (1997–2010). As noted in Card and Freeman (2004): 'Beginning with Margaret Thatcher and continuing under John Major and Tony Blair, these reforms sought to increase the efficacy of labor and product markets and limit government and institutional involvement in economic decision making' (p.9).

This book attempts to understand the crisis through the lens of this longer perspective. In our view, whatever the nuances of policy difference between Thatcher, Major, Blair, Brown and the coalition, the general direction of travel towards a more market-centric society has been unwavering. It is our contention that this has involved an unbalanced approach which has been destructive of economic capacity as well as social cohesion (as perhaps the two are not unrelated). On the economic front it has resulted in a neglect of capacity building (because

1

the market cannot do this very well but was given the job anyway) and the creation of a mode of workplace relations that cannot deliver commitment. Economic performance has not in any real sense improved in the changed policy regime, but a high price has been paid in terms of intensity or work and patterns of inequality. We can do better.

The shock to the economy that occurred in 2007–8 is likely to have long-lasting effects. Economic growth as projected by Her Majesty's Treasury in the budget of March 2011 shows a full 10 per cent shortfall from the budget forecast of March 2007 and that shortfall is projected to persist *indefinitely* meaning a *permanent* loss of that output, through the recession induced loss of capacity. Since the onset of the crisis, the projections for recovery have worsened, with the likelihood of only anaemic growth for some years, even if the problems concerning the Euro are resolved. The result today is that the UK faces a serious lack of demand combined with a composition of supply that is unaligned with future demand conditions. The UK is over-committed to sectors that are not going to recover completely because they are bubble sectors, a situation that poses severe challenges for policy. Even if growth resumes, helped perhaps by the low value of the pound and a resumption of growth in Britain's major markets, we cannot be certain that previous trend growth will resume. This will not be helped by the loss of capacity in sectors of high productivity growth.

Unsustainable booms are not something new to Britain and even the long boom that ended in the 1970s was characterized by a process known as 'stop-go' with blame frequently being put on 'obstreperous labour management relations'.[1] The decisive policy break towards 'flexible labour markets', initiated during the course of the 1980s, was intended to transform economic performance. Some simple statistics may help in making a judgement here. Figure 1.1 shows the progress of overall economic output (expressed as year on year percentage changes) in Britain over the whole period from 1948 through to 2009, a period that divides roughly equally into the period before 1979, and the period of the great market experiment that followed. The period of stop-go is now clearly visible for the early period, but only twice did the stop actually mean zero or negative growth – in 1958, a period which saw an early but short-lived experiment in monetarism, and 1974–5, when the advanced economies were collectively affected by a severe oil price shock, magnified in the UK's case by a previous deregulation of credit markets.

---

[1] The transferred epithet is in Card et al (2004), p.1.

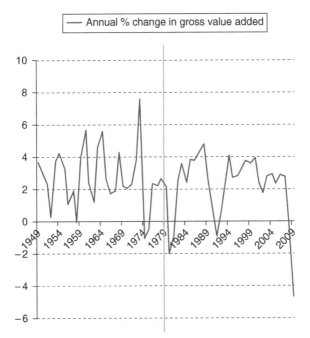

Figure 1.1   Year on Year % changes in aggregate economic output
Source: ONS 2010 Blue Book.

The 'stop' to economic expansion was however given a new meaning from 1979 onwards, when a change in the approach to economic policy heightened the risks of unsustainable growth. As can be seen from Figure 1.1, the era produced three major recessions (in the early 1980s; early 1990s and now), with the current crisis clearly quite unparalleled in post-war British experience. There is also evidence of an old-fashioned 'stop' phase corresponding to the bursting of the 'dotcom' bubble when the historically rapid rates of economic expansion toward the end of the millennium fell back sharply after 2000. Each of the recessions was of course different in various respects, not least in the mix of external and domestic factors in influencing events, but each occurred under a policy regime in which governments placed undue trust in market forces. Economic policy under Margaret Thatcher was based on the idea that controlling the money supply would be sufficient to tame inflation. The credit boom of the 1980s was the result of a widespread belief that there had been sea-change in Britain's economic fortunes which justified the surge in spending and property investment before it ended in a largely domestically induced recession.[2]

Remarkably similar things can be said of the seeds of the current recession, despite the increased relevance of global factors. Most remarkable was how an economy, once again experiencing such an obvious 'bubble' in housing prices, could also be simultaneously experiencing low inflation, deceiving many about the sustainability of growth. This was as true of 2007 as of 1989; on both occasions policy-makers apparently believed that control over consumer prices (using measures largely detached from the spiralling cost of house prices) was sufficient – bubbles just do not exist in low inflation market oriented economies. As one economic historian noted of the earlier boom 'Ministers trusted in the self-directing power of unrestricted free enterprise' (Dow 1999, p.359).

At a deeper level a central contention of this book is that over-zealous adherence to market solutions in Britain decisively changed what was deemed possible from public policy, encouraging a repetitive pattern of unsustainable upturns. It is not just that policymakers are content to let booms run on because of the belief that it is the job of the market to stop them. More particularly growth stops because the market does not work well enough to commit sufficient and early resources to meeting the anticipated demand, and so the economy runs short of capacity, generating domestic inflation or international imbalances. Many commentators and forecasting teams have even worried that, in this current uncertain and weak recovery, capacity shortages may already be fuelling inflation.[3] Of course some of the problem may in part be because the unbalanced nature of growth alerted business to its unsustainability so that investment was held back on that account. But it is also due to a learnt pattern of business caution in committing to supply. This has been a perennial problem in the UK. Business (at least outside of some sectors of finance) realizes that the downside risks represent their own potential loss, while the upside is in part a public potential gain. Our

---

[2] It is easy to imagine that the rapid rise in productivity growth in this period was seen, not as a one-off levels effect but rather as a permanent improvement in trend, thus leading to the surge in consumption, financed largely by second mortgages on appreciating homes. Indeed equity withdrawal from housing during the 1980s was enough to finance the entire growth in GDP, just as it did later under the Blair-Brown period of 1997–2009 (Froud et al 2011).

[3] Generally however commentators focus on labour supply and ignore the importance of capital constraints.

contention in this book is that while the proximate cause of current economic difficulties is the banking crisis and related international events, the vulnerability of the UK to such dangers has its roots in decades of misconceived economic strategy and policies. Indeed at the outset of the Thatcher administration the point was noted by the economist Lord Balogh:

> The fear of excess capacity, the dread of investing in new plant when the old would do, is notable. This means that the limits of expansion are reached in this country before they press on our foreign competitors. Thus, our improvement is interrupted at an increasingly early stage of the upswing.
>
> (Balogh 1979, p.199)

In the remainder of this chapter we look at three crucial questions of economic policy in recent decades. First, how and why do unsustainable booms emerge and to what extent is the current cycle similar or different to the previous one? Second, have the reforms over the whole period resulted in an enhanced ability of the economy to deliver productivity growth? Third, what can be said about the distribution of any productivity gains?

1.2 Repetitive patterns? The tale of two cycles

As we have seen, the modern market era has seen three major recessions and so far just two recoveries (see Figure 1.1). While we find several important similarities between the two completed cycles – which we call the Thatcher cycle (1979–90) and the long cycle (1990–2007) – there are also some important differences both in respect of the way that demand was allowed to develop and the extent to which capacity to meet that demand was adequate.

The sources of demand

How far has unsustainable domestic demand fuelled booms and led to subsequent problems of readjustment in the recession? First, it is important to consider the distinction between the growth of domestic demand and what the economy actually delivers in terms of real output. Domestic demand comprises demand from the private sector – household consumption and gross capital formation, to which the government and other public sector bodies contribute a small and declining share, and government consumption. The latter is comprised of expenditures which eventually result in acts of *individual* consumption – for example expenditures on education and health – and a smaller total which reflects government expenditures on items of *collective* consumption – for example defence. The aggregate balance between domestic demand and domestic production is indicated in Figure 1.2. It can be seen that in the earlier 1979–90 cycle, domestic demand ran ahead of domestic output (measured here in market prices) only in the final few years of what became known as the 'Thatcher-Lawson' boom, comparatively late in the cycle. In the later cycle domestic demand *persistently* grew at a more rapid rate than domestic output especially after the late 1990s when a rise in the real exchange rate made life extremely difficult for exporters. When demand rises faster than output it implies that imports of goods and services are rising more rapidly than exports, resulting in the pattern shown

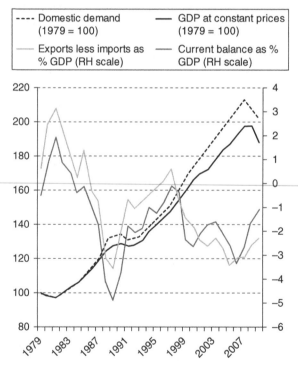

Figure 1.2 Domestic Demand and Output in UK 1979–2009
Sources: ONS 2010 Blue Book and 2010 Pink Book.

in Figure 1.2 which also records measures for demand, output and the current account.[4]

But does such a persistent and growing current deficit matter? A major cause of concern in the early decades after World War II was certainly the balance between exports and imports of goods and services – which more or less threatened foreign exchange reserves directly. Nowadays, the capital controls of that period have disappeared and a huge banking and financial system in Britain (loosely 'the City') provides services which enable the economy to finance such deficits for long periods. But an important question remains – the deficit needs to be financed – how, and with what implications? In fact it may be financed in many ways. One possibility is through the creation or acquisition of corporate assets (mainly take-overs) which exceed similar investments overseas. These types of transaction form the major component of what is known as Foreign Direct investment (FDI) – a subject of great importance to which we will return in later chapters. However in the period being considered, Britain has generally run a *deficit* in this subset of international transactions, as can be seen from Figure 1.3. It can also be seen that the swings in FDI became much more significant in the later business cycle. The net impact in both cycles has therefore been to *exacerbate* the potential impact of the current account deficit as shown in Figure 1.4 and hence the imbalance between exports and imports cannot be explained by the overall desirability of domestically owned corporate assets.

The growing payments deficit represents the UK's contribution to the global imbalances which have been increasing since the East-Asian financial crisis of the late 1990s. In fact Britain's current account deficit (in relation to GDP) was by no means the largest in international comparison, being rather smaller by the time of the global recession than that of Spain, and about one half of that of the US.

A persistent deficit of the sort experienced in Britain raise potential difficulties in regard to its financing. In addition to the danger that the necessary borrowing may be short term and thus may be withdrawn at

---

[4] The current account differs from the goods and services balance of payments by including transfers and other income creating transactions such as net interest and dividend flows and the profit remittances of British owned assets overseas (like exports, a credit) and those such as the profits outflow of foreign owned multinationals (a debit). Because the current account shows a trend improvement over the goods and services balance it may be inferred that net income transfers have been increasing as the UK has become more reliant on overseas rental income.

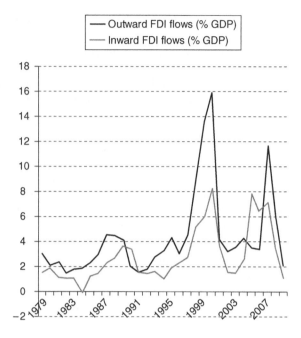

Figure 1.3   Inward and Outward flows of Foreign Direct Investment as % of GDP
Source: ONS Pink Book 2010.

short notice, the monetary inflows that result from such deficits provide a means by which domestic banks expand credit and provide the fuel for asset price rises (most obviously in housing) and make for lower real interest rates. Indeed recent research by Barrell et al (2010), using data from the OECD covering the period 1980–2008, has shown a significant contribution of current account deficits to the probability of banking crises in the OECD, over and above that arising from deregulation and capital adequacy.

The sources of domestic demand expansion are consumption, by both households and government, and investment. These are illustrated in volume terms in Figure 1.5 for the major components of demand.[5] The upper panel displays the 'Thatcher cycle' (1979–90) while the lower panel displays the 'long cycle' (1990–2008).

---

[5] Investment includes inventory which generally contributes substantially in the early stages of any recovery in GDP.

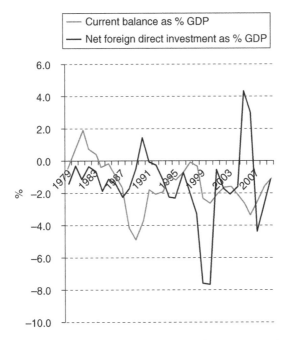

Figure 1.4   The Current Account of the UK balance of payments and Net Foreign Direct Investment as % of GDP
Source: ONS Pink Book 2010.

There are clearly both similarities and differences between the sub-periods. Household consumption, by far the largest component of domestic demand, was an important element in the recovery from the 1979–82 recession, where the collapse in investment was particularly severe. In the up-turn, it is also clear that investment surged in the later 1980s. By 1990, real household consumption was 40 per cent above its level in 1979, compared to just less than 30 per cent for domestic output as measured by GDP at market prices. Volumes of investment eventually grew to 50 per cent above their level in 1979, but only as a result of a powerful late surge. In the second cycle after 1990 investment was delayed even further and proved disappointing throughout most of the period, as we discuss further in comments on the supply conditions of both cycles in the next section.

Turning to differences between the cycles, an interesting contrast is provided by the two series for government consumption. *Collective* government consumption – which includes defence expenditures and

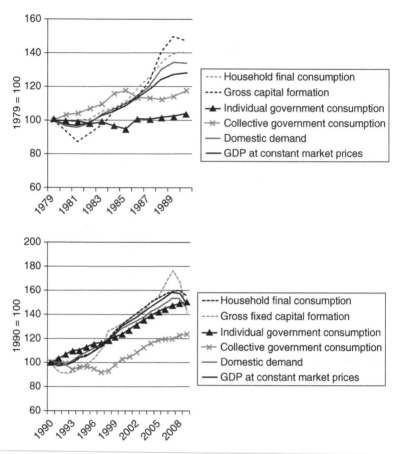

Figure 1.5   Sources of Domestic Demand Growth in the 1979–1990 and 1990–2007 cycle

Sources: ONS Blue Book 2010 and authors' own calculations.

police – rose rapidly in the early years of the Thatcher cycle, while falling back after 1985. By contrast, individually consumed public services such as education and health (known as individual government consumption)[6] rose hardly at all throughout the cycle. Here it must be stressed that these are *volumes*, intended to be indicative of the quantities of the relevant services being produced, and quite consistent with

---

[6] Note that these categories refer to government purchases of goods and services, and not to transfer payments such as social security benefits.

rising expenditures on government spending in *real* terms, where cash expenditures are deflated by conventional measures of the price level such as the Consumer Price Index or GDP deflator. Of course it is cash expenditures which need to be financed, indicating that mounting fiscal deficits may owe much to a slower rate of productivity growth in services provided by government consumption, as originally suggested in Baumol's seminal paper (Baumol 1967). Between 1990 and 2007 nominal expenditures rose at 6.6 per cent and 4.8 per cent per annum for individual and collective government consumption respectively, accelerating somewhat under New Labour (7.3 per cent and 6.1 per cent per annum over the decade from 1997).

The later cycle, like its predecessor at least in its later stages, was primarily driven by domestic demand in the form of consumption and, lagging this, investment. Although this cycle leading up to the financial crash in 2008 was ostensibly successful in maintaining more stable aggregate output growth, it was building problems because consumption demand growth was only made possible by increasing consumer debt and the transfer of output to risky sectors. In this the most recent boom differed from the earlier experience of the late 1980s in that from 2004 onwards real earnings were stagnating – as indicated in Figure 1.6. In the five years to 2007, the growth in real average earnings was just 0.7 per cent per annum while real household disposable income, which reflected strongly expanding employment as well as other income sources, rose at just 1.3 per cent per annum. This marked a beginning of the phenomenon of the 'squeezed middle' as the share of income taken by the top 10 per cent and especially the top 1 per cent of households grew more dramatically. The increase in debt in this period can be taken as reflecting a need to borrow to maintain consumption.

The continuance of the 2000s boom, despite the faltering of productivity growth, was facilitated by deception on a grand scale. The wealth promised by financial services and the business services industries that fed it was not all truly income but in part derived from fictitious profits. This meant that the consumption of private consumers and the projected tax receipts of government were both based on the confidence instilled by mis-priced capital assets. Even if this was vaguely appreciated by regulators, another throw of the dice was all the more tempting when markets were not producing the results prophesied. Early intervention to stop these booms would in such circumstances have been an admission of failure. It was not only the bankers who felt that as long as the music was playing they had to dance.

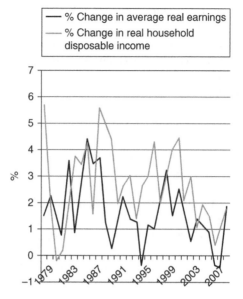

Figure 1.6   Stagnating Customer Incomes
Source: ONS.

With increasingly weak income growth, the expansion of consumer demand in the 2000s could only be financed by sharply increasing levels of indebtedness. In the UK, between 2002 and the onset of the financial crisis in 2007, equity withdrawal from housing amounted to 4 per cent of GDP implying that recorded growth was in effect capital consumption and that 'there was very little increase in national wealth' (Froud et al 2011).[7] As the boom of the 2000s developed, asset prices and real incomes started to change at increasingly divergent rates. The deceleration in earnings and incomes is evident from Figure 1.6. Note that the representative fall in income is larger than that shown since the share of income taken by the top 10 per cent and especially the top 1 per cent grew dramatically, with workers at median incomes and families struggling to record any income gains.

---

[7] Overall from 2002 to 2007, private borrowing including mortgages and credit amounted to about 9 per cent of GDP and over half of that was destined for consumption.

The story illustrates how the British economy had not lost its appetite for unsustainable growth. The economic cycle was claimed to be obsolete but, as with the earlier 1980s boom, consumption was sustained by a belief in tomorrow. Figure 1.7 shows the fall in the household savings ratio and the rise in consumer credit that resulted. By 2008, the savings ratio had reached historically low levels as consumption growth was maintained in the face of stagnant incomes.

The supply response

While unsustainable demand growth is an important feature in the explanation of how both cycles came to be cut short, the rising prices that are part of each cycle's end-game indicate that there was room for an appropriate supply response that could have contained inflationary pressure through encouraging adequate capacity to sustain the upswing longer. Public policy however was hostile to the view that supply (other than labour) needed to be actively managed; rarely deviating

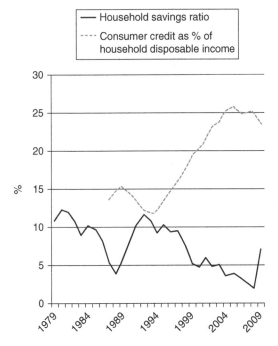

Figure 1.7 Rising Customer Indebtedness and the Fall in the savings ratio 1979–2009
Source: ONS.

from the view that sufficient capacity would be generated by market forces alone. Repeatedly, that has been called into question as firms have proved themselves more cautious than consumers. Capacity is first delayed and then subsequently created too late to prevent supply constraints and emerging price pressure.

Lagging investment after the recession was a common feature of both cycles. After 1979, the volume of investment did not reach the levels of 1979 before 1984; after peak investment in 1989, volumes did not recover to the same level until some seven years later. The reason for this has undoubtedly to do with business uncertainty in respect of where the market driven economy was going. Commenting on an investment survey more than three years after the 1990s recovery had started, an article in the *Bank of England Quarterly Bulletin* noted:

> [A] greater proportion of respondents have viewed a potential capacity constraint on output over the following four months as 'satisfactory'. In turn, this may reflect firms' uncertainty about the durability of the current economic recovery. In other words, firms have perhaps been willing to risk losing future output and perhaps sales, because they have believed that the sunk costs of investing represented too big a gamble. This explanation is lent some weight by the export-led nature of the recent recovery. Exports tend to be more volatile than domestic demand and this may have added to producers' uncertainty.
>
> (Cornelius and Wright 1995, p.273)

The question of the capacity stance adopted by the corporate sector of the economy has proved a serious issue in both of the market era cycles. The problem of tight capacity, evident in the Lawson boom of the late 1980s, re-emerged as a factor during the 2000s, creating inflationary pressure. Indeed as we write, and despite the deflationary help of downward pressure on nominal earnings growth and mounting unemployment, inflation has remained buoyant. This is in keeping with the view that British industry has learned how to maintain pricing power by adopting tighter controls on investment and reining in capacity expansion more than in earlier periods. Certainly, capital investment has been notably weak in recent years (Benito et al 2010). In theory, capital investment and supply generally should respond to the rate of return, and a sharpening of economic incentives has of course been a fundamental aim of economic policy in the market era. Labour market reform and a restoration of profitability were considered to be adequate supports for increased investment. This however has proved to be an illusion. None of the labour market reforms or anti-union measures seemed sufficient to alter the low investment climate in the UK, as noted in Card and Freeman (2004, p. 48):

> Despite the decline in unionization rates in the United Kingdom and the apparent shift toward more cooperative relations with employers, the rate of growth of capital per worker (or capital per hour) did not accelerate in the United Kingdom relative to West Germany or France. Either the underinvestment effect was relatively small before the reforms of the 1980s and 1990s, or de-unionization and an improved industrial-relations climate have had little effect on the investment calculus of U.K. employers.

Nor did the restoration of profitability appear to help. As the upper panel of Figure 1.8 shows, the long post-war boom that ended in the 1970s was associated with a declining rate of profit, quite possibly to crisis levels (Glyn 2006). The recovery in the profit rate during the Thatcher cycle is clearly evident, as is the fact that this recovery has not been reversed in the subsequent cycle.[8] The basis of the recovery in profitability stems from the apparent 'willingness of workers to accept a lower share of national income'.[9] This may be inferred from the second series in the upper panel of Figure 1.8 that shows a trend rise since 1980 in the gross operating surplus as a percentage of value added (the share of profit).

The lower panel of Figure 1.8 indicates that improved profitability did not result in any overall increase in the share of GDP devoted to fixed investment (as measured at current prices). Typically, this is measured in gross terms as shown here by the solid line. It suggests that the Thatcher cycle did end in something of an investment boom, with the investment share close to a post-war high. But it came too late to prevent the emergence of supply constraints that saw inflation rise to an annualized 9.5 per cent in her last year in office. Such a surge in investment was less marked in the subsequent cycle, though there was again a brief spike towards the end of the cycle.

It is also important to consider what had been happening to net investment, though this variable is difficult to measure due to the need to gauge depreciation. Here it can be seen that official estimates of the

---

[8] The series displayed is for the total private sector and therefore includes the impact of the substantial privatization programme.

[9] Kneller and Young 2000, p.1.

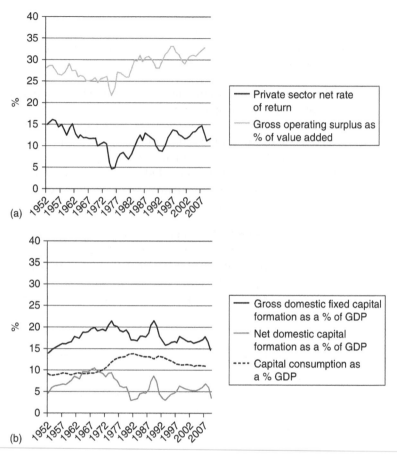

Figure 1.8   The Recovery in Corporate Profitability and Cautious Investment
Sources: ONS; Glynn (2006); and the authors' own calculations.

resources that the economy needs to devote to maintaining its capital stock, that is so-called capital consumption, underwent a considerable increase between the 1970s and 1980s, leaving the net investment share of GDP rather more depressed in the later cycle than the share of gross investment would suggest.

We recognize that there are other measures of fixed investment that could be used. Gross domestic fixed capital formation is the broadest possible measure of fixed investment and includes both fixed investment by general government and investment in dwellings. 'Business Investment' is a category that is often used in official presentations, but some part of this has been replacing investment spending by government from the 1990s (through for example the Private Finance Initiative) and so is particularly unsuitable for analysing longer run trends. Moreover there is every reason for including government investment in any assessment of the balance struck between consumption and investment in the market era.[10]

The disconnect between investment and profitability was particularly notable in the years leading up to the great crash. For non-financial companies as a whole, the share of profits in income and net investment in income diverged continuously, with the former rising while the latter fell. And although profit share in manufacturing tended to be squeezed by the high exchange rate, it should be remembered that manufacturing is much more highly geared than most service industries so that it will have benefited from the falling real cost of debt capital – which more than halved from the late 1990s to the onset of the great crash.

Fixed investment did, of course, grow during both booms but in each case from a very low base. Any capacity–building investment in anticipation of demand was hampered by business uncertainty given the belief that the market was the best form of planning.[11] The natural tendency therefore was towards caution. Even in the Thatcher boom between 1985 and 1989, the UK corporate sector invested twice as much in financial assets at home and abroad as in domestic fixed investment (Dow 1998, Table 9.7). Corporate investment became even more cautious in the later cycle than in the Thatcher era, with evidence of a downward break in the desired ratio of spare capacity by manufacturing firms from the late 1980s (Driver and Shepherd 2005).[12] Put simply, firms appeared to learn how to retire capacity early in a recession so as

---

[10] An assessment is also sometimes made in terms of investment at constant prices, but it is by no means clear what a ratio of investment to GDP signifies when measured in this manner. The price of some investment goods has fallen considerably compared to other components of GDP (led by ICT equipment) with an implied allocation to lower productivity use and also a step change in depreciation rates for shorter lived assets. The structures component of capital exhibits quite different behaviour however. Arguably the current price measure accurately reflects the constraints encountered by decision-makers and is therefore the appropriate measure in the current context.

[11] In the Thatcher period, it proved especially difficult for business to form a view of future prospects for the UK, with some arguing that the 'removal of manning restrictions only had a once-and-for-all effect' on productivity growth (Bean and Symons 1989, p.72).

[12] Other work shows that in the period up to the financial crash it was the larger manufacturing companies that were most cautious in their investment commitments (Driver 2007).

to maintain pricing power. This can be seen from the speed at which the percentage of firms working below capacity returned to normal after a peak. In the 1980s recession the peak was 85 per cent, which took four or five years to recover down to 50 per cent. In the 1990s the peak was around 70 per cent and took three or four years to recover. In the major recession following the financial shock of 2007, the peak was not as severe as the 1980s recession and took only two to three years to attain 50 per cent, though it rose again subsequently as the recovery stalled.

The flip-side of the caution being exercised by the business corporation is the extent to which it is prepared to borrow to finance investment. Here, the difference between the two cycles is palpable.

Figure 1.9 confirms that – for all non-financial corporations – the share of the gross operating surplus taken up by fixed investment fell after its peak in 1989, while net lending continued to rise. Compared to the Thatcher-Lawson boom, there would be no repeat of the financial deficits of those days. Financial balance sheets of UK based corporations were more than healthy at the start of the recession.

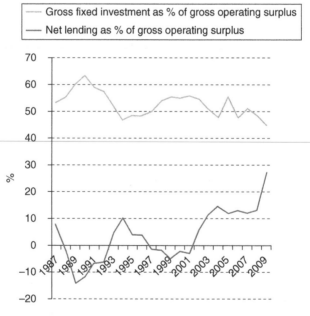

Figure 1.9   Non-Financial Corporations–gross investment and net lending as a % of gross operating surplus 1987–2009
Source: ONS 2010 Blue Book.

Sluggish capital investment and the failure of markets to correct it has been a perennial theme of economic commentary in the UK for more than thirty years. Yet it has proved impossible to address successfully because it would mean a challenge to the premise regarding efficiency of markets. When an approach is not delivering it is not easy to jettison it – rather the tendency is to effect 'one last push' in the same direction. Even if, as time went on, the limits of market forces were dimly understood, it was scarcely practicable to reverse the entire policy stance of successive administrations. The trick that was attempted instead was to reinforce the message of market friendly policies, repeating the effort that Lawson had made in the 1980s to alter the state of market confidence and increase the responsiveness of supply to demand (Dow 1999, p. 359). It was this policy that was brought to bear during the Blair-Brown administration with its relaxed approach to the huge disparities in income and wealth that were then emerging at the top end of the income distribution. It was evident also in the approach to corporate governance where serious reform was rejected in favour of continued emphasis on shareholder value.

A permissive regulatory approach, a belief in markets, legal constraints on labour unions and a burgeoning reliance on financial services to create chimerical capital were all parts of the jigsaw of events that came apart in the first decade of this century. The political theorist Colin Crouch (2011) has summarized well the underlying – but contradictory – approach:

> Government reduces ... employment protection rights so that employers are more willing to hire them ... workers might not be able to insure themselves against labour market risk but they can fund their consumption through second mortgages and credit card debt, making them less dependent on their labour income.
>
> (pp.21–2).

A major theme of this book is that this excessive and continuing reliance on labour market reform, rooted as it was in the economic record of the 1970s, has long since run into the zone of nil or even negative returns. At the same time there has been a widespread neglect of other supply-side issues that relate to capital investment and other sunk costs, so that a climate of short-term fix rather than long-term commitment has been allowed to dominate – the 'fast buck'. We elaborate on this theme in later chapters but here we continue our introductory comments by examining first the productivity record of the period and then the record on distribution and equality.

1.3   The productivity record

We begin with a comparison between the post-1979 'market era' and earlier decades. Figure 1.10 shows a number of indicators of output growth (as measured by gross value added), population and input growth for the period 1950–79 and for the subsequent market era from 1979.

The overall rate of output growth achieved since 1979 was 2.2 per cent per annum compared to 2.6 per cent in the earlier period. But the later period is affected by the financial crisis, so we take 2007 as an end-point, before the recession started. As shown in Figure 1.10 this results in growth at just 2.4 per cent per annum, a little short of that achieved between 1950 and 1979. It is important of course to consider how this growth has been achieved.

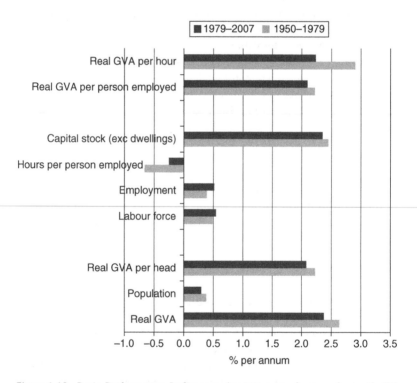

Figure 1.10   Basic Performance Indicators: Average annual rates of growth (%) 1950–79 and 1979–2007

Sources: Maddison (1982); ONS Monthly Digest; and EUKLEMS dataset.

Population growth has recently been very rapid, but remained slightly below that of 1950–79, so that GDP per head in the two periods is quite similar (2.1 per cent per annum as against 2.2 per cent per annum). Participation in the labour force grew in both periods (indeed becoming a major focus for policy in the later period), so that the rate of growth of real output per person employed was almost identical. The rate of unemployment too was rather similar in both 1979 and 2007 at about 5 per cent of the labour force, almost double that for 1950.

Labour productivity growth on a per *worker* basis was a little over 2 per cent per annum in each period. However, in the earlier period there was a more marked reduction in average working hours so that labour productivity growth measured per *hour* of labour input was noticeably faster. The degree of similarity in the data for the two sub-periods is nevertheless surprising. The inability to detect a decisive break in UK productivity growth from 1979 onward should not be taken as evidence for the widely held view that the UK economy grows at a constant rate no matter what policies are followed. It needs to be remembered that growth from the early 1950s was much higher than in the inter-war period. Moreover as we write, there is no clear indication of what new trends might emerge out of the financial crisis. Nevertheless the similarity in the periods pre- and post-1979 should put to rest the idea of a Thatcher miracle that is still sometimes entertained.

Arguably simple time-period comparisons for a single country are misleading. After all, Britain's growth performance in the early post-war period is generally regarded as being weak by international standards, and thus perhaps it is better to track comparative performance over time. In terms of GDP per person hour, the picture can be seen in Figure 1.11 which shows relative productivity levels in both 1950 and 1979. In 1950 (upper panel) UK productivity was behind only the US and the resource-rich economies of Canada and Australia. But, by 1979 the UK had been overtaken in terms of the productivity of its labour force by a large number of economies, including Germany and France, that were engaged in vigorous 'catch-up' by adopting standard but advanced technology. How far was the pattern reversed in the market era since 1979? Figure 1.12 (top panel) shows post-1979 annual *growth rates* in output per hour worked, obtained from the EU-KLEMS database. The growth rate of productivity (as measured by real gross value added per hour worked in all industries) was around the median for the UK, and only slightly below France and Germany, suggesting that there may be some truth in the idea that the market era at least contained Britain's relative decline.

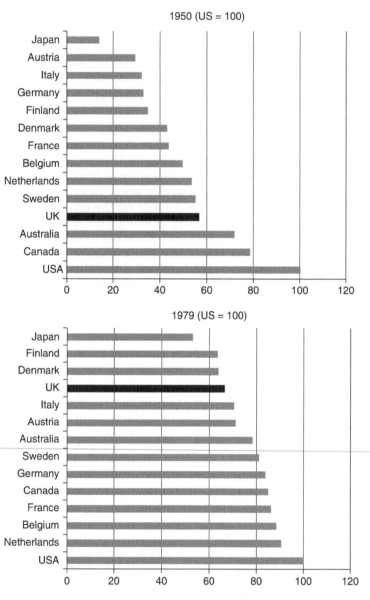

Figure 1.11 Relative Productivity as measured by GDP per person hour
Sources: Maddison (1982).

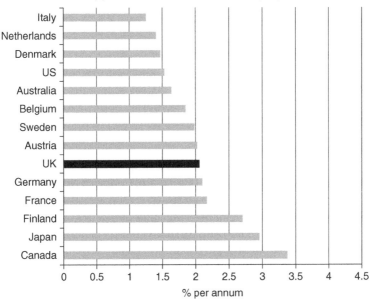

(a) Growth rates 1979–2007 in GVA per person hour

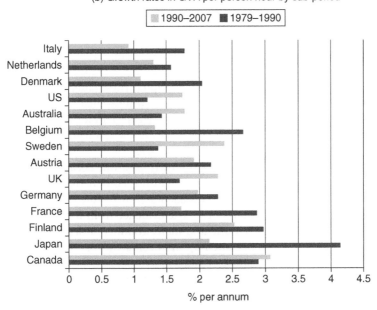

(b) Growth rates in GVA per person hour by sub-period

■ 1990–2007   ■ 1979–1990

Figure 1.12   Annual average growth rates of Gross Value Added per hour worked 1979–2007
Sources: EUKLEMS database, November 2009 release, March 2011 update Canada data until 2004; Japan until 2006.

The lower panel of Figure 1.12 contrasts the two sub-periods since 1979 corresponding to the two economic cycles we have identified. A number of features stand out, but the UK in the second cycle managed to improve productivity growth a little compared to the earlier one, in common with other so-called liberal market economies – here represented by the US and Australia – while countries in the Eurozone without exception experienced a clear retardation, quite limited in the case of Germany, but very marked in others such as Italy and Belgium. If this is some systematic 'variety of capitalism' effect, it is rather a subtle one as illustrated in the case of Sweden, which underwent an acceleration of productivity growth in excess of that of either the US or UK.

Comparisons of productivity *levels* between economies are tricky when there is a need to compare economies with quite different overall price levels and price structures – or indeed industrial structures or demographics. There are several large scale attempts to make appropriate price adjustments – by the OECD for its member organizations – and for the International Comparisons Programme (ICP) which creates the data for the well-known Penn World Tables. The latter are based on calculating GDP in 'international dollars' using a form of averaging of prices across many economies – ranging from the most advanced to some of the least developed. While the data from both sources has been much used in studies of cross country growth, it is less helpful for the current comparisons than those supplied by the OECD who estimate Purchasing Power Parities (PPPs) on the basis of the price structures of the member economies, the majority of whom have similar and high levels of GDP per capita. These latter data are used by the Office for National Statistics (ONS) to create annual comparisons of productivity levels. The latest are shown in Figure 1.13 for the G7 economies in 2010. Both measures suggest that the UK still lags behind other large European economies and the G7 average.

Evidently, the neat patterns of the early post-war decades in which there was nearly unanimous convergence on US productivity levels and where Britain's relative decline was such a clear feature, are no longer evident in the modern market era. The evidence from the overall productivity record is a mixed one and many commentators have tended to argue that at least some catch-up has been achieved, thus offsetting the pain of recessions and lost output. We do not, however, regard these arguments on UK comparative productivity as wholly convincing, partly because of the flattering effects of the UK financial bubble on profitability and growth. This is now being unwound in the wake of the financial crash so that the UK appears to be experiencing a deeper and longer recession than many comparator countries, and a slower pace

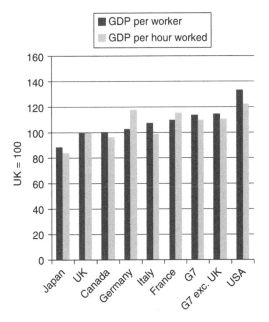

Figure 1.13 Labour productivity for the G7 economies in 2010

of investment recovery than even those of the previous two recessions. Of course some of this may stem from inappropriate macroeconomic policies – cutting too hard and too fast – but irrespective of this, there will be a permanent loss of capacity due to necessary reforms in banking and to the reliance of other high productivity sectors on demand conditions that have disappeared. Shrinking the banks will have a knock-on effect on other important supply industries. On our rough estimates, over a quarter of business services output[13] – which was one of the star productivity performers of the long boom – feeds directly or indirectly into the banking sector.[14] Nor should it be forgotten that many

---

[13] These were based upon the Office for National Statistics (ONS) analytical input–output tables. Since the most recent of these were for 1995, they probably represent an under-estimate.

[14] Stephanie Flanders in a review of the Institute of Fiscal Studies *Green Budget 2012* notes commentary from Goldman Sachs that: 'the official story that we have permanently lost at least 7–8 per cent of our national output in this crisis implies that the past few years have done more lasting damage to our economic potential than either World War II or the Great Depression': http://www.bbc.co.uk/news/business-16835450

comparator countries had their own difficulties, making a temporary catch up in UK productivity in the long boom difficult to interpret. Of note here is Germany's attempt to construct a unified economy, while elsewhere in Europe subdued demand conditions in the run-up to the Euro introduction and immediately after reflected attempts to achieve convergence of the Eurozone economies.

But in any event productivity comparisons are not the only ones that need to be borne in mind. Any introductory economics text will point to the limitations of GDP as a measure of welfare, and the retrospective assessments of the UK market reforms in Bean and Symons (1989) and Card et al (2004) make clear that they regard the reforms as a trade-off between productivity growth and inequality that needs justification. It is by no means certain that there is in fact a trade-off between inequality and efficiency, with some studies rejecting a negative correlation between the two (Corry and Glyn 1994). Nevertheless before returning to the main concerns of the book, we consider what the market era has done for the distribution of incomes, especially for the basic economic unit, the household.

1.4   Growing inequality

The distribution of productivity gains across households is clearly of enormous importance in any assessment of the market era. As suggested earlier, income inequality increased substantially during the 1980s. This is confirmed by a whole raft of measures. The spread of household incomes increased as a result of earnings disparity in the workplace, a changing distribution across occupations and a growing polarization of households into the 'job rich' (more than one earner in a household) and the job poor (no such earner). Figure 1.14 shows the well-known summary measure of income inequality across UK households – the Gini coefficient – for three measures of 'equivalised' household income[15] – original income (all income from private sources), disposable income (after addition of cash benefits and deduction of taxes) and post-tax income (which also takes the evidently regressive expenditure taxes into account). A sharp rise in all three measures is clearly evident during the 1980s, which is never reversed in the subsequent decades.

A further picture of the overall distribution of earnings emerges from an examination of the Households below Average Income Survey (HBAI) income data. From these, Joyce et al (2010) derive the growth

---

[15] Income is adjusted for household size and the fixed costs of households.

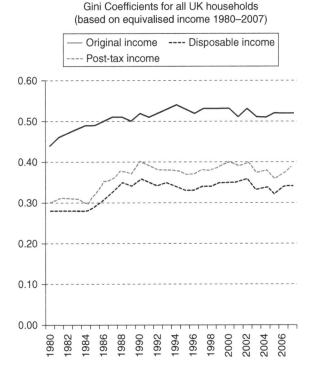

Gini Coefficients for all UK households
(based on equivalised income 1980–2007)

Figure 1.14   Increasing inequality among households
Source: ONS.

of household real incomes[16] by income quintiles over different political administrations as shown in Figure 1.15. The sharp ascending profile in the Thatcher era is once again very clear, but was partially reversed under Major. There was a fairly equal growth across the quintiles in the first Blair administration (1996/7–2000/1) but there was 'progressive' growth in the second (2000/1–2004/5). The final period may perhaps be described as an anaemic version of the Thatcher decade, but with the mean real income of the poorest 20 per cent of individuals actually falling. Not one of the quintiles grew by even 1.5 per cent per annum over the period, with the growth of incomes in the top quintile being the fastest at just 1.3 per cent per annum, the only group whose income grew by more than 1 per cent per annum.

---

[16] After Income Tax, National Insurance and Council Tax.

Figure 1.15 does not give the full picture. Top incomes have been an increasing source of controversy in recent years. Here we need to consider a more detailed picture of earnings growth. Figure 1.16 shows the percentage growth in incomes by percentile, comparing two sub-periods, 1979–96/7 and 1996/7–2008/9. The sharply increasing profile is still very much in evidence for the earlier period, but the latter period shows an interesting contrast, with faster real income growth among the bottom 30 per cent of the distribution and amongst the very highest incomes, some way beyond the 90th percentile. Indeed from roughly the 30th to beyond the 90th percentile real disposable income appears to have grown at rather less than the macroeconomic benchmark of

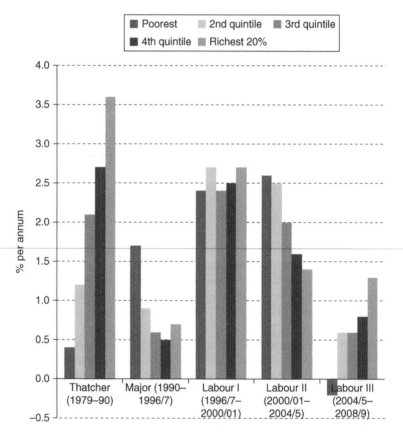

Figure 1.15 After tax income growth among quintiles of household groupings
Source: Joyce et al (2010).

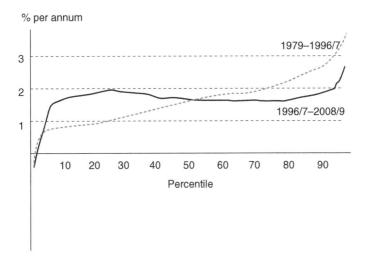

Figure 1.16   Growth in real incomes by percentile of household income distribution
Source: Joyce, R., A. Muriel, D. Phillips and L. Sibieta (2010) 'Poverty and Inequality in the UK 2010', *IFS Commentary C116*, reproduced by kind permission of the Institute for Fiscal Studies.

2 per cent per annum. Within the top 10 per cent, two categories of income growth are important – corresponding to the City of London and to corporate executive remuneration – with both affected by stock exchange valuations. Income Data Services record a huge rise in the real earnings of CEOs after 2003, with remuneration more than doubling in the top 100 companies and almost doubling in the next 250, between 2003 and 2007. This needs to be contrasted with the stagnation of real earnings of all employees at precisely the same time. Notwithstanding the hit to these earnings in the financial crash, they remained higher than 2004 levels (National Equality Panel 2010).

Contributing to an increasing inequality of household income has been the impact of the same phenomenon in earnings from the work-place. Two drivers of inequality have been identified – the role of skill biased technical change (see Katz and Autor 1999 and Machin 1996 for UK evidence) and that of international trade where labour intensive imports replace labour intensive domestic production (Wood 1994). Although the debate has not been conclusive, because the two may be connected, the consensus today is that skill-biased technological change – of which information technology is the leading exemplar – played a dominant role. This involved a general type of cross-industry technological and organizational advance which, at unchanged relative wage premia for labour force skills, shifts the relative demand in favour of skilled workers. The result is either increasing earnings inequality or, where unions bargaining for unskilled manual workers remain strong, rising unemployment among unskilled workers. This seemed to fit observed national patterns in which unemployment rose in the unreformed economies of Europe, while the market friendly economies saw rapid rises in earnings in inequality, especially marked in the US where real earnings in the lowest deciles actually fell for an extended period of time.

If these increases in economic inequality are perceived as an inevitable outcome of pro-market economic policies, optimists might hope that it would open doors for a new generation of able contenders operating on a new level playing field. Here, however, the evidence is less than encouraging. Recent research by Blanden and Machin (2007) compares birth cohorts of 1958 and 1970 and looks at their earnings in their early thirties, considering the extent of mobility compared to parents when in their teens. Astonishingly, they find that inter-generational 'stickiness' was higher for the latter cohort, which was entering the job market in the 1980s, the decade of profound change.

1.5   A preview of the arguments

The opening chapters of the book show how free market policies have been pursued in the UK in preference to an interventionist supply-side approach. The main exception is labour market reform where there has been heavy intervention to contain the power of organized labour, increase labour supply and lower the share of labour.

Chapter 2 considers the evolution of economic policy in the UK, especially during the formative period of the 1970s and into the 1980s, when the emphasis on labour market reform was taken to new heights. We chart the emergence of the new models that analysed work-place bargaining as a game between labour and capital. Initially at least, the new macro-models emphasized wage push as the key determinant of the high levels of unemployment. The standard economic view became that any productivity gain from capital investment would be captured by labour and thus was irrelevant to employment creation.

In **Chapter 3** we consider the idea of competitiveness, which in our view provides a useful way of thinking about economic policy, not least because it allows for a broader, more democratic debate about the underlying strengths and weaknesses of the UK economy than the type of macroeconomics which focuses so heavily on simply constraining labour cost. The balance of payments constraint that can transmit inflationary pressure is best viewed as a real economy issue of productivity and non-price competitiveness. Such considerations lead to an analysis of the role of manufacturing, and the engineering sector in particular. We argue that competitiveness depends crucially upon capital investment as well as research and development, since the innovation that drives competitiveness is usually embodied in advanced equipment and processes with widespread linkages throughout the economy. Here, there are important questions for policy regarding the role of engineering in the supply chain in the production and use of investment goods. The challenge is to combine productivity growth with output growth and here the picture has not been encouraging.

Chapters 4 and 5 of the book are largely concerned with the issue of capital investment and its importance for economic growth. **Chapter 4** identifies a downward bias to investment, from the point of view of social welfare resulting from spillover effects. It also develops an argument that the information limitations involved in most investment decisions inevitably impart an arbitrary element to the overall investment climate which requires attention to be paid to issues of behaviour and expectation. The market on its own will often result in too little investment, too late.

In **Chapter 5** these issues are addressed with a focus on understanding the *pattern* of bias in capital investment. The issue here is which industries or sectors are affected and how. There is a treatment of the composition of capital between tangibles and intangibles, between cost-saving and innovation investment, and between domestic and inward investment.

Chapter 6 locates the British economy in the context of the globalization wave that began after the establishment of flexible exchange regimes in the 1970s and particularly following the liberalization of capital flows in the 1980s. We show how all administrations of the period we study welcomed these developments without question, from the liberalization of financial services in the 1980s to the drive to attract foreign direct investment in the later years. The effect on the macroeconomy and industrial structure was to relegate to the sidelines any interventionist policy deemed at variance with the free markets and flexible labour regimes. This agenda spilled over into the corporate sphere with the acceptance of shareholder value as the only respectable theory of corporate purpose. The results here were to make the executive manager a simulacrum of the representative shareholder. A manager's own capacities to grow a company organically were suppressed in favour of an imperative to extract surplus as large and as early as possible in return for vast compensation packages.

Chapter 7 argues for a new direction in corporate governance policy. It surveys the various reformist agendas of the interventionist shareholder, the universal shareholder and that of enlightened shareholder value, all of which are found unlikely to be effective. The requirement for corporate governance in an innovative economy is to put power back in the hands of those with the knowledge and interest to grow the company organically. It is doubtful if this can be done without a system of democratic managerial involvement which will need a change in company law.

Chapter 8 concludes the book with a look to the future. It considers the principles that can underpin growth and cautions against some simplistic remedies. It illustrates principles for growth with a set of concrete recommendations for institutional reform and policy action.

2
Investment, the Labour Market and Economic Policy

2.1 Introduction

A major goal of economic policy in the market era was to transform the labour market. Far more than any other advanced economy, and beginning with the high unemployment decade of the 1980s, British economic policy has centred on the creation of a flexible labour market, to the exclusion of much else, with the exception perhaps of the search for a credible anti-inflationary monetary policy. By flexibility in the labour market we do not mean to include all policies such as skills training and the flexible use of labour within the firm – which were never a priority – but rather the process of increasing the willingness of workers to supply labour at a wage justified by the prevailing level of productivity. That approach has now become so much part of the current consensus that it is hard to recall that it displaced other more broad-ranging concerns over growth that headed the agenda in earlier periods. In this chapter, we ask how this transformation became accepted and commonplace. How did it happen that an orthodoxy emerged that downplayed – almost to the point of neglect – the positive contribution of capital investment, research and development (R&D) and technology in favour of a worldview that prioritized labour market institutional reform?

For economists working in the classical tradition such as Smith, Marx or Ricardo, the neglect of capital investment in particular would have seemed strange. Even the neoclassical view gives an important place to capital accumulation in that more capital added to the production process is expected to raise output and productivity levels. To be sure the standard case – before new growth theory complicated the picture somewhat – assumes 'diminishing returns', as when extra computing

33

power ends up being applied to low-level tasks. This means that new capital adds to productivity in a progressively weaker fashion so that in the very long run the *growth rate* of output will not be increased. But the long run here can be shown to be very long indeed. For reasonable parameters, any economy would experience several *decades* of faster growth following an initial boost to capital investment (Bombach 1985) before settling down to a rate determined by the underlying technological possibilities.

Standard applied accounts of UK economic growth at least up to end of the 1970s also emphasized the contribution of capital investment to both high rates of economic growth and high rates of employment. According to one Treasury insider in the 1970s there was unanimous assent for the view that low investment was 'a major drag on our growth and a reason for our lagging behind our competitors' (Gieve 2006, p 442). The economic historian R.C.O. Matthews (1968) asked why Britain had had much fuller employment after the war? This followed from his earlier work on the business cycle which, like Keynes and Kalecki before him, identified investment as a largely 'exogenous' component of demand that created growth. In his 1968 piece he identified a higher ratio of investment to full employment output as the chief reason as to why Britain had not returned to the depressed conditions of the inter-war years, though this was simply a way of saying that economic policy had achieved a balance that allowed for a virtuous cycle of investment and growth.

So a puzzle remains as to why and precisely how capital and technology were written out of the picture for the UK in the period with which we are concerned. This theoretical transition was made without any great fuss or fanfare so that the manner of the change has received comparatively little commentary while its explanation has been similarly neglected. In section 2.3 we will first explain the 'how' and later, in section 2.4, the 'why'. First however, we consider the historical context.

2.2　The macroeconomic climate and the NAIRU model

Macroeconomics at the time of the first Thatcher government was struggling to respond to the way in which the world had changed in the previous decade. The demise of the fixed-rate Bretton Woods system[1]

---

[1] Strictly of course the term 'fixed' is a misnomer since the system prevailing until 1971 did allow discrete exchange rate adjustments for reasons of 'fundamental' disequilibrium in an individual economy's balance of payments. The system was generally accompanied by considerable capital controls.

complicated national adjustment mechanisms that had allowed interest rates to target domestic demand. Commodity price shocks in the early 1970s had resulted in very sharp rises in inflation – reaching 26 per cent in the UK in 1976. The rise in inflation coincided with unemployment remaining stubbornly high, indicating that the standard Phillips Curve relationship linking unemployment to price inflation was no longer stable. Indeed the problems appeared now to be positively correlated with the emergence of 'stagflation' caused, it was argued, by strong trade unions defending wages from imported inflation even as growth and productivity slowed. This gave rise to the concept of 'real wage resistance' in wage bargaining, referring to the possibility that the union 'target' wage in the bargaining process constituted a well specified command over consumption goods and services.

The new pressures from the supply-side put orthodox Keynesian ideas on the back foot. They were under attack globally, first from a simple questioning of any long-run trade-off between inflation and unemployment and later from the more complex charge that no credence could be placed in a model that did not assign to agents the ability to respond to public knowledge. The public mood too was affected by a realization that there were economic challenges ahead, something that had already been explained to the nation by prime minister Callaghan in 1976.

> The cosy world we were told would go on forever, where full employment would be guaranteed at the stroke of a Chancellor's pen ... I tell you in all candour that that option no longer exists, and that, insofar as it ever did exist, it only worked in each occasion by injecting a bigger dose of inflation into the economy.
>
> (cited in Eccleshall and Walker 1998, p.352)

Callaghan's apparent acceptance of simple monetarism as an analysis of the post-war period may well have been the uninformed consequence of employing a partisan speechwriter. More importantly however it signalled the end of an essential element of the post-war consensus in which the inflationary implications of a full employment policy were considered soluble through democratic negotiation and appropriate policies for prices and incomes. The same ideas were later used by the Conservatives as a peg from which to hang the severely deflationary policies of the early 1980s. Monetarism was basically a theory of price inflation with an assumption of labour market equilibrium. Thus it was not a theory of unemployment as it had no serious understanding of labour markets that was distinct from the operation of any other market. It was nevertheless a useful fig-leaf with which to disguise a political agenda (see for example Glyn 2006, p.28).

Nevertheless by the early 1980s, unemployment had clearly risen to levels that were worrying even to a doctrinaire government. The rise in unemployment at this time was – on the evidence of Figure 2.1 – quite outside post-war experience and was more on the scale of the rises seen in the early 1920s and 1930s. Moreover as can also be seen, this was accompanied by a further spike in the rate of domestic inflation.

For academic economists the challenge was to explain unemployment in an inflationary situation and, at least in the UK, it became evident that some rudimentary institutional context of labour markets needed to be added to the theory.

The 'New Keynesian' response to the issues of the day was to fashion a theory of unemployment based on the type of wage bargaining that characterized the vast majority of manual workers. In this context, the competitive sector could play little role as a possible cushion for workers laid off through 'excessive' wage bargains. Unemployment required a treatment of labour market institutions to determine whether, for example, trade unions or high benefit levels contributed

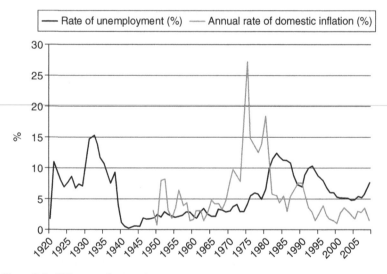

Figure 2.1   UK unemployment

Sources: ONS for deflator; for unemployment: OECD and Maddison (1982) for data before 1975.

most to aggressive pay demands. Armed with such a model it was hoped to embed the short-run notion of demand management with an overarching long-run model with classical properties (McDonald and Solow 1981). The intention was to transcend the economics of both Keynes – whose effective demand analysis was seen as relevant solely to the short run – and the 'classics' who believed that the problem of unemployment was essentially one of 'too high' real wages, for which strong trade unions were seen as the culprit.

The New Keynesian ideas took root in two remarkable conferences held in 1985 and 1988 that had been organized to try and understand the rise in unemployment in many (if not all) European economies. These will be referred to as Chelwood Gate I and II. The proceedings were published respectively in Bean, Layard and Nickell (eds. 1987) and Dreze and Bean (eds. 1990). Several of the contributions, including that of the British, to Chelwood Gate I introduced the idea that unemployment was determined by the struggle between capital and labour over shares of output. The essence of the argument is that unemployment is the mechanism by which competing claims for the national cake are reconciled.[2] This insight, popularized by the expression 'battle of the mark-ups', results in an 'equilibrium' unemployment rate at which the real wage demanded by workers exactly balances the inverse real wage desired by firms who, operating under imperfect competition, set prices. In equilibrium, the realized real wage and the mark-up of prices on wages equals that anticipated by the firms and workers. There will be no tendency here for the rate of inflation to change and hence the equilibrium level of unemployment became known as the 'non-accelerating inflation rate of unemployment' (NAIRU or u^*). In non-equilibrium situations, inflation would be rising or falling and unemployment will need to adjust so as to resolve competing claims between workers and owners.

The simplest versions of the model involve a pair of relationships. On the one hand, workers seek a real wage that is greater when employment is full and when their bargaining strength or other factors determining their 'target real wage' is high. On the other, employers tend to accept lower price-mark-ups on cost when there is more unemployment (that is the mark-up on cost is pro-cyclical) or when firms' monopoly power is constrained by competition or regulation. The institutional context is given substance with a principle known as the 'right to manage' under which when unions set a wage, employers then set prices and choose the numbers employed

---

[2] An earlier formulation of a similar idea is Rowthorn (1977). For an account of its relationship to different schools of economic thought see Stockhammer (2008).

(with an eye of course on product demand). The model can be expressed by a pair of equations determining the wage required by workers and the price margin required by employers which is represented by the inverse of the workers real wage. Thus we have, writing u for unemployment:

WAGE SETTING: Target real wage of workers

$$(w/p)^T = w_0 - w_1 u \tag{1}$$

and

PRICE SETTING: Target real 'inverse' wage of employers

$$(p/w)^T = \pi_0 - \pi_1 u \tag{2}$$

Note that when employers aim to set prices at a particular level they are simultaneously choosing the amount of output they plan to sell and the amount of labour they will need to employ to fulfil the plan (labour demand).

Since the left hand side of (2) is the inverse of the left hand side of (1) the equations have a simple solution for unemployment which is often referred to as the non-accelerating inflation rate of unemployment (NAIRU):

$$u^* = (w_0 + \pi_0)/(w_1 + \pi_1)$$

While this equilibrium level of unemployment seems to be fixed by parameters, we will see later that the real interest lies in the parameters themselves and how they are determined.

The price setting and wage setting relationships can be combined as in Figure 2.2 which has now become familiar in many of today's textbooks. Here the diagram is shown in terms of employment e rather than unemployment u, but for a fixed labour force L, these are related since $e = L - u$. The intersection of the two curves defines a level of employment at which the pricing behaviour of firms and the target real wage are reconciled, that is there are no price or wage 'surprises', and the rate of wage and price inflation become constant. It is in this sense that the level of employment e^* and real wage $(w/p)^*$ are said to be an equilibrium, and the corresponding level of unemployment follows directly if the labour force (L) is fixed. Thus we arrive at the NAIRU[3] given by $u^* = L - e^*$.

---

[3] It is well known that the NAIRU is actually a misnomer. When the rate of inflation increases, it is the price *level* which has accelerated.

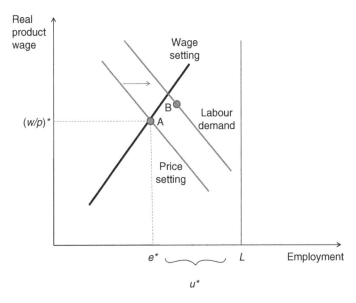

Figure 2.2 A short-run demand stock

But how does an economy reach the level of unemployment determined by the NAIRU? This is conceived as a 'medium-run' phenomenon. Most versions of the model require a policy response by the government or monetary authorities, reacting to the rate of inflation, for the actual rate of unemployment to tend toward the NAIRU. In Figure 2.2, consider an economy starting from equilibrium with the real product wage (that is the wage in terms of output prices) = $(w/p)^*$, and which faces a surprise increase in aggregate demand. This shifts the price-setting (labour demand[4]) curve to the right as shown. However in more favourable bargaining conditions, wages rise faster than anticipated, and so the real product wage rises. The economy moves to a point such as B. Workers have however also been surprised – prices have also risen faster than anticipated – so the actual real wage is below the target real wage, given by the wage-setting line. So B must be *below* the wage setting curve which implies continued upward wage and price pressure.

---

[4] Although the two terms – price setting and labour demand – are used interchangeably and both describe a relationship between employment and the real product wage, this is not a traditional labour demand curve in which competitive producers choose output on the basis of a given real product wage.

A number of reasons can now be advanced as to why an increasing rate of inflation will reverse the increase in demand. The most likely and realistic mechanism is action by the Central Bank to control inflation through monetary policy.[5]

The model just outlined does not as yet really answer many of the more interesting questions about unemployment and its determinants. First we need to know more about the bargaining process or whichever variables inform the setting of wages and prices. The story here is that workers' representatives have to think through a highly complicated narrative about the effects of pressing for higher wages. How strong is their actual bargaining power? What will happen to employment? These are questions that can only be answered once the effect on prices and output and thus labour demand has been calculated. The effect on prices is determined by the extent to which the employer wants to pass on the higher costs to consumers, something that depends on the responsiveness (elasticity) of consumers to price rises and the existing share of labour in production (which determines how important labour costs are for profits). They may also need to consider how much workers lose by becoming unemployed, something that will depend partly on the benefit level.[6]

An indication of the complex chain of influences on the equilibrium unemployment rate or NAIRU is shown in Table 2.1.

We can make intuitive sense of this table by seeing how the result is built up block by block. As illustrated in Table 2.1, u^* is determined by four main forces, external to the economic model itself. These are labour organization and demographics (those which affect bargaining strength), the labour share of output (technology), the real benefit level (or the next best job offer such as the 'casual' wage) and competition as reflected in the sensitivity of price to output (that is the price elasticity of demand).

Beginning with level 1 of the diagram, the wage-benefit mark-up is determined by the bargaining power of workers and the resistance of employers. Employers resist wage demands when it impacts their profit

---

[5] Mechanisms which do not involve policy interventions include a loss of price competitiveness in international markets where the nominal exchange rate is fixed, or the impact of price rises on real money balances (the so-called 'Pigou effect').

[6] In more complex models it will also depend on the likelihood of re-employment. As economists are not always multidisciplinary, important questions about the alternative wage such as whether unemployment feels different when it is a communal or individual experience, have rarely been addressed.

Table 2.1 Influences on the natural rate in the bargaining model

Variables in bold are determined outside the model				
LEVEL 3	**Labour Supply/ Unionization**	**Price Elasticity**	**Labour Share of Output**	
LEVEL 2	Relative bargaining power	Effect of higher wages on profits [and/or employment]		
LEVEL 1	The wage-benefit mark-up		**Real Benefit Level**	**Price Elasticity**
OUTCOME	The natural rate of unemployment (NAIRU)			

(through a high labour share of output) or when it is hard to pass on costs (due to high responsiveness to price). A higher labour share will make employers more willing to carry out policy that otherwise would have to take the form of unemployment (possibly induced by government or the Central Bank) to secure price stability. However if the labour share is fixed in the model, as is often assumed, it cannot affect equilibrium unemployment.

The reason why price elasticity of demand features in both Level 1 and 3 is that it influences both the price mark-up on wage costs, and the wage mark-up on benefits. The latter influence arises because a lower (absolute) elasticity implies a lesser effect on profit from a higher bargained real wage. In the end, the NAIRU only depends on bargaining strengths, the labour share, the benefit level and price elasticity.

The model just described is often known by the authors of the standard textbook on unemployment based upon it (Layard, Nickell and Jackman 1991 henceforth LNJ). It constituted an enormously impressive achievement in that it became accepted orthodoxy for more than two decades, permeating the ideas that students learned in the classroom from high school to doctoral level. It was a strikingly pluralist model in the sense that, as Stockhammer (2008) has shown, it can be interpreted as New Keynesian, Post-Keynesian, Marxist or Classical. However it is strikingly narrow in its choice of assumptions, particularly so for the version popular in the UK, which differed from many US and European accounts in insisting on the irrelevance of capital investment for unemployment.

The model details have been criticized in various ways and it has been subject to some empirical tests. One major question is whether a stable NAIRU can be identified to which actual unemployment tends to revert? Alternatively is there some process whereby the NAIRU itself becomes dragged along by the prevailing unemployment in a ratchet effect that economists called hysteresis? This idea had already been discussed at Chelwood Gate I, where the participants were well aware of the persistence of unemployment during the 1980s in many advanced economies. Indeed many of the factors creating the 'wage push' of the 1970s and which had helped inspire the model had gone into reverse: union powers in Britain and elsewhere were on the wane, while import prices as well as the price of oil (where Britain had become an important producer) had moderated, helping to reduce consumer and wage inflation. By the middle of the 1980s it was pretty clear that equilibrium rates may have followed actual rates in an upward direction. Thus Chelwood Gate II paid increasing attention to the *dynamics* of the NAIRU theory. Here, the problems with the whole approach became more evident as it became increasingly difficult to differentiate the theory empirically from demand-led explanations in a context where the NAIRU was itself responding to actual labour market conditions. Several studies also suggested that the NAIRU model could not be substantiated as a dynamic system (Fair 2000). The result was that more and more features were heaped on the model, including interaction effects (Blanchard and Wolfers 2001) and labour market 'catalysts' (Wadhwani 2001). None of this means that the battle of the mark-ups is totally wrong or that unemployment does not discipline wage demands, it simply means that the model is deplorably narrow and that productivity enhancing policies should not be discounted in containing unemployment (Wilkinson 2000; Schettkat 2003).

Stockhammer (2008) makes a vital point in distinguishing between the NAIRU model (some features of which are uncontroversial) and what he calls the NAIRU 'story', which is an interpretation of the equations in which additional restrictions on the value of the parameters of the model imply conclusions that do not necessarily follow from the full model itself. In that way the use of the model becomes an ideological statement. Indeed it may well have been this, as much as technical virtuosity, that contributed to its appeal and impact. Layard and Nickell (1987) cite from the 1985 White Paper that 'the biggest single cause of our high unemployment is the failure of our jobs market, the weak link in our economy' (HMSO, pp.12–13). For the NAIRU authors this was *the* problem for which policy was required. As shown in the next sections, the NAIRU model was bent towards that end and away from a broader consideration of other enduring problems in the British economy, including both low capital investment and a persistent problem of the international competitiveness of its goods and services. The policy conclusions which follow from the series of papers in the LNJ textbook left little doubt about the implications for policy: unemployment benefits of limited duration, stronger job-search tests and generally 'active' labour market policies designed to increase the employability of those out of work. For those in work, a reduction in their employment protection should ensure that the balance is tilted toward hiring rather than not firing. Little scope is seen for work sharing or early retirement or public sector employment, and so on. In this framework, hysteresis was acknowledged to imply a short-run role for demand but the focus of attention was on long-term unemployment, which was seen as requiring active labour market policies for those out of work.

2.3 Capital investment: A vanishing trick

Identifying the centrepiece of economic policy with labour market reform needs to be justified. An obvious challenge – in the context of persistently high unemployment – is why competing claims on income cannot be reconciled at lower levels of unemployment through a faster rate of labour productivity growth, which in any school of economics depends on capital investment. For those rejecting this scenario, a theoretical model was required in which labour productivity growth somehow becomes irrelevant to the employment outcome. This is exactly what is achieved in the LNJ model outlined above. But how precisely were both investment and productivity excised from the picture?

Capital investment, R&D and other contributions to productivity make no difference to the long-run or natural unemployment rate (NAIRU) because if productivity improves with higher capital intensity, any resultant lessening of pricing pressure is cancelled out by a corresponding upward effect on wage pressure.[7] This restriction is a feature of the NAIRU model popular in UK academic and policy circles but one which is often absent in US and European accounts (McAdam and McMorrow 1999).

There are a large number of objections that can be made to this feature of the model – arguments that directly contradict the irrelevance of

---

[7] Technically this means that productivity effects enter the pair of equations (1) and (2) with equal and opposite sign. Another way in which capital is written out of the model is that the variable u stands for both labour utilization and capital utilization though the relationship between these variables is itself of interest (Driver and Hall 2007). Finally it may be noted that the model accords no influence for capital investment on the price elasticity of demand though both infrastructure and private investment may be expected to play such a role (Rowthorn 1995; Pickelman and Schuh 1997; Driver and Shepherd 1999, 2005; Arestis and Sawyer 2005).

capital investment. At this stage, we will just mention three of the most popular criticisms related to the transmission of productivity effects.

The first critique centres on the relevance of the model for the post-1980s period. By the time the LNJ arguments were formulated, the bargaining framework – so characteristic of the post-war years up to the 1980s – had already become less representative. The bargaining model is not applicable where union coverage is low so that, for example, it has never directly been applicable to the US. As Westaway (1997) argues, where there is a secondary, competitive labour market which clears, 'shocks to labour demand will have permanent effects on unemployment and the concept of the [natural rate] will not be very helpful for policy' (p.19). This is important because the bargaining model became less relevant to the UK after the dramatic retrenchment of manufacturing and the defeats suffered by trade unions in the 1980s. Nickell et al (2005) show collective bargaining coverage in the UK falling from 70 per cent to 40 per cent in the 15 years from 1980 and indeed this trend applied to all workers in the private sector by the late 1980s (Forth and Millward 2002). LNJ argue that their model does not necessarily rely on bargaining or trade unions and that the same results may be reached by an 'efficiency wage' model, where wages are set by employers to guarantee loyalty and commitment 'as with the union model, productivity changes have no impact on $u^{*\prime}$ (p.152). It may be possible to mimic the rising wage setting curve of Figure 2.2 for the case of efficiency wages. However it is not at all clear that this model can then be used to argue for the irrelevance of capital investment and other productivity variables. In many circumstances a higher capital intensity increases the scope and intensity of the efficiency wage effect as LNJ appear to accept: 'in firms that are more capital intensive ... the importance of having the work well done [is greater] so that firms paying efficiency wages have an incentive to pay more' (p.193). Such workers are therefore more valuable to retain in the firm. This suggests that capital intensification may indeed progressively *increase* the NAIRU, according to the logic of the model, though LNJ do not draw this conclusion, perhaps because it would call into question the plausibility of the whole approach.[8]

---

[8] In any case the argument based on efficiency wages is double edged; exactly the reverse interpretation to that in LNJ is made in Dreze and Sneessens (1995). They question whether, without productivity increases, wages can be maintained sufficiently to preserve efficiency and even LNJ admit to short-run effects on unemployment from productivity falls (p.171). Since such falls could require nominal wage reductions, the adjustment could be lengthy (Akerlof et al 1996).

A second critique concerns the timescale over which the NAIRU is believed to be of importance and the precise real wage over which a bargain is being struck. The model – and the vertical axis in Figure 2.2 – is specified in terms of the real *product* wage, that is the wage in terms of the price of output of the typical producer. The worker is of course interested in what the money wage will buy in terms of consumption goods and services, that is the real *consumption* wage. The difference between the two depends upon factors contributing to what is sometimes known as the 'wedge'. This is composed of both indirect and direct taxation, taxes on employers on their wage costs and, most importantly in the context of their rapid rise in the 1970s, import costs relative to domestic costs and prices. Many elements of the wedge are subject to long-run trends – such as the fall in import prices relative to the GDP deflator between the Korean War and the late 1960s, or the contribution made by imports from China more recently. Between 1980 and 2009 for example, the rise in import prices was only 2.3 per cent a year compared with just under 4 per cent for output prices, and was duly reflected in a lower rate of growth of the price level for final consumption expenditure. External shocks originating in this way can be thought of as similar to productivity shocks. For LNJ, the elements of the wedge need to be treated in a consistent manner with capital investment and productivity. So the wedge too has to be limited in its impact on the NAIRU – a tricky proposition since it assumes, among other expectations, that 'workers' marginal valuation of leisure ... [is] unaffected by the wedge factors' (Melliss and Webb 1997, p.11). In fact, there is abundant evidence that workers real consumption wages do not fully reflect tax or import shocks (whether favourable or unfavourable) on wage pressure (Chan et al 1995; Arestis and Biefang-Frisancho 2000). Melliss and Webb (1997) note that the effects can be 'very prolonged'. Nevertheless LNJ feel that they can ignore such inconvenient effects because they are not, in theory, permanent.

> Note that, if these were permanent effects, the impact of a rise in competitiveness on price setting would enable firms to set a higher mark-up on costs and therefore to improve permanently their profit share, ceteris paribus. Equally, a permanent effect of competitiveness on wage-setting implies that workers are able to offer real wage resistance indefinitely. Neither is perhaps very plausible, so we may suppose that, in the end, these effects disappear. However, as we have already seen, real wage resistance effects may influence unemployment *for at least a decade*, so investigating their 'equilibrium' consequences is an appropriate strategy.
>
> (LNJ, p.386, our emphasis)

A decade is of course a long time in the history of a household, worker, firm or economy. In the view of Sargent (1995) the positive effects of investment on employment can be stretched somewhat to cover the 'medium-run' over the years of the 'Golden Age' of the 1950s and 1960s. Sargent shows that in this period, the impact of investment on productivity growth consistently ran ahead of the real wage aspirations of the work-force and its union representatives. In Sargent's view the favourable conditions for an investment policy to work (including collective bargaining) might have shrunk somewhat over time, but there was no case for the 'super-pessimism' implied in LNJ.

LNJ do in fact have another argument of sorts to support the irrelevance of productivity variables for equilibrium unemployment. If unemployment is mean-reverting in the long run they claim that it cannot be determined by productivity variables. But as unemployment itself is a malleable concept that changes over time it can indeed be affected by productivity (Hatton 2007; see also Ball and Moffet 2001). In any event many of the structural variables argued by LNJ to affect the NAIRU are themselves likely to be non-stationary.

A third criticism of the claim that capital investment and other productivity enhancing steps have no effect on unemployment takes issue with the technical specification of the model, in particular the production function (Rowthorn 1999a, 1999b, 2000). The LNJ model assumes a production function – linking output to inputs – under which the share of labour remains constant when the capital intensity varies.[9] With other production functions, where the labour share is free to vary, there is scope for productivity changes caused by higher capital intensity to contain unemployment. In this more general model, labour takes a larger share of output as capital intensity rises (the elasticity of substitution is less than one). The clever – perhaps too clever – argument here is that rising labour shares offer a mechanism for containing inflation. Given a rising labour share, employers should resist wage demands to a greater extent because of its greater effect on profit; this effectively

---

[9] Technically the production function is 'Cobb-Douglas' and the 'elasticity of substitution' equals unity in this. The share of labour is an important variable in the LNJ model (see Table 2.1) because it helps to determine the wage mark-up which is given by a weighted sum of the elasticity of the real wage with respect to employment (ε_n) and with respect to profit (ε_π). Even if the former elasticity is zero because workers do not bargain over employment, the labour share clearly affects ε_π since an incremental change in wages with a higher labour share will impact more on profits.

lowers the unemployment that the Central Bank will have to sanction so as to control wage pressure.[10]

The above three critiques call into question the LNJ dismissal of policy variables other than structural labour market ones. However these arguments, while of some interest from a technical point of view, may be overly detailed in that they do not really engage with what the model – and indeed the whole approach – was attempting to capture. The technical features of the LNJ model perform the function of demonstrating to those who care about such things that it is possible to translate an argument for labour market reform into the language of economics. But perhaps the specifications of the model were never intended to be taken that seriously. Rather, the project was to design policy based on *political economy* considerations, while leaving just a short-term influence for demand management.

Indeed the exact details of the economic model are of so little concern to LNJ that they are prepared to concede even the most central points. In comments that are both revealing and puzzling they explain that the justification for capital irrelevance implied by the production function is only for illustration – the real assumptions come from a set of prior stylized facts. Thus in comments written in advance of the Rowthorn critique, LNJ affirm their standard view that under Cobb Douglas assumptions, unemployment in the long run is independent of capital accumulation and technical progress. But they do not insist on the underlying assumption, suggesting instead that 'Indeed *the same is true without Cobb Douglas* ... if the real rate of profit and relative factor shares remain stable' (p.105, our emphasis).

LNJ then make the interesting claim that in the 'very long run' there is a required rate of return on capital so that real product wages are determined by this and the degree of product market competition. Thus the 'ratio of distributive shares is fixed *regardless* of the production function' (emphasis in original). The implication would appear to be that shares are determined by political economy considerations – rather as if the whole of Table 2.1 were truncated to begin at level 1. This helps

---

[10] Rowthorn's point is that capital intensity operates as a roundabout form of incomes policy but you have to be a strong believer in the bargaining model (it may not work for efficiency wages) and in the link from labour intensity to employer wage resistance to make this a centre-piece of theory. Empirically there is no evidence that the labour share rises with capital investment: indeed the reverse seems to be true in contradiction of both LNJ and Rowthorn (Driver and Munoz 2010).

us to understand better the argument they are making – it clearly does not depend on the exact technical specification of the battle of mark-up equations.

Nevertheless the political economy approach raises a new problem. The assumption of constant distributive shares might have been a stylized fact up to the 1970s (as argued by Kaldor 1961) but it proved more stylized than fact over the long run as was evident by the time that the LNJ model gained popularity. From the Penn Tables for the period 1950 through 1990, when LNJ was published, the labour share for a number of important countries – including the UK – appears to be integrated of order one. This suggests that the share had not been reflecting a unitary elasticity of substitution or that other influences on the labour share have been in play (Blanchard 1997). More recent data confirms this pattern. Indeed the rate of profit and the share of profit have been rising in capitalist economies for the last thirty years and certainly since the publication of LNJ (1991). Also surprising is the reference to a constant required rate of return. To some extent this could be regarded as fixed globally under international capital mobility that prevailed from the 1980s. Nevertheless cross country differences in required rates of return exist and are often large. The same is true for the cost of capital which varies considerably over time and across countries. Indeed so great was the US disparity with Japan in this regard that the US government sent up a special commission to examine the reasons for this in the early 1990s. The LNJ model excluded capital investment and technology using explanations that can only be regarded as odd and at variance with the facts on the labour share, as is clear from Figure 2.3.

What is evident from all this is that the LNJ model, far from being flawed by this or that technical assumption, was addressing the problem of unemployment from a political economy perspective, with a strong prior presumption that labour market reform was the answer. But this only deepens the puzzle as to what thought process lay behind the dismissal of any importance for *capital investment and other supply-side issues.*[11]

---

[11] Empirical evidence from a number of sources indicates a link between capital accumulation and employment (Rowthorn 1995; Glyn 1998). One route is via market share effects in export markets, with unemployment responding to the relative rates of capital accumulation (Malley and Moutsos 2001; Carlin et al 2001). Direct testing of the LNJ model without capital accumulation effects also shows it to have poor explanatory power (O'Shaughnessy 2001).

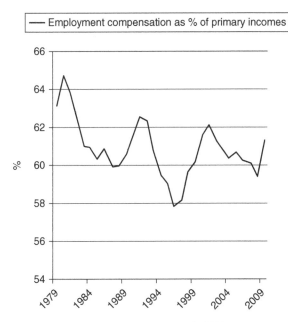

Figure 2.3 Labour share of national income 1979–2009
Source: ONS 2010 Blue Book.

2.4 No market failure – no role for investment policy

It is perhaps understandable that in the early 1980s, economists worried about excessive capital intensity, relative to the growing army of unemployed. Rising import prices appeared to require a lower feasible real wage, so that capital intensity – at least for the whole economy – would need to fall rather than rise. Disequilibrium unemployment would thus last as long as it took to redeploy or retire capital and to reduce real wages. Of course, since it is not easy to reduce capital intensity, future employment would be constrained by the capital expansion required to sustain labour intensive production. Creating capacity was a problem with no easy solution because it required a precondition of improved profitability and confidence. The best that could be hoped for then was to contain real wage growth which would have the effect of reversing capital-labour substitution and of course *reducing* labour productivity (Dreze and Bean 1990, p.60). Policy makers were reluctant however to commit to such a strategy as it would probably have required planning a dual-sector approach with labour intensive expansion in some sectors complementing a technological push in others so that economic dynamism could be sustained. While such an approach was considered under the National Economic Development Office 'New Jobs Exercise' in the 1980s, it did not progress very far.

In any event, the notion of excessive UK capital intensity must be seen in relative terms. The proportionate growth of capital per worker from the 1970s to the 1980s was no greater in the UK than in Germany or the US while, at the same time, the level of capital stock per worker in the UK was about two-thirds that of the US and half that of Germany and Japan at the end of the 1980s (Bond and Jenkinson 1996). Across Europe the notion of unemployment resulting from too high a level of capital intensity became increasingly untenable during the 1980s. The utilization of capital increased along with profitability at the same time as unemployment greatly increased. This was the issue addressed in a thoughtful piece by Charles Bean (1989). Bean recognized that investment had been depressed in the 1980s not just in the UK but in Europe generally and that it would have to rise by more than 20 per cent (to the rates characteristic of the early 1970s) to facilitate a reduction in unemployment. Nevertheless his conclusion was that:

> [T]he required resurgence in investment will arise automatically, so that capacity shortages are likely to be a temporary phenomenon at worst. The real obstacles to a rapid return to full employment lie elsewhere, *particularly in the labour market*. The presence of such transient capacity shortages during any sustained recovery does not, by itself, justify policy measures discriminating in favour of investment, for *there is no obvious market failure involved*. (our emphasis)

Bean's argument on the automatic responsiveness of capital investment and the lack of any associated market failure is one of the clearest indications of the mind-set that gripped policymakers, especially in the UK, not just at that time, but for a long while thereafter. What happened to investment under this policy of benign neglect?

Five years after Bean's optimistic piece, the Bank of England conducted an informal review that suggested firms were being over-cautious in their investment plans – effectively their required rates of return remained higher than would be expected from economic calculation alone. The report (Wardlow 1994) went on to note that growth in investment had played only a small part in the recovery. Far from investment rates returning to the levels of the early 1970s, they did not even match the upturn after the severe 1980s recession. Among the explanations discussed by the Bank were that that firms worried about sustainability in demand, debt and their financial position.[12] As ever, the tone was diplomatic. The fact that companies were, even by the mid-1990s, maintaining excessive required nominal returns in the face of lower inflation posed a risk – but only a hypothetical one. The appropriate strategy was to maintain course and to press on with the labour-reform, low inflation agenda: 'A further period of monetary stability may, however, be needed before a more fundamental adjustment in [investment] behaviour becomes widespread' (p.254).

As time went on however, some alarm bells began to sound over the neglect of capital investment. Barker (1999), by then a member of the Bank's Monetary Policy Committee but previously chief economic adviser at the CBI, looked back on the 1990s and concluded that concern over lower levels of private investment in the early 1990s had 'fallen on stony ground in government circles' (p.301). And when the Cabinet Office issued a tendentious paper in 1996 explicitly defending the UK investment record, it was responded to in a careful rebuttal by Oxford economists (Bond and Jenkinson 1996).[13] By 2001, the Department of Trade and Industry had reinstated the theme that UK investment levels per worker were low relative to competitors but noted early signs that 'greater macro-stability and growing confidence were beginning to reverse this' (DTI 2001, p.37).

The next few years generated discourses on innovation, the new economy and the importance of technology – issues that we review in detail in Chapter 5. But little of substance was done to address the perennial under-investment in capital and R&D. As time went on it became increasingly clear that UK private investment was indeed stuck in a cautious mode that threatened growth prospects. The Deputy Governor of the Bank of England addressed the 'puzzle of UK business investment' in a major speech at the end of 2006. As he ruefully acknowledged, business investment had by then suffered three episodes of a triumph of hope over experience – the early 1980s, the early 1990s and the end of the century dot-com retrenchment. The puzzle that formed the title of the lecture (Gieve 2006) was

---

[12] An interesting addition to the list was the view that low inflation was constraining investment as it did not allow much flexibility to widen margins to reflect product quality. The latter explanation was to be 'borne in mind' but 'needs to be refuted'.
[13] The DTI paper suggested that intangibles and service industries were increasingly important, that utilization had increased in manufacturing necessitating lower investment and that UK business investment (a difficult category to standardize across countries) was a higher share than for some competitors.

how could such propitious circumstances – a three-decade reduction in macroeconomic volatility, an historically high ratio of financial surplus to GDP, and unprecedented low borrowing costs – have ended up with the lowest whole-economy investment rate since the 1960s?

The culprit could perhaps be that a higher required return in the UK had choked off investment, but Gieve admitted that he remained puzzled how this could be compatible with globalized markets, where the government remained committed to stable and low inflation rates. The thinking here was entirely compatible with the LNJ view of stable required return and with Bean's observation of 'no obvious market failure'. As had by now become a ritual in such critiques, optimism lay in the latest quarterly indicators. Could this cyclical upturn 'be the start of a long term increase?' Gieve asked of the current year's first half investment statistics, just a year and a half before the financial crash extinguished such hopes with what the Bank itself described as an 'unprecedented decline in business investment' (Benito et al 2010).

The emphasis on labour market reform to the neglect of other issues had detrimental effects on the UK economy for a surprisingly long period of time. A major neglect in the early period was any consideration of structural unemployment caused by the mismatch between unemployment and vacancies across skills and regions, which required targeted investment in skills and capital. Structural unemployment was regarded as an inconvenient distraction from making the NAIRU case and was dismissed on the flimsiest of evidence that would be challenged only gradually (Wood 1988; Manacorda and Petrongolo 1999; Webster 2000; Rowthorn 2000).

Some supporters of the NAIRU approach argue that it brought down the levels of British unemployment. This is debatable. While some forms of labour flexibility such as part-time work may have increased job prospects for many in the UK in contrast to more rigid approaches in much of Europe, it is not clear that this had anything to do with the NAIRU, which remains a contentious approach. Nor is it clear that the UK labour market, where over a million workers are now employed in call-centres, is even analysable within that model. As for the statistics of unemployment, it is perhaps more relevant in the British case to focus on labour activity rates, given the drive in the 1990s to get unemployment off the books and onto the sick register (Webster 2000). Here the story is of very little change over thirty years of labour market reforms.

From the late 1990s, the rhetoric but not the reality of economic policymaking changed with increasing reference to non-labour supply-side issues such as technology and innovation. But the previous overarching policy was never seriously questioned. In 2002 one of its architects wrote in *The Guardian* newspaper 'I'm pretty happy with what we said then. Policymakers think along the lines we set down. They certainly do here [Bank of England]. They do in the Treasury'.[14] He was surely not wrong then and might still be right were it to be repeated today. The evidence however is increasingly pointing to an alternative view. Stockhammer and Klar (2011) confirm with a panel of OECD countries that it is capital accumulation rather than labour market institutions that best explains the variation in unemployment.

2.5 Conclusions

The British version of the NAIRU model is a triumph of injecting a prior partial worldview into a seemingly general model that can be used to illustrate a chosen policy. All the better that the policy fitted in with prevailing ideology. It would be too much to claim that the theory has silenced discussion on important matters such as investment led growth but it has certainly diverted attention away from such alternatives.

---

14 Stephen Nickell, *The Guardian* 26 January 2002.

3
The Question of International Competitiveness

3.1 Introduction

The economic constraint that has preoccupied policymakers in recent decades has been that of wage and price inflation. The policy response – structural reform of labour markets and monetary policy rules – is credited with giving rise to the 'great moderation', a reduced volatility of output and price inflation. The success of this approach was accepted by many until the great financial crash, though not everyone was entirely sure. As the head of the US Federal Reserve explained (Bernanke 2004): 'if the Great Moderation was largely the result of good luck rather than a more stable economy or better policies, then we have no particular reason to expect the relatively benign economic environment of the past twenty years to continue'. Just so – looking back, good luck, including the effects of cheap imports from China and elsewhere, does seem a strong contender, but even without such retrospective vision, the great moderation needed to be questioned; success in reducing volatility and inflation was bought at the expense of a falling labour share, more severe recessions and increased inequality which implies new problems.

We explained in Chapter 2 how inflation came to be seen as *the* constraint on growth, preventing the Central Bank from taking a more accommodating stance. Since wage costs are, apart from external influences, the main component of inflation, this approach directs policy attention to labour market reform. So the labour share suffers in the pursuit of growth.[1] What is new about this approach?

---

[1] Melliss and Webb (1997) comment that worker insecurity has increased over the years and insofar as it reflects longer-run factors and institutional changes it will 'exert downward pressure on the NAIRU' (p.25).

In one sense there is nothing new – it is a continuation of what went on before the NAIRU approach was invented. All economies face constraints and, in the case of the UK, the main constraint up to the 1980s appeared to be the balance of payments. Britain could not grow faster than its exports could finance the imports that were needed for consumption and the requirements of industry. If exports were not growing rapidly enough, the constraint could be met, under fixed exchange rates, only by reducing the import bill, the main means of which was to reduce aggregate demand. Under flexible exchange rates a successful devaluation requires lower real wages to relieve the balance of payments constraint.

It may seem from the foregoing that the same policy answer was available for the case of a balance of payments constraint as for that of an inflation constraint: a reduction in the real wage. But in fact this is not how the balance of payments constraint was always regarded. National competitiveness has often been seen as a broader issue than how cheaply you could pay your workforce (Oughton 1997).

As explained in a US policy document responding to a competitive threat from Japanese firms:

> Competitiveness for a nation is the degree to which it can, under free and fair market conditions, produce goods and services that meet the test of international markets while simultaneously maintaining and expanding the real income of its citizens.
>
> (US Presidential Commission on Industrial
> Competitiveness (1985), Vol. II p.7)

By the early 1990s, even the OECD had begun to express itself in these terms, defining the 'structural competitiveness' of a country with reference to technology and systems of innovation as consisting of:

> R&D and of successful appropriation of external technologies ... [It is] ... more than a simple sum of the collective or 'average' competitiveness its firms; there are many ways in which the features and performance of a domestic economy, viewed as an entity with characteristics of its own, will affect, in turn, the competitiveness of firms.
>
> (OECD 1992, p.243)

Viewed in this way, as we argue below, competitiveness provides a useful lens for a much wider policy debate, as indeed it had in an earlier era, which we now consider.

3.2   National competitiveness in the era of balance of payments constraints

National competitiveness is too often seen in terms of wage restraint rather than productivity growth in establishing the 'real exchange rate'. A broader definition takes account of factors other than relative wage growth, including quality enhancement and 'non-price competitiveness' stemming from skill upgrading, technology, capital accumulation and the coordination of firms' activities.

Up to the early 1980s, competitiveness policy in Britain was to some extent seen in this way, as cooperative and concerned with much more than wage restraint. Institutions such as the National Economic Development Office (NEDO) promoted joint employer–labour initiatives to improve export performance and national competitiveness. Technology programmes organized around sectors or international collaborations supported by the state were seen as key to ensuring that the private sector would join in. Policymakers had not yet given up on the notion of competitiveness based on the idea that 'we were all in this together' and that a consensus view was important.

The era of balance of payments constraints was thus characterized by policy responses more varied and nuanced than in the more recent inflation constraint period, which has been dominated by rules-based monetary policy and by labour market reform. The earlier period had an emphasis on competitiveness as a shared national project, which disappeared from the UK agenda (and the textbooks) sometime after the 1980s.

The background to the pre-1980s view that rectifying payments deficits may not always require a reduction in the real wage, may be found in the literature of the time. Kaldor (1978) had noted that the rising export share of Germany and Japan was associated with currency revaluation and apparently *rising* relative unit labour costs – later dubbed 'Kaldor's paradox' by Fagerberg (1988). In a formal model, Thirlwall (1979) assumed that exchange rate variations in the long run more or less cancelled out differential wage and productivity growth, so that the growth of an economy's imports and exports depended only upon two key *income* elasticities, the elasticity of demand for imports with respect to domestic income (m) and the elasticity of demand for exports with respect to world income (e). If (assuming initial balance) an economy's trade balance is neither to improve nor deteriorate, then it follows that the growth of imports should equal that of its exports:

$$m\ \Delta Y_d/Y_d = e\ \Delta Y_w\ /\ Y_w \quad \text{where } Y_d = \text{domestic income,}$$
$$Y_w = \text{world income}$$

If this equation is satisfied then the growth of domestic output or income is fixed as a proportion of world demand by e/m. If for example, $m = 0.9$ but $e = 0.45$, then an economy may grow only one half as fast as the rest of the world without its current balance of payments deteriorating. In fact these numbers are not just hypothetical since they correspond to early econometric estimates of UK income elasticities in trade for the period 1951–66 (Houthakker and Magee 1969). Thirlwall himself used such an approach to explain cross-country differences in growth rates (see Thirlwall 1979 and Fagerberg 1996).

As an explanation of differing growth rates the idea of a balance of payments constraint worked at least for the decades up to the 1980s and was reincarnated by Krugman as the '45 degree rule' (Krugman 1989). When combined with the nature of the stop-go cycle discussed in Chapter 1, it provides a useful starting point for explaining Britain's poor growth performance in this period. But while the correlation between economic growth and trade elasticities is suggestive, the direction of causation is far from clear and the typically high income elasticities for imports reported for Britain may well be related to insufficient investment in both physical capacity and skills (see for example Temple and Urga 1997). Nor does the model extend readily to more recent periods. No doubt deregulation of international capital flows has been an important factor, where, as discussed in Chapter 6, Britain has been able to finance considerable payments deficits in the market era (post-1979). Of importance too, has been specific favourable conditions for the trade balance from the late 1990s, including terms of trade and net investment income that are unlikely to be durable (Coutts et al 2007).

More recent evidence on income elasticities is presented in Hooper et al (2000) using data on all merchandise trade up to 1994. They find that while the income elasticity of demand for UK exports is much higher (at 1.1) than the Houthakker-Magee study, the import elasticity had also grown to 2.2, the highest of the G7, leaving the ratio of the elasticities approximately unchanged compared to the earlier estimates. But the question remains as to what determines *e* and *m*? Both Kaldor and Thirlwall had suggested that they reflected underlying 'non-price' competitiveness – factors that are likely to be shaped by technological change that influence product development. Other influences include the reliability of service and support, delivery time and the ability to supply. Swann (1998) provides a general discussion of the role of quality and competitiveness with a review of some of the empirical evidence for Britain.

The results in Hooper et al also show that the estimated *price* elasticities are also much higher for UK exports than for other members of the G7 (−1.6 for the UK and −0.3 for Germany), suggesting that UK exporters may have continued to cluster in price sensitive market segments, a finding recently confirmed by Barrell and Pomerantz (2007). This process may have been reinforced by phases of devaluation of sterling when a lower exchange rate seems to encourage entry in lower quality, price sensitive market segments (Brech and Stout 1981). While policymakers who trusted to market forces may have been happy to allow the balance of price-sensitive and non-price-sensitive sectors to adjust of its own accord, much theoretical work in modern trade analysis supports a more interventionist approach towards the product mix.

3.3   Technological competitiveness

Industrial leadership in technology may be thought of as establishing a productivity advantage in a number of 'progressive' industries or segments within industries, in a way that allows for growth in export markets without a fall in the wage share. As suggested by Fagerberg (1988) in his seminal article on international competitiveness, the requirements are threefold:

- First, there is the technological capacity to generate innovation.
- Second, there is the ability to 'catch-up' when domestic firms are operating away from the technological frontier.
- Third, each economy needs to establish the physical capacity to embody many of the innovations and sustain reliable supply.

There are now many studies which have sought to examine trade shares using an augmented export demand equation which includes some measure of relative technological capability and proxies for the other two factors. In principle perhaps, relative technological capability should be simply reflected in unit costs, but it appears that in practice there is an independent explanatory role for technology where that can be measured. The literature has tended to use R&D and patent counts in order to supplement the export demand equation. Business expenditure on R&D is the most common indicator and it has at least been subject to a process of international standardization in the Frascati Manual (OECD 2002).[2]

Fagerberg's original paper estimated the importance of each of these three factors outlined above for total export market shares – in addition to the impact of relative unit labour costs. Using a sample based upon whole economy data for 15 industrial countries for the period 1960–83, his measures of technology use both civil R&D and external patent applications to provide proxies for the growth of technological activities. Fagerberg's results show how the model can account for Kaldor's paradox by decomposing the predicted change in market share for the UK, US (big losers in market share) and Japan (the pre-eminent gainer) for the same period as Kaldor's original investigation (1961–73). In the multivariate framework, the expected sign on relative unit labour costs is correct, but the impact is swamped by variables representing technological and physical capacity. Fagerberg's estimates suggest that by far the largest contribution to changes in the share of exports was a low investment share of GDP, with in the case of Britain the growth of technological capabilities and the potential for catch-up acting (slightly) in the opposite direction.

Empirical exercises relevant to the UK include Greenhalgh (1990); Buxton et al (1991); Greenhalgh et al (1994); Swann et al (1996); Carlin et al (2001); Barrell and Pomerantz (2007). The study by Carlin et al is directly relevant to the thesis being developed in this book in providing

---

[2] The measure tends to reflect only expenditures taking place with the formal R&D departments of large corporations and so ignores the widely acknowledged contribution of smaller firms and much of incremental innovative steps in industries such as mechanical engineering. A more serious defect is that it tells us little about its direction – is it aimed at product innovation or process innovation – or is it aimed more modestly at imitation, reflecting the 'two faces' of R&D (Cohen and Levinthal 1989). Furthermore there are issues relating to whether it is privately and publicly financed especially where the demand is defence-related. Output-based measures of innovation include intellectual property, usually captured by patent counts. Patent use varies considerably across industries and there is a highly skewed distribution in their value. It is now common to weight the raw patent count by citations or to use international patents. Other measures of technological capacity include data on industrial standards – documents specifying technical characteristics relating to products and processes – as well as more direct survey-based measures of innovation.

a direct comparison of measures of investment, R&D and patents as explanatory variables in a disaggregated study of OECD export market shares. They find that whereas shares of R&D and patents have little or even perverse explanatory power, the investment share is significant, suggesting that the technology variables tend to act through investment, or at any rate are not independent of it. This seems consistent with the argument that it is the diffusion of innovation, particularly that embodied in ICT equipment, that is of most relevance (Hughes 2008). Of course it is important to recognize the variable manner in which capital investment embodies innovativeness (Cantwell 2005) and some argue that the function of capital has largely been displaced by R&D for countries at the frontier (Aghion 2006). Useful information on this is provided for Italian industry by Evangelista (1999) in an extension of previous work on technological classification by Pavitt. The results suggest that innovativeness is embodied to a much greater extent than previously thought, corresponding to about two-thirds of industrial output, though with some advanced sectors primarily based on disembodied knowledge capital (p.177).

3.4   The competitive contribution of manufacturing

Any attempt to bring about an 'investment led' expansion – which we argue for in this book – needs to be considered in relation to the exports needed to finance it. Otherwise it would likely lead to a deteriorating external position as other consumption components of demand increase and would imply inflationary tendencies. While FDI investment might obviate this dependence on exports, we are talking here about an investment exercise that is aimed at generating externalities – an opportunity that inward investors may not see as their priority.

The capacity to export depends to a large extent on manufacturing industry. As Figure 3.1 makes clear, manufacturing exports make up over half of the total (55 per cent out of a total for all exports of goods and services of £371 billion in 2007). This is rather larger than the combined exports of sectors such as banking and finance (£46 billion), professional and business services (£53 billion) and insurance (£4 billion). However as Figure 3.1 also shows, manufactured products have sharply declined as a share of total exports, by value from 69 per cent to 55 per cent over the period 1992–2007 (roughly the period of expansion in the economy). Over this period, the growth in service exports in certain areas has been quite dynamic (BIS 2010a; Coutts et al 2007). Nevertheless manufacturing exports will in the future have to take a larger share if, as expected, the finance and related sectors shrink and other trends such as energy

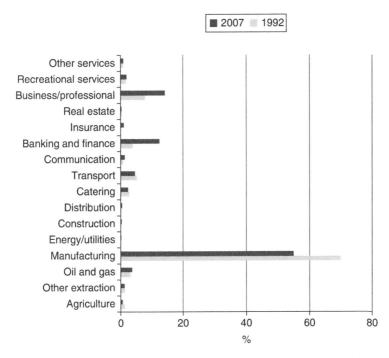

Figure 3.1 Distribution of UK exports of goods and services in 1992 and 2007
Source: ONS Supply–Use Tables.

imports turn less favourable). Furthermore net investment income has been buoyant because of the composition of overseas assets with the foreign capital stock paying twice as much as assets held in the UK by foreigners; this is however not a stable feature of the balance of payments and can change suddenly (Rowthorn 2009).

A turnaround in manufacturing exports of this magnitude is difficult, given the structural changes that have occurred. From the early 1990s, manufacturing output grew by a paltry amount, less than 1 per cent per annum, despite the fact that 1992 was in a period of recession, and 2007 represented the peak of the boom. This was the lowest growth among 18 industrial economies.[3]

---

[3] According to US Bureau of Labor Statistics on manufacturing. Note that since the trade in UK manufactured goods is approximately in balance, there may be potential for import substitution, although the increased exports themselves will make intensive use of imports.

A focus on manufacturing may be justified on several other grounds than its capacity to export. Of particular significance is the likely regional spread of the jobs that may be created, and also the favourable distribution of incomes that may result (see for example Rose (2007) who also notes the potential for extended development of industrial clusters when strategic commitment by government is strong as exemplified by the Toulouse aerospace cluster). These beneficial outcomes arise in proportion to the scale of the manufacturing sector so that this quite reasonably becomes a policy target. Manufacturing plays a special role in advanced learning and in particular it conducts the lion's share of business expenditure on R&D (BERD). Figure 3.2 shows that manufacturing maintained its

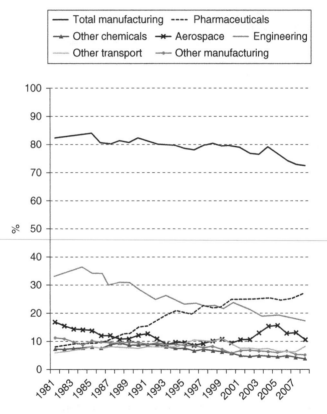

Figure 3.2 Manufacturing Shares of Total Business Expenditure on Research and Development in UK 1981–2008
Source: ONS; figures for 1982, 1984 interpolated.

share of total BERD for much of the period since 1981 though it fell quite sharply in the run-up to the financial crash.

Figure 3.2 also indicates the extent to which R&D composition has changed over what we have been calling the market era. One of the important and most familiar stories here is the substantial rise of pharmaceuticals R&D. Pharmaceuticals accounted for less than 10 per cent of *total* BERD in the early 1980s (although still higher than the rest of the chemical sector), but by the end of the period had climbed to over one-third of manufacturing R&D and over a quarter of all business R&D. Less well known has been the trend fall in the share of the engineering sectors of the economy, which constituted over one-third of total R&D in the early 1980s, but less than 20 per cent today, reflecting a trend fall of just under 1 per cent each year in real terms from the early 1980s.[4] This reorientation across sectors may represent an effect whereby the UK comes to specialize more in codifiable innovations, as reviewed in Chapter 4. Arguably upstream sectors such as engineering create more vertical spillovers, between producers and users, than do other sectors such as pharmaceuticals and chemicals, though of course it is hard to value the distinct types of spillovers involved in each case. Intersectoral flows of innovations that distinguish between innovations 'used' and innovations 'produced' show that spillover effects on UK manufacturing industries tend to originate from innovations generated by the engineering industry (Robson et al 1988; Geroski 1994). The result here, obtained from an analysis of the Science Policy Research Unit (SPRU) database on major innovations is shown in Figure 3.3 (upper panel). A similar result using a different methodology was obtained for later data (Driver et al 2006). The most plausible explanation is that technology often tends to be embodied in capital investment, so that: 'major flows of knowledge embodied in specific products seem to flow between producers and users of specific innovations (particularly those originating in Engineering)' (Geroski 1994, p.105).

But these kinds of vertical spillover are not necessarily automatic. Collaboration along the supply chain is an important feature of competitiveness that often requires an effective means of communication

---

[4] In *nominal* terms, engineering R&D (which includes non-electrical, electrical and electronic machinery and equipment, as well as instruments) grew by just 2.9 per cent per annum between 1981 and 2008 as against over 10 per cent for pharmaceuticals. The usual price index used to deflate R&D spending is the GDP deflator, which grew by 3.8 per cent per annum over the same period.

(a)

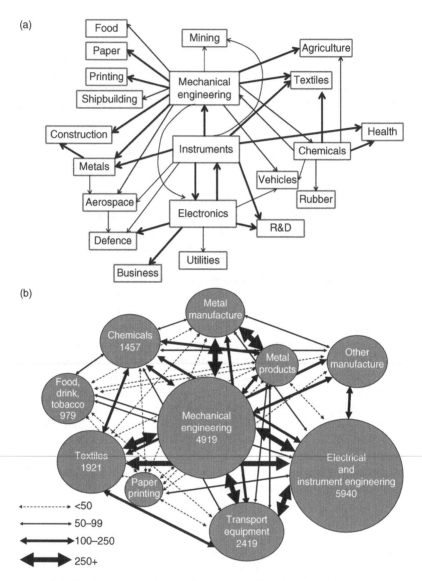

(b)

Figure 3.3 The Inter-sectoral flow of innovations based on the SPRU dataset
Sources: (a) Geroski (1994) by permission of Oxford University Press.

between user and producer. This makes the role of industrial standards particularly important.[5] Standards mediate between codified repositories of knowledge (metrological knowledge for example) and exploitation and application of that knowledge via proprietary technology. Standard setting gives firms the confidence to invest for example through agreed procedures for validating claims about product characteristics that reduce transaction costs and uncertainty.

Following Swann et al (1996) a number of studies have used 'counts' of industrial standards – documents created through a consensual process and which detail technical specifications of products, processes and so on – and found that they can explain both trade flows (Choudhary et al, 2012) and productivity performance (DTI 2005). Using the PERINORM database it is possible to identify documented standards which appear to be relevant to more than one industry, sharing thereby a means of communication. In Figure 3.3(a) we once again see the role of engineering as a hub for learning processes, this time within manufacturing. The size of the arrows indicates the number of standards documents linking the different sectors while the size of the bubbles corresponds (very roughly) to the total number of standards relevant to a sector. The role of engineering (mechanical, and electrical and electronic instruments) in *both* these regards is clear. Both diagrams in Figure 3.3 show a similar structure of effects. The evidence here is consistent with that from repeated UK Innovation Surveys which indicate the importance of both equipment suppliers and technical standards for innovation.[6]

The arguments developed above suggest that the size of the manufacturing sector is fundamental for national competitiveness. The size of manufacturing depends upon both exports and the demand for manufactures arising from domestic investment and consumption, which stimulates both imports as well as domestic production.

---

[5] Today public (so called de jure) standards now mainly come from international institutions, and are especially important as an element of EU harmonization. The size of demand still matters for Britain's decisions as to whether it is worthwhile participating in the standard setting process. Standards have fixed costs attached to their development, once again suggesting that the size of manufacturing matters.

[6] In the 2009 survey, outside sources of information internal to the enterprise, users and suppliers (of equipment, materials or software) were considered more important than competitors and 'other' sources (such as external R&D or universities). Of these others, 'technical industry or service standards' were rated the most important.

For exports it can be argued that the decline relative to comparative countries that characterized the pre-1979 period, has been arrested. As Figure 3.4(a) indicates, Britain's share of OECD (rather than world) manufacturing exports, which had been falling continuously in the post-war period, had stabilized by the middle 1980s. Moreover Figure 3.4(b) shows that the pattern of trade is broadly 'progressive', with shares being higher than for aggregate manufacturing in R&D intensive industries (those defined by the OECD as being 'high tech') and lower in the 'low tech' industries. Looking at net exports in the lower diagram 3.4(c) (the export–import ratio) also shows a similar pattern, although note that the ratio of total manufacturing exports to imports fell below one in the 1970s and has remained there ever since. But there is a twist. An important reason for a slower growth of manufactured imports is the slow growth of manufacturing itself, since the latter is of course an important user of manufacturing imports. The good news from the export–import ratio therefore partly reflects the lack of growth of manufacturing output.

The apparent strengthening of UK trade performance has not however been reflected in any significant growth of the aggregate size of manufacturing, as measured by output. Here we compare the growth performance of manufacturing over the two cycles that we identified in Chapter 1. We also infer some changes in the dynamism of manufacturing growth by looking at the extent to which productivity performance feeds into growth in a virtuous cycle.

In Figure 3.5(a) we show a scatter plot of output growth (value added at constant prices) between both 1979–90 and 1990–2007 across 31 UK manufacturing industries, taken from the EU KLEMS database. Aggregate manufacturing output growth is recorded in these data as being 0.9 per cent per annum in the earlier period, and actually *slowing* to 0.6 per cent over the later period. This slower growth in manufacturing in the latter period appears to be fairly universal across the industries with only a small proportion of those industries recording measurably higher growth in the later post-Thatcher period. Moreover the data does not suggest any strong competitive selection effect operating across industries, international or otherwise, with the inter-quartile range in the growth rate data narrowing considerably (from 3.8 percentage points to 2.4).

To understand better what is happening, we investigate the relationship between output growth and labour productivity growth (as measured per hour worked) across industries. This is shown as a scatter diagram for the earlier period in Figure 3.5(b) and for the later period in Figure 3.5(c). In the earlier period, despite the clear outliers (tobacco and 'other

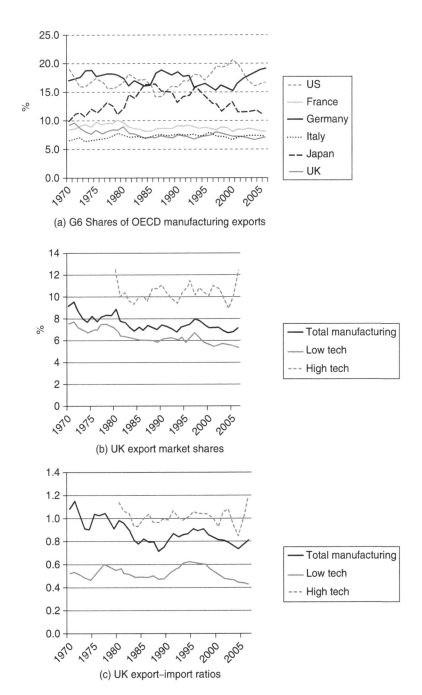

Figure 3.4 UK shares of world trade and export-import ratios
Source: OECD 2010.

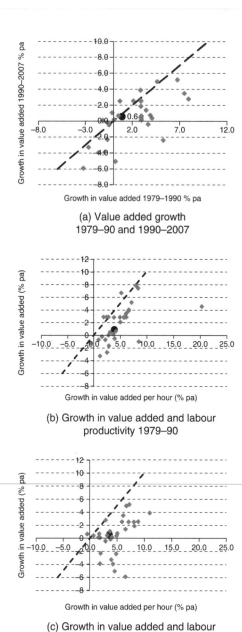

Figure 3.5 Value added and labour productivity growth in UK manufacturing 1979–90 and 1990–2007

Source: EU KLEMS Growth and Productivity Accounts: November 2009 Release, updated March 2011.

instruments'), the scatter shows a positive association. This relationship appears to have broken down in Figure 3.5(c), with a large number of industries combining substantial productivity growth and negative output growth. There are of course multiple interpretations for what is clearly a two-way relationship, but substantial productivity growth in the absence of output growth suggests that one part of the story is that investment opportunities made possible by the productivity growth itself are not being taken up, for reasons to be explored in the remainder of the book. This possibility is entirely consistent with that of increasingly cautious investment behaviour at the level of the economy as a whole, to which we drew attention in Chapter 1. For manufacturing, substantial variations in real exchange rates may have exacerbated the problem. In any event, understanding the fact of slow and increasingly non-existent output growth in manufacturing is important if manufacturing is to fulfil the function that many commentators now desire.

3.5 Conclusions

The debate on national competitiveness is important because it allows us to move away from abstractions about the market to consider industrial policy and the effects of such policies on different sections of society. In much mainstream economics, competitiveness is conceived as just a question of an appropriately defined 'real exchange rate'. This approach ignores the potential for a more progressive debate. While unit labour costs that make up the competitiveness indicator can be contained either by lower labour costs or by higher productivity the latter is clearly to be preferred where distributional concerns and whole economy issues are to be considered. In addition productivity improvements not focussed on cost also count. Attention must therefore be paid to strategic issues of improving performance in a systems-wide way and of expanding production in areas of high opportunity for coordinated growth. It is impossible to do this without considering the *capacity* and growth of the internationally tradable sector of the economy, where manufacturing, despite its relative shrinkage, continues to offer the greatest potential.

The arguments in this chapter suggest that we should not rely too much on international rankings of competitiveness, such as the World Economic Forum's Global Competitiveness Index (GCI) which assesses country long-run growth prospects. In our view the hold that such indices have on policy tend to stifle progressive debate, through an assumption that appropriate competitive policies can be read off from some world view and that the policies of individual states can and should be subject to external validation by this rulebook. There needs to be a pluralist approach to the design of industrial strategy that is based on deep knowledge of the reform possibilities in particular national contexts, and the advantages and disadvantages of different specific approaches. For example it is unlikely that the analysis of this book that documents the shortcoming and disappointments of the market era would be recognized as valid by such external ratings bodies. In the remaining chapters, we argue that narrowly defined cost competitiveness will not resolve the problems of the unbalanced economy.

4
Capital Investment: A Neglected Issue

4.1 Introduction

The lack of concern for capital investment among UK policymakers is to some extent puzzling because, as noted in Chapter 2, it provided a mainstay of economic beliefs up to the 1980s, and remains important for growth theory. What exactly are many economists objecting to when they criticize the 'exaggerated belief in the importance of promoting investment' (Crafts 1991, p.89)? At one level the argument is hard to follow because there is a clear correlation between investment and other inputs that are indeed thought to be important. According to Crafts himself, any long-run success of 1980s policies was limited, because of the neglect of training and technology solutions 'for which the present (Conservative) government has a distaste' (p.95). But saying this, while dismissing the importance of capital investment, requires a convoluted argument. What does promoting investment mean if not associated acceleration in technology and training? Are firms likely to invest in irreversible expensive equipment without ensuring that it can be well used? Is not one of the obstacles to such investment that workers can be poached after training? And what is technology but a broad form of irreversible investment? The correlations between forms of investment are high. For example, the correlation between training and machinery equipment and software is 0.39 for manufacturing and 0.58 for services (Bulli 2008, Tables 3 and 4). Only 5 per cent of firms invest in training without at the same time acquiring machinery or software, compared with 35 per cent who invest in both (*ibid*, Table 9). The classic article of Finegold and Soskice (1988) on a low-skills equilibrium argued that investment in training would only work if it were paralleled with changes in work practices and technology.

Antipathy to investment-led growth seems to have been based less on substance and more on form. What is feared perhaps is not the investment itself but the interventionism that would be required to bring it about in the UK. Also at issue is the effect of investment on class relations and the distribution of power. Investment is often linked subjectively to corporatism, subsidies and power structures where change is delayed and distributional concerns are privileged over growth.[1] Corporatist arrangements sabotage the 'realization of the gains from technological change' (Crafts 1991, p.82) as the 'new bargaining models' that underlay the NAIRU approach were said to make clear. Oulton (1995) explains that 'if investment is at least partially irreversible, then any agreement today on wages and conditions risks a hold-up problem tomorrow. The union cannot guarantee that it will not attempt to skim off the firm's profit from its planned investment. Knowing this, the firm invests less'. Although such arguments have been disproved by events (Card and Freeman 2004) they may have been influential in downgrading the case for public support for capital investment.

At its core, the objection to an investment-led approach has nothing to do with investment as such but with the social relations that characterize high capital investment. But even if one grants that such a view made some sense at one time for the UK, it can scarcely be said to have any purchase at all in the current context, well after the weakening of organized labour in the 1980s and the bending of political purpose to serving global capital interests and finance (Glyn 2006). The last three decades have indeed seen redistribution toward profit privileged over investment and growth.

Another plank of the anti-investment case is that even if investment were shown to be central to growth, it would nevertheless be unnecessary to pursue proactive policies because capital markets are efficient, thus ensuring an appropriate and automatic response of investment to incentives. While the first argument has at least received some discussion, this second one has largely gone unchallenged outside of specialized circles. In contrast to much of the literature, we take the view that it is *because* capital investment does *not* respond in optimal fashion to market signals that its strategic role has a claim to our attention. It is difficult to make a convincing case for investment simply on its intrinsic properties for example on the grounds that it is 'twice blessed' because of its simultaneous

---

[1] Crafts sees rent-seeking as extending to regional influence 'there was frequently a very strong element of regional policy in support for investment' (p.89). That may be true but the true failure here was one of inept policy design rather than the regional focus.

contribution to supply and demand; most commentators would say that investment-led growth inappropriately substitutes investment for consumption, something that would be true but uninteresting without market failures. We agree here with the economic commentator Samuel Brittan that consumption is just as good at filling a hole in demand as investment, provided that investment is not inhibited in any way, because in that case investment will adjust to any consumption stimulus. However the multiple market failures that characterize capital market investment explain the key role that needs to be accorded to this variable. This contrasts of course with the proposition that only labour markets exhibit failure on account of the features of monopoly and hold-up that characterize labour relations. Such views, while commonplace among economists, clash with modern business thinking which locates success in the hard-to-imitate capabilities that firms build up and on which many of the investment opportunities that arise are predicated. Yet this 'resource-based view' is now the dominant strand in understanding business strategy and it implies that a monopoly of resources is characteristic of all business exchange; economists' pre-occupation with labour markets is misplaced and incorrectly understates the role of firms as ongoing institutions. The real question for capital investment and associated resources is how to plan them in the absence of future markets in illiquid assets and the fact that any self-equilibrating forces are weak or perverse as Keynes recognized when British industrialists of the 1920s and 1930s were showing a similar reluctance to invest as those of today (Keynes 1937, p.115).

Capital markets are characterized by disequilibrium to a greater extent than other markets because they are characterized by a combination of sunk cost and higher uncertainty due to long-lived irreversible assets, where resale prices average around a quarter of the purchase price (Asplund 2000). The resulting complexity results in rules of thumb or heuristic rules, given the difficulty of calculating firms' own optimal responses to shocks in each period, but also in second-guessing the responses of others.[2] Such complexities have rarely featured in mainstream investment models which are characterized by representative agents adjusting smoothly with rational expectations along an infinite horizon path. The poor estimation and forecasting performance of such models has made this approach difficult to sustain and there is now some recognition that investment may require more explicit treatment of how expectations are actually formed (Chirinko 1993; Nickell and

---

[2] Rationality can be imposed by assuming particular forms of conjectural variation as in Spence and Porter (1982) but it is hard to accept such solutions under bounded rationality; focal point solutions may be superior.

Nicolitsas 1966; Mairesse et al 1999). Nevertheless apart perhaps from some work on financial constraints, there has been little appetite to revisit the issues left in abeyance with the dismissal in the 1990s of market failure in capital investment noted in Chapter 2.

Market failure attaching to investment decisions should be obvious from the aftermath of the great financial crisis. Interest rates are, as we write, at historical lows, while firms are hoarding cash and are reluctant to invest. These corporate savings are not like a 'sack of potatoes; savings not immediately taken up to create capital simply vanish in reduced income' (Vickrey 1993). Such features help explain why, in contrast to the ideal of equilibrating markets, the predictions of economic models, and the hopes of economic commentators, British investment responded sluggishly to the economic recoveries of the early 1980s, the 1990s and the current uncertain period of hesitant growth.

4.2   Company decision-making: Routines for investment

There is a strong *a priori* case that economic principles can offer little more than broad guidance to corporate executives or company boards, struggling to assess the merits and risks of particular investments. As any industrialist knows, the information requirements to make investment decisions in real assets are formidable, but disguised by an outward show of 'pretty, polite techniques for a well-panelled boardroom' (Keynes 1937, p.115). In contrast to these complexities, the textbook approach to capital investment appears disarmingly simple. Future net cash flows arising from any project are estimated, and the sum of their discounted value is compared with the initial cost of the project to provide a net present value of future earnings (NPV); an acceptable project is one with positive NPV. For example, a simple project with investment c in year 0 and return π in year one would have a net present value of $-c + \pi/(1+r)$ where r is the discount rate that penalizes later cash flows.[3] As any manager knows, such

---

[3] For the polar opposite case of infinite lived assets depreciating at rate δ, replace the second right-hand term by $\pi/(\delta+r)$, using the assumption that the future cash flows are predictable from the present. Economic purists may argue that 'the right criterion has never been to invest if NPV is positive' (Caballero 1999, p.22). Of course this is technically correct but few 'managerial economics' texts that inform business managers have concerned themselves with the difficulties of an optimal investment path that includes irreversibility constraints. As noted in Abel et al (1996) the NPV rule may be interpretable as correct but it is then very difficult to apply in practice. See the discussion of real options below.

calculations are fiendishly complicated in practice. First the estimation of cash flows, either real or nominal will become increasingly uncertain the longer the horizon, unless the industrial context constrains the outcome – as in regulated industries or where long-term contracts can be negotiated. Otherwise forecasts have to incorporate expectations of others' expectations, which can only be achieved by inventing a consensus.

Economic and accounting practice recognizes the difficulty of predicting long-term outcomes. Beyond a certain horizon it is conventional to approximate the remaining value of the project with a hand-waving formula for the 'termination value' that assumes steady growth. One experienced observer estimated that this termination value frequently accounted for over half of the total project worth and simply tends to amplify any errors in the early years analysis (Christensen et al 2008). Errors in the chosen discount rate can have a dramatic effect on project value but there are serious debates as to how to calculate it. This discount rate is supposed to reflect the alternative use of funds to the provider of finance who assesses the risk of the marginal impact of the project on the overall holdings of the ultimate investor. Known as the capital asset pricing model (CAPM), this approach is controversial because ignoring project-specific or firm-specific risk runs requires stringent assumptions that are not generally valid. The respected finance academic Rene Stulz has concluded that 'firms do not apply modern capital budgeting as it is usually taught in business schools' for very good reasons (Stulz 1999, p.4). Quite sensibly, firms would never accept large volatility for small expected gains if it involves betting the company. In practice, firms tend to finesse formal financial theory and pay at least some attention to 'total risk' rather than just the risk component that affects their owners' portfolio. This is entirely appropriate because a firm close to financial distress finds it hard to enter into contracts or to take advantage of valuable opportunities. In practice however it makes decision-making a matter of judgement rather than strict science.

Despite the fuzziness of the risk concept, many large firms *formally* adopt the convention that the discount rate (or cost of capital) be determined by the CAPM or some variation of it. The calculation here involves an assessment of how the inclusion of a project in the investor's portfolio would influence its overall return and such estimates are subject to both wide margins of error and structural breaks over time making it difficult to arrive at a reliable forward-looking number. Empirically, there is little convincing evidence on the ability of CAPM models to capture risk in an adequate way (risk and return in practice are often negatively correlated [Fama and French 1997]). More recent research concludes that 'the picture that emerges from the UK research is every bit as bleak as that which emerges from the Fama and French US study. Cost of capital is estimated with large errors' (Gregory and Michou 2009). Moreover as noted in a classic study by Graham and Harvey (1999), even if the model were correct, for most US firms 'it is not clear that the model is applied properly in practice' (p.201).

Additional problems arise because different sources of finance need to be combined to obtain an overall discount rate and that entails a view of the appropriate (or feasible) mix of debt and equity and retained profit. Here again there are academic disputes and suggestions of behavioural biases; 'executives rely heavily on practical, informal rules when choosing capital structure' (Graham and Harvey 1999, p.189).

A further concern, particularly for long-lived projects, is that the practice of discounting with a constant rate rests on shaky foundations. In most cases the construction costs are not subject to the same risk as income flows. Some infrastructure projects for example have front-loaded risk and most long-lived projects have risk characteristics that change with time and outcome. In classical NPV calculations these complexities are often ignored and there is only one envisioned path through the decision tree, corresponding to unconditional expected values. This reduces complexity but at a cost of realism – it is more sensible to deal with risk by modelling the possible contingencies by simulating possible decision paths according to the statistical distribution of uncertain variables outside the control of the decision-maker. A minority of firms in capital intensive industries have tended to pursue this approach through the use of scenario simulation, monte-carlo or dynamic programming analyses. More recently this has been taken a step further in the 'real options' approach to capital investment where project appraisal is modelled in a more realistic, but also more complex manner (Busby and Pitts 1997). Here the decision at the outset has to reflect the flexibility of the firm to adapt to changing information that would alter the optimal progression of the project (for example to expand or abandon) as time progresses.

Depending on the path chosen through the decision tree, the risk (and therefore the appropriate discount rate) varies. Furthermore the expected outcomes now have to be seen as conditional since not all paths through the decision tree are optimal or even feasible. Real options approaches can deal with these issues by amending the NPV criterion. In turn however that entails a string of extra assumptions so that it is easy to tweak any NPV calculation in any desired manner. The decision criteria that result may either be more or less strict than conventional NPV rules. For example emphasizing the irreversible nature of decisions will tend to increase the trigger or 'hurdle' rate of return to start the project. Identifying the potential of an investment to permit follow-on projects will lower the hurdle rate. Perhaps because of this flexibility, few firms have sanctioned the use of real options as anything other than one of a battery of investment decision routines.

In short, even without considering further complications around tax, working capital, dividends and inflation, it is evident that the investment decision is so complex that it is difficult just to write down an agreed set of rules. The decision routine has so many degrees of freedom arising from deviations from different sets of theoretical assumptions, that it can only be operationalized by conventional practices that may vary from firm to firm. The process is generally better described as a matter of 'muddling through' than it is about utilizing any one set of clear guidelines. Far from market failure being an occasional aberration of such a process it is hard to think of a more likely case of badly functioning markets than where the participants themselves – the buyers and sellers – have only a vague idea of true valuations. Here as ever, rationality is bounded, leading to heuristic rules (Hodgeson (ed.) 2007; Akerlof and Shiller 2009; Fazzari 2009).

4.3   Investment and economic theory: A loose fit

The discussion so far has pointed to the circumstantial evidence for market failure in investment. Put simply our argument is that firms do not and cannot know the rules of investment because such rules do not exist in a complete form. Neither can they know with any certainty what rules others will follow except that they also are likely to be bound by some conventional assessment. To be sure this argument does not rule out a weak form of rationality where decision-makers use available information, however partial, as best they can. Nor does it show conclusively that investment markets are any less rational than others where decisions may also be taken on less than perfect information. For those who see our arguments so far as speculative and simply confirming the *possibility* of market failure, we next relate some evidence that is more concretely linked to the processes and outcomes of investment appraisal. Two sets of observations are examined here. First we look at direct survey evidence of how firms self-report their investment decision-making methods. Second, we briefly assess the ability of economic models to capture variation in investment.

Self-reported survey findings

The complexity of investment theory reviewed earlier creates the potential for a variety of responses to the same stimulus. There is ample evidence that this variety is realized in practice, thus confirming a degree of autonomy for investment decisions. Were decisions characterized by clear and robust rules, it would surely be reflected in some commonality in approach by firms and conformity with the textbook approach. But even firms in very similar circumstances use different criteria to value investments indicating that there is a large measure of arbitrariness in the decision. Repeated investment surveys over the years in both the UK and US indicate that firms do not rely on a single metric in their investment decisions but simultaneously use a range of approaches that may conflict – including NPV, internal rate of return and payback. An even larger range of methods appears to be used by US firms where at least a quarter of reporting managers claimed 'always or nearly always' to use one or more of the following techniques: IRR, NPV, Payback, Sensitivity Analysis, Earnings Multiple, Discounted Payback and Real Options (Graham and Harvey 1999). Some behaviour is difficult to understand including the popularity of payback (third in importance). This cannot be justified as proxy for maintaining liquidity because its use appears uncorrelated with financial status. Rather the popularity of payback is to some extent linked with age, tenure of CEOs and whether or not they possess an MBA, though that is hardly evidence that it represents simply a lack of sophistication. For large UK firms, Arnold and Hatzopoulos (2000) showed that despite increasing diffusion of advanced methods, most firms supplemented these with older methods that were perceived to have 'qualities that modern techniques seem unable to provide' (p.622). Firms' decisions are thus based on some unspecified weighting of possibly conflicting criteria that allows for considerable subjective judgement. Firms also use a wide range of methods of adjusting for risk, many of which are at variance with established financial theory (Alkaraan and Northcott 2006).

Were companies to pursue a classical NPV approach it would follow that investment would be pushed to the point where the required rate of return on new investment would equal the cost of capital. Yet a range of studies have shown that this is not the case. A Sloan Business School study using a sample from the Fortune 500 shows that most companies use a real hurdle rate (required investment return) much higher than the real cost of capital. Intriguingly moreover, the hurdle premium over the cost of capital was negative for a substantial proportion – about a quarter of the total. The authors were unable to explain this pattern by any correspondence with financial and structural variables that might proxy for risk (Poterba and Summers 1995). A separate study for the US confirmed this diversity with approximately 40 per cent of a sample of over two thousand business units reporting hurdle rates more than five percentage points different from the cost of capital, split equally between firms above and below that benchmark (Driver and Temple 2010). Here it was possible to pin down some reasons for these variations. Firms pursuing a lower hurdle rate were seen to be pursuing aggressive strategic targets. Firms that were adopting high hurdles were to some extent perceived as sheltered – and taking advantage of weak competition – in that the recent entry of a major competitor discriminated against observing this category. A smaller but more recent study of US Chief Financial Officers indicated that firms use hurdle rates approximately twice their cost of capital. Variation in CAPM explains only 10 per cent of the hurdle rate cross-section variation, which is better explained by growth prospects that determine the option to wait (Jagannathan et al 2011). Others however have queried the extent of options thinking in business and certainly there is much variation in practices adopted by individual firms. This degree of autonomy by managers and boards thus makes the investment decision to some extent arbitrary and subject to non-economic forces such as corporate culture or swings in business sentiment.

The econometrics of investment

Were investment to follow closely the textbook approach and were that to be an adequate guide to practice, we would expect a well determined investment function to be capable of being specified and estimated. Yet, given that forward looking expectations reflect the poorly articulated and understood decision methods of other firms, there is little theoretical basis for the assumption of rational expectations that generally underlie these models. Extensive testing over the decades has failed to produce good out-of-sample forecasting superior to survey methods. Quite distinct models of macro-level investment appear to be superior for different decades and for different forecasting horizons. One recent comparative study of US forecasting models for the thirty years up to 2005 showed evidence of multiple structural breaks in all of the forecasting models examined (Rapachi and Wohar 2007).[4]

---

[4] Akerlof and Shiller (2009) suggest a complex non-formal assessment of the last half-century of US business investment: 'when loss of confidence causes stock markets to fall, there will be a fall in investment. But if the stock market is falling because of inflation, while the economy remains otherwise strong, then most likely investment will also remain strong' (p.146). This may well fit the facts but as the authors note it is scarcely compatible with economic theory as we know it.

A persistent puzzle has been the perverse or insignificant effect of interest rates and other components of the cost of capital such as fiscal incentives, at least in the short run (Blanchard 1986; Sumner 1999).[5] Profitability tends to perform better than the interest rate in investment equations but traditional economics gives profitability 'virtually no status as a relevant analytic category' because it is – in theory – equilibrated with the interest rate, itself determined by personal savings propensities (Gordon 1995, p.70). An alternative and more credible perspective is to see personal savings as endogenous to the income created when *companies* respond with varying propensity to profitability. This variable propensity of investment to profits (and indeed stock prices) asserts the autonomy of the company investment decision over the savings one (Bhaskar and Glyn 1995; Glyn 1997).[6] The key point is that investment has an autonomous component driven by time-varying and national business sentiment so that: 'when companies actually decide how much to invest, the psychological factors underlying investment play a major role' (Akerlof and Shiller 2009, p.143). We might add that these psychological factors take on a cultural form as they are generalized in social settings and networks.

4.4   Market failure and spillovers

So far, we have been concerned with the assessment of private benefits from investment projects, arguing that there are only weak forces that make for market efficiency. Here we extend the argument to the more conventional form of market failure that occurs when there exists a wedge between private and social rates of return, reflecting spillover benefits or externalities which are captured by agents other than the firm itself. Put simply, the firm that invests may not reap the full benefit of the investment so that the incentive to invest is insufficient to ensure commercial approval for all projects that would increase total welfare.

---

[5] While careful econometric treatments have shown interest rate sensitivity (Gilchrist and Zakrajsek 2007) it is hard to disentangle firm-specific interest rates from other influences such as default risk. Others have found markedly different elasticities depending on the component of the cost of capital, with different effects also found for different capital assets.

[6] Glyn (1997) uses profit share as an indicator of future profitability which is often captured instead by some version of Tobin's Q. In Glyn's estimates, the investment response to profitability appeared to weaken after the 1980s, reflecting perhaps the uncertain trajectory of demand given a deepening distributional struggle between capital and labour, and global imbalances.

Spillover benefits can arise in a number of ways. Most simply, it is possible that some portion of the gains from investment cannot be protected by law or company strategy and will end up in the pocket of consumers through lower prices, suppliers in higher rents, or competitors who can free-ride on first movers. Another form of spillover can occur through information flows, whether of science or know-how. Technical knowledge spillovers may be of particular benefit to growth because it is a free resource that may have many uses (Jaffe 1986; Griliches 1992). Some case-study evidence suggests that social returns from investment in knowledge may be more than twice private returns (Mansfield 1984, 1990; Greenhalgh and Rogers 2010 collate results). Because of this externality, most countries offer significant public incentives to R&D and other forms of innovation expenditure.[7]

Spillovers can arise naturally through 'thick-market' effects where the density of market transactions either speed up information flows or permit fixed costs to be spread over a larger base.[8] Any impetus to growth could thus be amplified by spillover effects, though the process might be more self-sustaining when it originates on the supply side. In the UK, policymakers have tended to accept the case for spillovers arising from technical innovation but regarded externalities related to capital investment as quantitatively unimportant. However the evidence here is ambiguous. Oulton (1996) found that output growth in total manufacturing increased productivity in individual sectors, so that: 'a *prima facie* case can be made for externalities operating at the level of aggregate manufacturing' (p.111). The question is whether the origin of these spillovers lies in

---

[7] Spillovers may be horizontal within industries or regions or vertical between industries. Vertical spillovers between producers and users appear more important than horizontal ones between competitors (Geroski 1991; Gorg and Greenaway 2004). Spillovers are sometimes envisioned as taking place in geographical clusters where knowledge exchange is argued to be enhanced by local contact and where specialization can raise productivity. Some argue that a degree of absorptive capacity or initial capability within firms is necessary to obtain spillover benefits and that the same applies to regions hosting inward investment (Girma and Wakelin 2002).

[8] Critics argue that spillovers may simply reflect the measurement problem involved in identifying unobserved variations in inputs. In particular, firms may be utilizing unmeasured services from either workers or their capitals stocks (for example Basu 1996; Burnside 1996; Sbordone 1997). Despite these important contributions, some studies have remained robust to the criticisms. For example Paul and Siegel (1999) find evidence for both short-run and long-run thick-market externality effects in US manufacturing after taking account of all utilization change.

capital investment. Support for a technological influence from investment comes from studies on the effects of information and communications technology (ICT) investment in the US and UK (O'Mahony and Vecchi 2003). These findings are also consistent with the sectoral analysis of externalities that identified an effect from equipment investment and the mechanical engineering industry output on total factor productivity for the UK as emphasized in Chapter 3 (Driver et al 2006).

Internationally, the role of capital investment externalities in promoting growth finds support in 'statistical and anecdotal evidence for their importance at the microeconomic level' (Romer 2001, p.70). Despite this, as Romer notes, the issue has been 'largely ignored' reflecting an apparent willingness to elevate occasional negative results to accepted knowledge. Bernanke and Gurkaynak (2001) also conclude that 'a country's rate of investment in physical capital is strongly correlated with its long-run growth of output per worker' (p.12). The fact that capital accumulation leads to higher growth – not just a higher level of labour productivity – is consistent with external effects (p.37).[9]

Subsequent UK work on spillovers has almost entirely been concerned with testing for those which arise from foreign firms locating in the country, although it is important here not to confuse additional investment from the impact of ownership change. The implicit view – from the mid-1980s onward – appears to be that the only good investment is a foreign one, though the reasoning is seldom explained. There is some basis to take a positive view on FDI but it needs to be heavily qualified.[10] Some studies have shown spillover gains, particularly related to vertical relationships (see the survey Gorg and Greenaway 2004). Whatever the exact source of these gains it seems to involve physical investment in facilities and associated routines of production. The gains reflect 'the

---

[9] Some authors see equipment investment as more important than structures, particularly for developing countries. See however the reasonable criticism of DeLong and Summers (1991) in Oulton and Young (1996) and the cointegration study for advanced countries in Coakley and Wood (1999).

[10] Different categories of inward investment have different aims. Those that reflect technology-based ownership advantage (as where R&D intensity is higher for foreign firms) tend to bring gains but there are no gains associated with FDI based on technology-sourcing (Driffield and Love 2007) pp.460–73. In a separate study Driffield et al (2009) show that the proportion of inward FDI with higher research intensity and competitiveness has trended sharply downward largely due to an increase in technology sourcing. Other work shows that more than a quarter of US or EU large companies have not established any R&D facilities in the UK compared with 5 per cent for UK firms (DTI 2005a).

international transfer of firm-specific assets [that] are embodied in new capital investment' (Driffield et al 2009, p.181). It should be noted that these are the spillovers that are routinely dismissed as irrelevant in the context of domestic investment. This contrast may be explained by economics being the discipline of choice for those concerned with domestic investment while management resource-based theory is more to the fore in foreign direct investment. The notion of firm-specific ownership advantages originated in the study of foreign direct investment. FDI can bring spillover gains because of the leakage of some sets of firm-specific advantages as firms collaborate or engage in supply links or become part of a common labour pool. But the notion that this process only applies to foreign multinationals inward flows of capital rather than, say, to expansion or diversification by domestic multinationals seems unwarranted, or at any rate has not been generally seen as a research issue.

Spillover effects from capital investment arise when *second-mover advantages* exist. First mover advantages, by contrast, arise when a lead innovator can generate super profits from captive consumers, for example if they are locked in due to high switching costs. Alternatively, on the supply side, a technological lead for a first-mover may prove enduring due to patents, learning effects or advantages of scale (Porter 1982) or preferential access to the supply of a complementary input. In contrast to these first mover advantages (that tend to accelerate a firm's investment) there are many cases where it is the second mover, or follower firm, who gains more. For example the configuration of a new process, the logistics of its installation and expansion into new markets all create information that will be available for follow-on competitors to use (Lieberman 1987). Assuming that information lags are no longer than those for R&D, such spillovers will occur within months (Mansfield 1987; Levin et al 1989). The follower firm can then free-ride on the rival's trailblazing expenditures in: advertising (insofar as it is generic), market research, customer education and regulatory approval. In effect the market is often created for the second-mover and leakage of valuable information will reinforce the advantage. Other gains come from savings on the supply side – worker training, the creation of industrial standards and routines and the construction of specialized supply sources. Installation experience can be built on and mistakes avoided. All of this suggests a dominant effect for such second-mover advantages (Cottrell and Sick 2001). If that is so, the externality acts as a depressing force on investment; the expected private returns of the lead firm would have to equal the social return to trigger enough investment. The issue here, essentially, is that private capital investments have some of the characteristics of public goods and may thus be under-supplied. As a pioneer researcher of market failure noted in a somewhat neglected early comment: 'As long as activities have even a trace of publicness, price calculations are inefficient' (Bator 1958, p.377).

4.5　Market failure and financial constraints

Investment can be limited by access to credit or other financial constraints. This has been a long-standing concern in the UK leading to tensions between finance and industry. There have been repeated worries about the restrictive nature of bank credit, the finance gap for smaller firms unable to access capital markets, the short-termism of City institutions and the historical the role of the City in resisting downward pressure on sterling, especially in the period of fixed exchange rates. We assess these arguments in Chapter 6.

While recognizing the importance of finance for investment, we nevertheless wish to distinguish them from the broader concerns of this chapter. The correction of financial distortions is often mistakenly seen as a silver bullet for investment led growth. In our view that is not the case. In a perceptive comment just months before the onset of the great financial crisis, Samuel Brittan wrote that 'Excessive credit, undue risk-taking and dubious ventures are different concepts, but in practice overlap to a disconcerting extent'.[11] The problem with the UK economy in the preceding years had not been excessive caution in respect of bank credit nor a conservative attitude to risk, but rather the 'dubious ventures' that it bankrolled. While there have been periods (including the present one and the recessions of the early 1990s and 1980s) where companies have suffered a credit squeeze, the charge cannot be made to stick for the run-up to the financial crisis (Tucker 2003). Nor can the story easily accommodate the incidence of pension holidays in the 1980s and 1990s when companies took advantage of inappropriate estimates of future liabilities to tap previously unavailable cash flows.

Much of the work on finance constraints and investment has been a product of the New Keynesian school of economics. The theory rests on a set of assumptions regarding asymmetric information between firms and investors. The inability of investors to make a separation between good and bad projects leads to the possibility of credit rationing, higher cost of equity, misallocation across projects and a preference for

---

[11] See the review of Elliott and Atkinson (2007) in 'An economy on fantasy island', *Financial Times* 25 May 2007: http://www.samuelbrittan.co.uk/text276_p.html

internal funds (Fazzari and Variato 1992; Fazzari et al 2008). But the story of investment finance should not be limited to the constraints posed by a reliance on internal funds. Company boards make decisions on how much to retain for reinvestment and how much to pay out to investors. Put differently, income available for reinvestment is not a passive variable for many large firms but a decision variable that is decided by the political economy of the period and the degree of autonomy for executives relative to investors, a subject we return to in Chapter 7.

4.6 Conclusions

In this chapter we have examined some of the objections to the view that capital investment is worthy of a special place in economic analysis and that capital expenditure should be supported by public policy. Some of these objections are built on outdated views that policies to stimulate investment will end up strengthening the hold-up power of organized labour. Others objections rely on a textbook image of investment as a process with no obvious market failure. This view is untenable; market failure can be shown to occur in many different ways.

We have highlighted the information deficiencies in the capital allocation process that confers a degree of freedom on the decision-maker leading to a behavioural response. We have argued that these responses are often inconsistent and capricious. At the same time, complete instability is rare, so that the value of convention appears functional. In the UK context company boards have tended to authorize an adjustment of capital that is too cautious and hence too slow. Beyond the general idea that market forces are only weakly equilibrating there must be some specific features of the industrial environment that inhibits stronger risk-taking, a subject we take up in the next chapter.

The existence of spillovers gives added importance to capital investment but these are often neglected in favour of those spillovers arising from disembodied technology. We have defended the notion of capital investment spillovers in this chapter, particularly where second-mover effects are present. These considerations serve to strengthen the competitiveness case for an investment led strategy made in Chapter 8. Market notions such as that of the 'level playing field' are particularly strong in the UK climate and lead to a presumption in favour of light industrial policy. However this is not always appropriate where spillovers and externalities exist.

Finally, we considered financial frictions. There is little doubt that finance asymmetries exist and create difficulties for investment decisions. However it is hard to argue that it should be the centrepiece of investment theory.[12] We agree with Crotty (1996) that there is a need to better explain *the firm's demand* for financial capital. This will require attention to the capricious nature of investment decision-making, already discussed above in relation to Keynes' (1937) *Quarterly Journal* 1937 article. A theory grounded in conventional expectations and their breakdown seems best placed to explain the twin possibilities of insufficient credit and excessive credit. Finance matters but it should be considered as part of an interaction whereby investment decisions are shared between executives and investors with the balance of influence between them itself subject to variation and evolution (Fazzari 2009). We return to this theme in Chapter 6.

---

[12] An architect of the theory Myers (2003) entertains some doubts while survey evidence is equivocal (Graham and Harvey 1999). For a good account of the controversy in relation to financial constraints and investment see Chirinko and Kalckreuth: http://www.econstor.eu/bitstream/10419/19585/1/200228dkp.pdf

5
Underinvestment or/and Overinvestment?

5.1 Introduction

In Chapter 4 we highlighted the potential for market failure in allocating fixed capital, one reason being the difficulty of investment decision-making under uncertainty. That argument in itself may not be enough to convince doubters of the case for a *negative* bias to capital investment. It may for example reasonably be claimed that the 'animal spirits' that replace conscious calculation may result as much in irrational exuberance and over-investment as in cautious inactivity. Arguments concerning spillover effects, while in our view powerful and persuasive, have also failed to fully convince because the emphasis in that literature tends to be on disembodied spillovers. A third argument relating to financial constraints has found more acceptance, but we have not emphasized it here because it is a complicated story that relates to the design of corporate governance as we discuss later in Chapter 6.

In this chapter we defend (in section 5.2) the hypothesis of a negative directional bias to investment, accepting that it may not be entirely general but requires specific conditions related to industry or asset type. First however in section 5.1, we consider a more basic objection against concentrating at all on fixed investment. It is often argued that physical, fixed or tangible investment is now a less important part of the forward commitment by firms in a modern economy and the reader may be troubled that this is so far not properly recognized in our analysis. It is now also commonplace that fixed investment has become *commodified* in the sense that it can be bought and installed in a 'plug and play' manner, at least for countries that have reached the technological frontier or at least, in the jargon, have sufficient 'absorptive capacity'. Being available to all, it is seen as being unable to confer competitive advantage to firms. The key to firms' success, it is argued, lies with other types of complementary investment such as organizational or marketing capacity. Since these forms of investment are said to have grown disproportionately over time, a focus on fixed investment is argued to understate the extent to which firms are building up capital assets.[1]

Certainly at firm level it is hard to fault the concept of broad capital as a strategic planning tool (Grant 2003). But we argue here that it is mistaken to translate this argument too readily to the macroeconomy. One objection is that much branding and some organizational capital involves anti-competitive behaviour and the creation of barriers to entry. For example individual firms may be better off after a price comparison site is established but the overall effect may be anti-competitive. We show here that much of the case for intangibles has been over-stated and that the particular importance of fixed investment has not been understood.

5.2   Investment broad and narrow

The distinction that is important for the current discussion is that between investment – the use of resources to create an asset which yields a return and 'intermediate consumption' – goods and services which are used up (or depreciate quickly) in the act of production. It is possible to alter our perception of the growth rate of capital by adopting different accounting conventions. The use of electricity to power a tool provides a clear-cut case of intermediate consumption. The distinction is important when interpreting measures of productivity such as GDP or value added per hour of work. National income accounting methods need to reach clear-cut distinctions between the two categories in an area where international standardization is important. In the last update of international accounting practice for example (United Nations SNA 93 and European System of Accounts 1995) both expenditures on dairy (but not beef) cattle were reclassified away from intermediate consumption to fixed investment, as with considerably more importance generally, were expenditures on computer software. The somewhat arbitrary nature of such conventions makes economic arguments even more difficult to resolve.

---

[1] There are in fact two distinct arguments here. One is that R&D and education is now more important than fixed capital; the other that a host of intangibles such as marketing, organization and other soft capital expenditures can substitute for fixed capital particularly in services. The latter argument has some merit (Aghion 2006); the former, we will argue, is meretricious.

Investment in intangibles and its measurement form a particularly important issue. As with any investment undertaken by firms, we must think in terms of both the social and private rate of return. The latter may well be served by expenditures which increase market share at the expense of rivals (sometimes called the 'market stealing' effect). The social rate of return may however, in such circumstances, be rather smaller. While quite a lot is known about the empirics and impact of research and development on productivity, our understanding of other intangibles is still limited.

Figure 5.1 shows a breakdown of spending on a variety of 'intangibles' by different types of asset.

These different expenditures are not really commensurable in that some are defined and recorded with greater accuracy than others and of course with different depreciation rates they have little correlation with capital stocks. The most measurable form of intangible investment is expenditure on R&D which is based on an internationally standardized definition. R&D occurs mainly in manufacturing and related sectors; it has a fairly close correlation with fixed investment and has tended, for the UK, to mirror both the weakness in the latter and of manufacturing, which as we saw in Chapter 3 has been growing more slowly than in many other advanced economies. Business expenditure on R&D performed in the UK (BERD) shows varying trends by sector, with

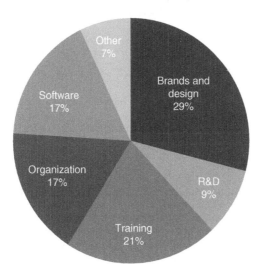

Figure 5.1 Breakdown of spending on intangible assets
Source: Marrano et al (2007, Table A1).

pharmaceutical and aerospace R&D intensity rising over time, matched by falls in sectors such as electronics. Total BERD, as shown in Figure 5.2, has trended down as a share of GDP over the last two decades in contrast to most other major economies (Abramovsky et al 2005; Bulli 2008).

An alternative measure of R&D is based on the international comparisons of large companies recorded in the R&D Scoreboard data.[2]

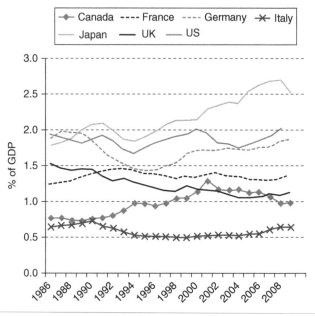

Figure 5.2   International Comparison of Business Expenditure on R&D as a % of GDP 1986–2009

Source: Department for Business Innovation and Skills SET statistics 2011.

---

[2] The data from the R&D Scoreboard reflects expenditure by large companies irrespective of location while the BERD data reflects expenditure in a country regardless of origin. The Scoreboard dataset is interesting when the focus is on company decisions or outward location of R&D while the BERD data is of interest for domestic productivity and inward flows. Both inward and outward R&D flows have grown more rapidly for the UK in recent years than for comparable countries. In terms of international comparisons, controversy exists over the appropriate definition of intensity whether real or nominal but it is hard to devise accurate cross-country deflators for R&D because of the quality of labour input which is the largest component.

These data tend to reflect the historical overseas expansion of UK headquartered companies and reveal a low R&D intensity relative to competitors such as France, Germany, Japan and the US. This finding however appears to be almost entirely due to the sector mix: the UK firms' global sales are concentrated in low R&D sectors (utilities, tobacco, forestry and paper) where it is argued that there is less scope for R&D investment (Bulli 2008). Some commentators have utilized this finding to argue that it also explains the domestic decline in R&D (NESTA 2009a, p.13). This does not appear to be the case: the decline in R&D as measured by BERD statistics cannot be explained in this way, except perhaps in comparison with Germany where the data reflects the latter's large auto sector. R&D performed in the UK seems to be comparatively low, not because of the sector mix, but because UK firms within most sectors are less likely to perform R&D at all. Indeed the top 100 spenders account for 80 per cent of the total indicating an unusual level of concentration (Abramovsky et al 2005).

R&D statistics clearly do not capture all innovation activity and they are often argued to give a biased picture due to the omission of engineering design and more particularly the failure to register novelty in some service sectors where innovation occurs more by organizational design or process reorganization. In particular R&D statistics do not fully reflect the innovation activities of small firms which lack any formal R&D department. One way of getting a broader picture of innovation is to utilize survey sources such as the EU Community Innovation Survey. But here too the data tend to show the UK in a poor international light. The National Endowment for Science, Technology and the Arts (NESTA 2006) reports that fewer UK firms are innovation active compared with the rest of the EU and particularly so compared with advanced EU countries and that far fewer UK firms had introduced a novel innovation by way of either goods or service than was the case in other EU countries.

Despite producing such convincing evidence of comparatively low innovation activity for the UK, NESTA found it impossible to reconcile this with the perceived superior 'growth' of the UK economy before the financial crash. How could the UK economy be doing so well with so little investment or innovation using conventional measures? The idea that the UK economy was experiencing housing and banking bubbles was not something that would have been easy to argue at that stage. It was simpler to conclude that the official investment figures were understating success by failing to capture much of the soft innovation and growth of intangibles. But the supporting evidence for this was thin and heavily lampooned in a prescient contribution by Atkinson and Elliott (2007). Self-reviewing their book, Elliott commented:

> Unlike Germany, Japan, Sweden – or even the US, which has a huge trade deficit itself – Britain is no longer an industrial nation. Is this worrying? Well, it scares the life out of me, but not it seems the government. The fantasy here is that we can cope with living beyond our means at a national level through the profits generated by the City and by building up Britain's 'knowledge economy'.
>
> (*The Guardian* Monday 14 May 2007)

Bigger guns were brought to bear. HM Treasury economists Marrano et al (2007) carried out research to show that 'traditional measures of investment may not be capturing the dynamic changes in the economy' (p.4), an idea that was then popularized in influential briefing documents such as NESTA 2009b. Marrano et al calculated that intangibles doubled as a ratio of tangibles in the twenty five years from 1980 resulting in an intangible capital stock about a third greater than that for tangibles. Using such revised systems of national accounting they were able to assert that broad investment was on a *rising* trend relative to GDP (Marrano et al (2007), Chart 3.4). The unstated implication was that the substantial fall in fixed investment as a ratio of output over the last thirty years may not be all that important. As in DTI (1996), policymakers had moved into denial mode.

NESTA (2009b, 2011) built on this research programme, assembling the elements of intangible expenditures into a category called 'innovation' which was, they claimed, responsible for two thirds of UK labour productivity growth from 1990 to 2007. It has always been a tricky and controversial task in economics to attribute productivity growth to factor inputs and especially to try to relate innovation gains to productivity. The standard – and heroic – assumption is that all inputs are paid at competitive rates. The contribution of different inputs to commercial output can then be distinguished quantitatively in an exercise known as 'growth accounting'. Were NESTA to have followed this orthodox if questionable route they would have attributed 20 per cent of labour productivity growth to their constructed innovation category. However they make the further assumption that anything not accounted for by other factors is also entirely attributable to innovation, thus arriving at the two-thirds estimate. Put differently they attribute all the residual in the equation accounting for output (usually referred to as our measure of ignorance or 'total factor productivity') to the direct effect of intangibles on output so as to arrive at their inflated estimate. This is surprising as Criscuolo and Haskell (2002) had previously identified the types of innovation input that impacted most on total factor productivity. In that study, the important factors were mainly related to capital investment rather than to intangibles.

Part of the recent interest in intangibles originates from the view that the manufacturing sector is unfairly flattered by traditional statistics and whether new ways of measurement are necessary to identify the 'new' or 'knowledge' economy. Output of the service sector has grown much faster than manufacturing in the UK in recent decades. Not just has there been a growth in financial intermediation but other sectors such as retailing and business services have grown with the latter doubling its real value GVA as a share of the whole economy in the twenty years to 2005 to around 15 per cent (DTI 2007b). By widening the categories of innovation to include activities performed in all sectors, the innovation opportunities implicit in the services sector will, it is argued, be put on an equal footing. But this way of thinking fails to acknowledge that the under-recording of some soft innovations such as design is by no means confined to services. Within manufacturing, there is a high level of complementarity between technological activities that are embodied in fixed capital and those that are not (Evangelista 1999). Data from DTI (2007b) show that the manufacturing sector has a higher total innovation intensity than business services or distribution even when innovation is broadened as a category to include all types of process and organizational improvements. Indeed for distribution, the comparison shows it to be lower than manufacturing on every single measure.

Overall, our take on the intangibles question is one of cautious scepticism. It is clear that much firm-level expenditure that creates future value for the firm goes uncounted. But whether it contributes to a build-up of capital – and thus should be capitalized – is less clear. Conventionally the issue is answered as to whether the benefits last more than one year, so that there is an *a priori* argument for considering capitalization (Awano et al 2011). Econometric work however has suggested quite low durability – with a majority of industries for example showing an annual depreciation rate for advertising higher than two-thirds (Landes and Rosenfield 1994).

Conceptually, it is not clear that longevity of benefits can be the main distinguishing point of expenditure and capital formation. For example, retail analysts tend to speak of companies such as Tesco as 'investing in price cuts'. Since market share may respond with a lag, would any loss in revenue arising from price reductions then count as 'capital'?[3] In any event, a proper depreciation rate depends also on the effects on rivals; there is a question of whether there is *any net accumulation* of capacity once the destruction of rival firms' capital is accounted for, making the social return effectively zero. It is difficult to argue that a duopoly's marketing expenditure for mutually protecting their brand should be put on the same footing as their expenditure on new products. How much of that marketing expenditure is on the creation of entry barriers and the protection of rents and how much on user information? If the costs of competing such as marketing are to be counted as capital then why not the public expenditure on law and security that underlies trade? Should we count as capital the anti-competitive expenditures aimed at the creation of barriers of entry, most of which concern intangibles? (Singh et al 1990). And should we then also cost the expenditure of investigating the appropriateness of these arrangements, through public monitoring and regulation?[4]

It is often argued that much unmeasured investment takes the form of new business models. But there is a big question mark over what to include in this. This may be illustrated by what gets counted in estimates of US intangibles; two major items are the business model of Dell Computers and the supply chain logistics of Wal-Mart (Corrado et al 2006; Oliner et al 2008). Such firm-specific intangibles give a market share advantage to these firms. But should they count in the estimates of aggregate capital? The aim of strategic change is to maximize the returns to owners and that that often involves the destruction of others' capacity: 'Giants like Wal-Mart have wide latitude to do as they wish to rivals and suppliers so long as they deliver lower prices to consumers'.[5] In respect of the Dell model, the strategy largely revolves around a division of customers between companies. Dell focused on high repeat

---

[3] Interestingly, such conundrums do not always depend on the tangible–intangible distinction. Consider two trading companies that keep rivals out by high territorial walls (physical expenditure). This can hardly be counted as part of the aggregate capital stock, but a costly negotiation scheme that reduced such expenditures (intangible) might well have a better claim to count as capital.

[4] Further difficulties arise with rent seeking activities: lobbyists, tax-avoidance lawyers and acquisition advisers have a less than certain relationship to economic welfare. Further digression on this point would lead us to consider the topic of productive and unproductive labour which is outside the scope of this book.

[5] 'Is Wal-Mart too powerful?' Bloomberg Business week 6 October 2003. For a different argument why such intangibles should not be classed as capital but regarded as an attribute of other factors see Cummins (2005).

buyers with stable demand and low service needs. The division of markets in this way may or may not bring overall gains but it requires the netting out of negative externalities on suppliers and competitors.

Clearly some intangibles do belong in the capital stock. It seems appropriate to capitalize R&D though the correct depreciation rate is difficult to evaluate. Here however much knowledge generated by R&D involves a private rate of depreciation which may actually be higher than the social rate of depreciation, as for example when knowledge about a process innovation is imitated by other firms. Also the stock of 'goodwill' has traditionally been recognized in company accounts. But it is true too that goodwill can be added to or subtracted from. For example the increased expenditure on organizational capital in the 1990s that involved delayering and middle management retrenchment cannot just be recorded as increasing the intangibles stock by the associated expenditure. Rather it seems to have soured labour relations and increased tensions of remaining middle managers as the intensity of their work has increased. The reneging on implicit trust that has characterized much recent organizational change surely also needs to be included if we were to go down this road.

Our first argument against over-emphasizing intangibles is therefore that some components of broad capital are not capital at all. To count as capital accumulation at macro level, the value potential of the new asset must be greater than that which it displaces, whether the asset be tangible or intangible. Expenditures aimed at defending market position from competitors can cancel out in the aggregate. We are thus led to share the scepticism of Atkinson and Elliott (2007) that the intangibles argument is hyped. There will be even more support for this now that so much of the intangible capital of the financial intermediation industry has been depreciated in an accelerated fashion.

Trends in intangibles

Intangibles have of course long existed as part of commercial practice. A second query on intangibles is therefore whether the phenomenon is indeed something new or trended (Grant 2003). Table 5.1 shows the nominal expenditure on different forms of 'capital' from 1990 to 2008. Even allowing for the fact that the financial crisis will have affected some categories disproportionately, these figures appear to show a rising ratio for intangibles. However the comparison should arguably be made in real terms – that is in terms of the volumes of capital being created. Here we may note that the fixed capital deflator – partly reflecting the radical declines in computing and electronic components – has moved

Table 5.1   UK tangible and intangible investment in £ billion

Investment type	1990	2000	2008
Tangible	67(100)	87(120)	104(126)
Intangible	56(100)	95(127)	137(148)

Source: ONS 2010 Blue Book for Deflators.

in quite different ways to the GDP deflator, which is more relevant for intangibles. Making the adjustment, we suspect that there was very little difference in volume growth between the categories 1990 and 2000, and while the difference is clearly far greater between 2000 and 2008, the more important feature here is perhaps the sluggish growth in *both* series. While intangibles actually fell some way short of the rate of overall expansion of the economy (1.9 per cent per annum as against 2.2 per cent per annum), the measure of tangible investment grew at a paltry 0.6 per cent per annum. This surely is the important story.

We have in fact been here before with inflated estimates of intangibles, often influenced by stock market bubbles. Intangibles were said to be behind the 1980s stock market boom in the US – as Tobin's Q, which measures the ratio of market value of a firm's equity to tangible assets, rose by 50 per cent in ten years (Blair 1995). The claim was repeated when Q value rose in the 'dot-com' boom (Hall 2000; Lev 2001) when the authors noted the 'declining importance of firms' physical assets' (Burton-Jones 1999), or even that 'physical assets are unimportant relative to human assets' (Rajan and Zingales 2000 p.214). Bosworth and Triplett (2000) were somewhat more cautious and suggested that an alternative explanation of the rise in intangibles was a 'speculative bubble in asset markets' (p.15). The latter explanation is supported not only by recent evidence but also by the historical finding that, for the US corporate sector, Tobin's Q is mean-reverting to a hundred-year mean (Smithers and Wright 2001). This strongly suggests that, despite a rising spend on firm-specific intangibles, the aggregate intangible capital stock is not trended relative to the tangibles in the long run.

To sum up this section, intangibles matter, now as ever, being an important part of broad capital, whether measured or not. But it is not reasonable to view intangibles as filling a hole created by lower accumulation of tangibles unless there is better evidence than that which has so far been offered that there has been a sudden and permanent acceleration of the need for intangible inputs. It seems irresponsible on the basis of flimsy evidence to conclude that the government should recast its innovation target from R&D to their broader measure of innovation (NESTA 2009).

The debate on intangibles has distracted attention from the issue of investment in general. Our approach is to focus on any category of investment that is deemed to suffer from market failure. As we will argue below it is only certain categories of investment (and we may include here some aspects of training and other intangibles) that can be considered prime cases for public policy because they are unlikely to be provided to the desired degree by private provision. In the next section we will give conditional importance to types of investment (in terms of policy prioritization) depending on theoretical arguments rather than tangibility or otherwise.

5.3   The direction of bias in investment

Our starting point in this chapter was to ask how and when capital investment would be biased downward. A degree of freedom is open to decision-makers but that only demonstrates the feasibility of bias, not its direction or extent. Decision-makers are capricious, sometimes creating bubble effects in a frenzy of competitive accumulation and sometimes exhibiting the contrary tendency of hoarding cash. It remains to be considered how and why one or another might predominate. Our argument is that any downward bias depends on three sets of factors – the *industrial context*, the *financial context* and the *business climate*. By industrial context we mean the specific characteristics of each asset and each sector. For example we argue that fixed investment assets in some sectors of the economy – and also some intangible assets such as R&D – are exposed to downside uncertainty in a way that leads to downward bias. We also show how investor relations in respect of finance would produce the same result. We postpone the more difficult question of the business climate to Chapter 6, where we address institutional features such as corporate governance regimes and system-wide influences that inhibit investment.

Objective industrial characteristics

When is investment biased down? One reason for investment to be unresponsive to growth and profits is the presence of risk, so that managers, investors or both are not prepared to commit. Risk is often diversified by investors, or at any rate appears to be so. However even where diversification protects an investor's portfolio of holdings, firm-specific risk is still important because of its affect on behaviour. In particular, the firm may envisage becoming cash constrained with adverse affects on flexibility, reputation, industrial relations and ease of hiring staff. The incidence and import of such firm-specific risk will depend on industrial and market conditions. Projects classed as irreversible, with long payback, slow depreciation, standard but uncertain profitability, will be those where risk judgements will be most cautious, even where the firm is large enough to internalize some failures. Irreversibility matters because the project, once committed, will be hard to abandon or sell on to another owner. Lengthy payback and slow depreciation mean that the window of opportunity for the occurrence of cash constraints is wider. Uncertain profitability may tilt the balance towards delay if information becomes available by waiting, and if the project's profitability is not judged to be much in excess of financing cost.

The list of characteristics just identified with cautious behaviour corresponds closely to the fixed investment and R&D asset classes, and in terms of coverage, to the manufacturing sector which makes intensive use of both types of investment. It is not surprising that UK manufacturing investment responds sluggishly to signals – capital intensive firms are understandably more concerned about the downside than the upside. Driver and Meade (2001) compare the speed at which UK manufacturing sectors close the gap between forecast need for capacity and actual capacity and conclude that firms are using adaptive rather than forward looking models. Driver and Whelan (2001) show that demand risk is a dominant concern of firms. A study of large manufacturing UK firms planning advanced manufacturing technology (AMT) showed that over half used a hurdle of 16 per cent or more and 80 per cent demanded a payback of three years or less (Abdel-Kader and Dugdale 1998). AMT at this time was sophisticated but hardly novel. Services firms are not immune from risks but they are more protected by their capital being more fungible (often structures or general purpose equipment) giving lower sunk costs.[6]

Critics of the argument that manufacturing investment has been held back by risk tend to cite the more stable macroeconomic conditions that prevailed internationally between the oil shocks of the 1970s

---

[6] There are thus distinct logical reasons why manufacturing should be given special consideration, contrary to Bhagwati (2010) and going beyond those considered in Chapter 3.

and the financial crises beginning in the late 1990s. But this rebuttal is flawed. The liberalization of trade and finance since the 1980s has produced large swings in trade balances and exchange rates and these, along with more variable energy prices have affected the UK as an open economy. Apart from Italy, the UK had the greatest fluctuations in volume and prices of exports in the 1980s (Eltis 1996). Volatility continued after the exit of sterling from the ERM in the early 1990s with effects on investment (Darby et al 1999).

Macroeconomic stability is in any case only part of the picture; firm-level uncertainty cannot be inferred from a climate of stable and low good price inflation or even a lengthening of the economic cycle. Nor can macro-level stability be a substitute for any micro-level uncertainty that it induces; there is some evidence that firm-level uncertainty has risen in tandem with the evolution of price stability with a negative effect on investment (Baum et al 2008; Temple et al 2001). The counterpart to a more variable exchange rate and more inflation targeting in the UK may have been a greater micro-level uncertainty. Baum et al (2009) argue that US firms increased their cash ratios sharply after the late 1990s to deal with heightened uncertainty. Put simply, the very competition and labour market pressures that help contain inflation had to some extent been achieved at the cost of a greater burden of adjustment on individual firms and consumers, a process that implies macro-forecasts have less relevance.

Increased uncertainty is thus one plausible candidate to explain a relatively poor investment record for UK manufacturing in general in recent decades, despite the low inflationary climate.[7] But there are also successful parts of manufacturing that have coped well with this challenge and that match or exceed the best global performers. A negative bias to investment does not seem to characterize all parts of the sector and this variety in growth and investment paths needs to be addressed. We suggest here that the observed variety across the sector can be explained by structural features that lead to a *heterogeneous response* to risk.

One distinction that is often made for the UK is between industries based on physical and chemical sciences, with the latter arguably more successful in the UK. Certainly the sectors are distinct in terms of technical skills and market characteristics (Crespi and Patel 2003). They have also performed differently – the long run trend in export share of

---

[7] In fact there are arguments that mild inflation is good for investment (Wardlow 1994).

chemicals and pharmaceuticals holding steady while that of engineering fell sharply (Eltis 1996). Eltis attributes the difference between the sectors to a greater tendency for the chemicals sector to pursue a retain and reinvest policy, that is, to adopt a higher intensity of fixed investment and R&D (p.190).

Sectors may be compared in their appetite for investment by looking at 'hurdle rates' – the required rate of return that firms demand on their marginal investment. A survey on investment propensities (CBI 2001) indicated mean hurdle rates in both the engineering and chemicals sectors at around 12 per cent corresponding to roughly equal financial betas for these sectors. However this disguised a much lower median figure for the chemicals sector. While 75 per cent of chemical companies recorded a real hurdle rate of less than 12 per cent, the corresponding figure for engineering and allied was only 44 per cent of companies.[8]

It does therefore appear that there are differences in the investment appetite of the UK's chemicals and the engineering sectors and differences of this magnitude cannot be explained by differential costs of capital. One structural reason for such a difference may be that the profits of some sectors are more securely defendable than others, for example by patents, giving rise to less perceived risk, so that the hurdle rate can be lower. The proclivity to patent is highest for pharmaceuticals and specialized chemicals whereas only some sub-sectors of physical science-based industries such as instruments fall into this category (Levin et al 1987). The argument extends to the other major successful sector of UK manufacturing – Aerospace. The large military component ensures that market risk is contained while the regulatory environment for civil aviation requires close cooperation between firms and public bodies.

In discussing circumstances in which investment is biased downwards, it may be noted that the industrial risk context not only affects the quantity of investment but also its type. Economists such as Eltis (1996) have identified a tendency for UK industry to focus on defensive, cost-cutting forms of investment rather than creating product variety in enterprise-type expansionary investment which inevitably adds market risk to purely technical risk. According to this view, firms

---

[8] The issue of engineering investment is long standing. A decade earlier a report by McKinsey (1988) found that UK companies having built up substantial cash surpluses by short-term actions 'found it difficult to identify attractive opportunities – or were simply unwilling – to reinvest in their electronics business at levels that would sustain rates of growth comparable to their non-UK counterparts' (p.12).

and sectors that are most risk-averse tend to focus on the safer end of investment. This involves incremental process changes where cost estimates are reliable and where results are immediate, in contrast to the more risky development of new products for new markets. The importance of product variety has now achieved the status of normal theory within economics with the acceptance of endogenous growth models. According to this theory, product variety creation has the advantage of being able to offset – for a sector or a whole economy – the diminishing returns that characterize investment at the firm level. The exact process can vary but the creation of thicker markets for previously custom-made or rare inputs can drive down input costs and improve macro-level productivity. It is thus damaging for economies to be biased away from this type of investment.

For Eltis (1996), the problem is that UK profitability is too low. But if product-variety increases productivity and profitability, how can 'the comparatively low rate of return on capital' be the 'root cause' of the loss of manufacturing capacity (p.191)? Of course retained profit is essential for re-investment but the proportion retained tends to be highly variable. It seems circular to blame low profitability for a focus on cost-cutting, where the reverse causation is commonly accepted. Low profitability is the *outcome* of an economy concentrating on cost-cutting investment, where the gains are low but predictable. While it is true that pharmaceuticals for example have demonstrated a virtuous circle of higher profitability *and* higher re-investment, the causality of such a relationship cannot be general because of the variable response of investment to profitability across sectors. Indeed profitability has risen sharply for the manufacturing sector and indeed the non-financial sector as a whole since the early 1980s without the benign effects predicted for growth and competitiveness (p.195).[9] The puzzle remains therefore as to why some sectors invest more than others in risky types of investment such as product development. If investors shun some 'unloved sectors' such as engineering where the stock price is relatively low in relation to profits (Abbott 2003), we are again left asking why?

We return to the question of the preference for the cost-cutting form of investment that characterizes so much of UK industry (Kenway 1996;

---

[9] Ten years after Eltis declaring conditional victory for UK reforms, Oxford Economic Forecasting was finding it 'puzzling that investment has remained so subdued given the continuing strength of corporate liquidity ... it is not entirely clear why firms are not spending more of their income ... [it] may ultimately be intended for mergers and acquisitions' (OEF 2005, p.52).

Kitson and Michie 1996). Evidence for this feature comes not only from industry observers but from econometric work that shows the main shortfall in UK private non-housing capital investment relative to other countries is in the category of structures that arguably corresponds to expansionary investment and new plant. The International Monetary Fund country report for the UK (2003) showed that structures investment was about a quarter less than a comparator set of twenty countries over a long time-frame. A similar effect showing a long-term downward trend in structures was observed, using cointegration analysis, in our own contribution (Driver et al 2005).

A formal analysis of the implications of a focus on cost-cutting investment is provided in Boone (2000). He argues first that limited managerial resources dictate a choice between the innovative product development and cost-cutting investment – firms do not have the management time to focus on both. According to this analysis private firms will tend to over-invest in cost-cutting but this will be more marked in some settings. In Figure 5.3, position A is likely to be chosen by private firms as compared to point B that would maximize social benefit. The discrepancy is greater for firms that pay efficiency wages to middle management staff that can be regarded as overhead labour. The intuition is that a social planner reduces unit wages so as to increase aggregate output while the private firm increases profits by reducing overhead labour in preference to competing on the basis of quality or marginal cost – which would be replicated by all players. It is the

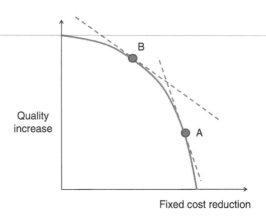

Figure 5.3   The trade-off between investment in product quality and in cost-cutting

relative weight of overhead costs – mainly middle management – that incentivizes private firms to devote resources to cutting these and this will be done (because of managerial constraints) at the expense of innovation in a way that is harmful to aggregate output and welfare.[10]

Boone's model is not the only explanation of how cost-cutting might prove excessive. Others have pointed to cultural and historical influences that emerged much earlier. Reflecting on the fading promise of the 1980s, the head of industrial finance at the Bank of England suggested that UK business had long been culturally adapted to low expectations:

> [O]ur greatest failing as a nation is concentration on successful and profitable management of gradual decline ... [investment] is still very much concentrated on cost-saving measures with a rapid payback.
>
> (Lomax 1990, p.213)

Whatever its origins, the preference for cost-cutting seems a generally accepted feature of UK manufacturing. But some may need to be convinced of the initial premise of Boone's model that there is a trade-off between cost-cutting and innovation.[11] Boone himself recognizes that there may be exceptions to the supposed trade-off, admitting that downsizing and quality improvements can sometimes go together. Fortunately there is good recent evidence on this. Mellahi and Wilkinson (2008) investigate a set of UK medium and large sized firms engaged in downsizing of various degrees that also obtained at least one new patent during the sample period. They find that high downsizing firms are four times more likely to abandon or reduce new product development than to intensify it.

Industrial characteristics and finance

Financial characteristics can also lead to heterogeneity in investment due to the varying degrees to which investors are happy to trust their funds with different types of enterprise. Appropriating profits and

---

[10] The discrepancy only exists when wages are in excess of the marginal product of labour in alternative employment, as say in efficiency wage models. The effect is shown to be largest in mature or weak firms as the fixed cost component is most significant in those cases.

[11] Note that Boone does not dispute that downsizing is good for the firm, in contrast to other literature such as Dougherty and Bowman (1995) that argues that it is good only in the short run.

preventing their erosion is a task that all firms face, but which is done in distinct ways in different sectors. While engineering and allied sectors clearly have ways of protecting the profits of innovations from competitors and suppliers, the manner by which this is achieved may be less transparent and convincing to investors than for other sectors where more formal means are available. Patents and other intellectual property devices such as copyright are more secure methods for keeping potential competitors at bay and thus offer a stronger basis for investor funding. Indeed this may explain why investors take care to understand the technical quality of these types of innovations. A report by the UK Innovation Advisory Board (1990) found that nearly all chemical sector analysts were science graduates but only a third of electronics analysts were as highly qualified, despite the high research intensity of the sector. From the analyst side it was felt that since share prices did not respond to electronics research 'a less deep understanding is needed' (p.7; see also Tylecote 2007; Tylecote and Visintin 2008).

There is thus a contrast between engineering and science-based industry in terms of disclosure to investors with secrecy being an important method of defending intellectual property in much of engineering. In pharmaceuticals by contrast, public disclosure of tests is often a prerequisite for obtaining regulatory approval. This contrast in transparency has a bearing on investor valuation of projects at the planning stage and thus affects the proclivity of firms' managers to carry out innovative projects as contrasted with simple cost-cutting ones.

The effect of transparency in making science-based industries more attractive to investors and thus permitting managers to commit resources is reinforced by the economic effect of real options, that is, the potential opportunities to exploit assets such as patents, zoned land or unique business ideas. As is now well known there may often be a financial case for carrying out initial stage projects even where the project is expected to have negative return. The issue here relates to 'follow-on investments' – those that cannot be carried out without the first stage being initiated, that is without an option being created. Crucially the follow-on stage does not require commitment (exercising the option) until the outcome of the first stage is known. Investment may therefore be boosted where managers have the confidence to use options thinking in this way.[12] Managers and investors may be disposed

---

[12] The textbooks often emphasize the opposite idea – that options justify delay since information arrives through waiting. In our view that is of less significance because managers already implicitly take account of this feature.

to these arguments depending on the structural characteristics of the sector. One key issue is whether it is possible to measure a project's option value: if measurement is impossible, managers will find it difficult to make a case. A further consideration is whether it is possible to trade the option. In the case of patent protected and codified forms of output it is possible to trade part-completed projects where their fit with the originator is less than planned. This possibility is not generally available to firms in engineering sectors where the nature of the technology is seldom transparent. Firms can still value options in-house but if the project requires significant external finance that is not sufficient. Even where financiers can be appraised of the project, that transparency would need to extend to any future hypothetical buyer for the abandonment option to be properly valued.[13] It seems reasonable to portray sectors such as pharmaceuticals where knowledge is codified as options-friendly in the sense that the nature of the risks are known statistically and that there are likely to be available bench-marks and comparators from which parameters of the valuation models can be estimated. Being measurable in this way such options are also more likely to be tradable in contrast to the more idiosyncratic and possibly secret risks associated with other sectors such as engineering.

There are other reasons too why the codified nature of much of the chemicals-sector innovation encourages investment and risk-taking. Codifiable discoveries allow first-stage research to be farmed out to competitive small-scale firms that share the initial risk but which cannot commercialize any discoveries without the complementary assets of the larger firm. Furthermore, the existence of patent protection creates a skewed distribution of returns with the prize of a large upside and the possibility of further follow-ons. This gives rise to a greater predisposition to invest than where returns are clustered in a narrow range.

Our interpretation of inter-sector variation in investment and performance is thus somewhat distinct from the story told by Eltis (1996), though we agree with him that investment is biased towards cost-cutting. Profitability is important for investment, but it is because profits are

---

[13] It is possible to trade risky pre-human trial projects in biotechnology, effectively valuing them as options and companies such as Celtic Pharma and Symphony have been involved in funding the development side of new drugs with the manufacturing rights to successes then sold on (*Financial Times* October 26 2007). The view that only some sectors are assessed with option value included is also supported by anecdotal evidence that techniques such as real options are used commonly only in a small number of sectors such as energy and pharmaceuticals.

easy to quantify and to be reliably protected in pharmaceuticals (with patents) and aerospace (with government contracts) that investment follows profits. Industrial environments where profit opportunities are not codifiable and quantifiable tend to be viewed with suspicion by investors who like certainty and transparency. Such projects then tend to be shunned by managers in favour of easier ways of making money, either through takeover activity, asset backed sectors or a reliance on the safer end of investment such as cost-cutting and short-lived assets.

5.4   Conclusions

The arguments above have suggested that specific characteristics of parts of manufacturing make them especially vulnerable to underinvestment. Exactly the same arguments apply to R&D given the large proportion of costs which are sunk and the long paybacks involved in uncertain projects. Arguments based on sunk cost and uncertainty do not give the full picture because there is considerable heterogeneity across industries and firms in the investment response to profits. And, of course, the propensity to engage in these activities varies across national boundaries and industrial cultures and time. We have gone some way to explaining the observed patterns in our discussion of financial conditions and in particular the ease of communication with investors. In the next chapter we broaden out this idea to consider the complex interactions between systems of finance, corporate governance and corporate culture in a way that allows for a deeper understanding of the UK investment climate.

6
Global Finance, Industry and Shareholder Value

6.1 Introduction

A key reason why the UK persisted with a pronounced pro-market stance – even after the Thatcher-Major years had delivered no increase in trend growth – was the intellectual climate that paralleled the emergence of a finance dominated global economy. We outline in section 6.2 how financial globalization shaped ideas on economic policy from the 1980s, and in particular macroeconomic and industrial policy. In section 6.3, we deal with the crucial question of how market orientation affected the institution of the *firm* so that the corporation as an institution no longer plays the relatively independent role in economic development that it once did.

6.2 Finance and the global environment

Throughout the twentieth century, Britain's economic policy has catered to the interests of the City of London. Nevertheless until at least the early 1980s, industry constituted a powerful counterweight. Firms tended to be financed out of retained earnings (Mayer 1988), so that decisions at company level were to some extent autonomous, especially when weak competition facilitated this. Finance was powerful but even in the UK for a great many years it was just one pillar of the economy.

All of this was to change in the 1980s and 1990s, not just in the UK but internationally as well. To understand this we must separate out the domestic fact of a finance-dominated industrial structure in the UK from the global forces that were making finance more powerful everywhere. The key was the increasing international mobility of capital that had been heavily constrained during the fixed exchange period up to the early 1970s. An important rationale for this early constraint was that a contrary policy – under fixed exchange rates – would have enforced common monetary policies on all countries – similar to the operation of a gold standard. An extreme form of globalization was thus avoided and countries were free, at least up to a point, to develop along separate capitalist lines with different institutional approaches to issues in finance, labour relations and industrial policy. Once flexible exchange rates were established after the break-up of the Bretton Woods agreement, capital controls were no longer seen as a necessary part of the framework resulting in a different and more highly globalized system (Rodrik 2011).

Capital mobility

Capital controls were lifted very early in the first Thatcher government to open up London to US investment banks. A decade later, by the end of the 1980s capital flows were unrestricted in all major European countries. The US and the UK, with their large financial services industries, were to the fore in pressing for further liberalization and they lobbied successfully for capital mobility to be a condition for OECD membership. Towards the end of the 1990s the IMF also committed itself to removing restrictions on capital flows internationally, something that up to then had not been part of the globalization programme which had focused more narrowly on traded goods. Trade negotiations had by then also become focussed on liberalizing services trade, in particular banking and business services which would particularly benefit those industries in the US and UK. The environment in which these changes operated is known as financialization.

The international capital markets were now dominant, but they did not work as economic theory had predicted; they proved highly volatile, with real exchange rates failing to regulate flows between debtor and creditor countries. Capital imports, often recommended for developing nations, became a feature of some developed ones, particularly after the Asian crisis of the late 1990s. Some countries such as the US and UK were permitted to run current account deficits, spending more than they produced and exporting less than they imported. Others such as Germany, Japan and China ran large surpluses. For some developing countries, current account deficits were possible to sustain as long as international capital markets were willing to underwrite the necessary capital inflows. Overall however these large imbalances contributed to global uncertainty.

Financialization and the macroeconomy

Financialization is a controversial subject with supporters and detractors. On the plus side, it can be argued that financialization creates deeper and more sophisticated financial markets, permitting access to new and innovative sources of funding at a lower cost partly due to higher ceilings on gearing (Ashworth and Davies 2001). Additional arguments are that it permits consumption smoothing over time and that equity financing in particular fuels growth as it permits greater risk-taking (Carlin and Mayer 2000). According to Rajan and Zingales (2003) vested interests prevent the emergence of new firms and thus the simultaneous liberalization of trade and finance is important for growth.

Critics have challenged many of these arguments. Baltagi et al (2009) argue that the gains to trade and financial liberalization tend to experience diminishing returns and that the greatest gains (and often the only positive ones in terms of stimulating private credit) come from liberalization cases that are starting from a fairly closed or autarchic position. This is important because capital flows have been much less directed towards developing countries under financialization than in the classic gold standard period (Schularick 2006).

Financial liberalization has also implied more volatility in capital flows than expected. Sudden changes in investor sentiment have resulted in reversals in capital flows such as those that affected Asian countries in 1997. International capital is a 'fair-weather friend' – only there when it is least needed as exemplified by the over-lending by banks that later profit from the ensuing distress (Rodrik 2011, p.124).[1] There are no adequate international regulatory institutions that replicate those at national level, as a result of which banking crises have correlated with periods of capital mobility. Recessions too were on average deeper in the flexible exchange period than in the preceding Bretton Woods era of fixed rates (Stockhammer 2010).

Financialization and the UK

For the UK, the effects of financialization involved:

- A crowding out of manufacturing and related sectors that accelerated the rate of deindustrialization relative to other advanced countries (Coutts et al 2007).

---

[1] Indeed it was a fear of capital flight that saw China and some other countries massively increase their purchase of US government bonds in the wake of the Asian crisis thus providing the liquidity to fuel the credit explosion in the years before the financial crash. Capital flight also affected Russia (1998), Brazil (1999), Turkey (2001) and Argentina (2001–2).

- Increased volatility of sterling with adverse effects on UK exports (Darby et al 1999).[2]
- A turn towards inward direct investment often in the form of acquisition, increasingly aimed less at productivity enhancement and more at obtaining resources for the acquiring firm, such as technology, brands and market position (Driffield et al 2009).

None of these developments would have worried those observers who had a strong sense that the market was always right. But sustainable growth in an economy, no less than in a single firm, requires the patient building up of capabilities. Industries cannot be knocked down one day and new ones created the next. Skills, equipment, reputation and networks cannot always be sourced externally. If transactions cost has any relevance it is surely in the understanding that coordination matters and needs investment. The transition to new industries that was needed in mature economies such as that of the UK, required a serious planning exercise. It is not enough to aim at stability in the price level. When businesses lock up capital for many years in capital projects they need to have confidence that markets (and suppliers) are going to be there for products and services years down the line. Such views were consistently ignored. Rather, policy encouraged flexible job contracts and flexible financing arrangements that implied uncertain markets for products and services. Financialization created high incomes for a few as we saw in Chapter 1, but the same phenomenon was weakening labour's bargaining power and creating less secure employment. UK profitability experienced a trend rise from the 1980s but investment was not matching this, indicating that it partly reflected regressive income distribution. This made broad based growth dependent on rising consumer indebtedness, particularly in the decade up to the financial crash. Consumer demand remained buoyed by asset price inflation but businesses may not have identified this as a sustainable path as the discussion on global imbalances and uncertainties in Tucker (2003) makes clear.

Redistribution of income away from wages was also an issue in the *type* of economy being created. In certain industries, low labour protection underpinned the rise in profits. Productivity increases here took a form that was unrelated to technical progress and therefore was

---

[2] In the period from 1980 to the formation of the Euro, exchange rate volatility for the UK considerably exceeded that of Germany and France and even Italy (DTI 2001).

by its nature bounded. It is only possible to increase the intensity of labour or to drive down wages and conditions so much or so many times. The process is limited and therefore raises doubts about the continuing growth path of demand in a way that is likely to discourage capital and skills investment.

If the prospects for demand arising from broad-based domestic income growth were low, why did the changed labour climate not lead to a large expansion of UK exports? We have already mentioned the volatility of sterling during the period, which discouraged exports. It seems unlikely, that currency volatility, however important, can fully explain this trend. Export success increasingly depends on quality issues rather than price competitiveness. This is especially true of products where advanced countries can hope to compete. As noted by Froud et al (2011) 'substantial depreciation of the currency is now necessary just to hold exports on their historical rate of growth' (p.27). To have delivered success in quality would have required increased investment and R&D in export-oriented sectors and a planning framework to facilitate this.[3] While the increase in profit share from the 1980s should – in textbook theory – have stimulated R&D and capital investment, the relation between the two was never strong for the UK and weakened further during the period.

This divergence between profits and investments – in capital and R&D – should have signalled a warning for policymakers. But the implied message was perhaps too discomforting to be recognized let alone elicit any response. A standard post-Keynesian view is that when investment responds weakly to profit margins unemployment can only be preserved by wage-led growth (Marglin and Bhaduri 1990). Policymakers would have been reluctant to accept this argument and indeed there may have been sound economic reasons for caution. There is a danger in lurching from Keynesian to classical unemployment if the only mechanism for signalling future demand is by raising current wages. In our view there is also room for an institutional approach to building confidence in the sustainability of *future* wage paths that can increase the propensity to invest. But this assumes a context of industrial planning with social partners to which current policy was (and is) hostile.

---

[3] Comparisons with the US on this issue generally give the misleading impression that the hi-tech sector there arose spontaneously from small enterprise and universities. In fact the original Silicon Valley which the hi-tech boom of the 1990s echoed was a product of quasi-industrial policy by the US Defense Department.

As seen in Chapter 3, the manufacturing sector was especially important for export-based growth. Here more than anywhere was evidence of lack of joined up policy and a failure to bring social partners together. Far sighted employers and their representatives had long recognized the difficulties faced by manufacturing and particularly by the engineering based industries. The damage inflicted by the recession of the early 1990s led to the setting up of a National Manufacturing Council (NMC) by the employers' body, the Confederation of British Industries (CBI), to coordinate policies for renewal. The first report of the NMC, CBI (1992) painted a realistic and blunt picture of investment output, productivity and the trade balance. It identified priorities such as investment, research and coordination of local supply chains. Perhaps the most interesting aspect of the NMC report was the way in which it allocated responsibility to both finance and industry. Finance was argued to be misdirecting loans to sectors such as property (up 800 per cent in real terms in a decade) rather than manufacturing (up just 50 per cent) so as to 'to gain short term profit supported by asset price inflation' (p.22). But there was also criticism about the manufacturing sector's own decisions. Criticism was made of dividends growing faster than profits and three times faster than investment in the preceding decade. Companies should not 'allow themselves to pay out an excessive level of dividend which ... cause them to abandon the capital spending required to secure their long-term competitive position' (p.23).[4]

This was strong stuff coming from the horse's mouth. But the critique was not pursued vigorously and was largely ineffective. In part, the CBI's change of approach was necessitated by the 'unfriendly policy stance' that manufacturing was faced with. As recalled by the Chief Economic Adviser at the CBI, 'there was a lack of conviction, as far as the government of the day was concerned, that there was a UK investment problem'

---

[4] The CBI were not alone in arguing the case for a stronger intervention to protect manufacturing. Following the peak of North Sea Oil production there were concerns over the lack of an industrial strategy particularly for manufacturing (House of Lords 1985). Economists such as Robert Rowthorn and economic journalists such as Will Hutton and Larry Elliot made powerful cases against the new orthodoxy of benign neglect. The CEO of Rolls Royce John Rose in a largely ignored contribution in 2007 went to some lengths to explain how a prosperous future for UK workers was dependent on maintaining a strong manufacturing presence. See Rowthorn and Ramaswamy (1997); Hutton (1996); Elliott and Atkinson (2007, 2008). See also video-link: http://www3.imperial.ac.uk/events/dennisgaborlecture to the lecture given as The Dennis Gabor Lecture 'Why Manufacturing Matters' by Sir John Rose, Imperial College, 15 November 2007.

(Barker 1999, p.301). The tenor of the NMC was to change radically over the coming years to a more up-beat and optimistic assessment despite the continuing problems that the sector actually faced. This language presaged a growing tendency for much of the manufacturing sector to pursue productivity growth *at the expense of expansion*; the voice of manufacturing increasingly came to represent the winners from this strategy, as others downsized their activities in the UK. British industrialists had ceased to criticize the City culture by the 1990s as 'CEOs and finance directors of quoted companies now shared the same time-scales and priorities of the financial institutions themselves' (Kristensen and Zeitlin 2005, p.175).

The New Labour era

We can agree with Crafts (1991) that the Conservative administrations of the period under examination had a 'distaste' for economic policies based on training and technology. But what of the New Labour years that followed? Were the political trends of the late 1990s and onward more favourable to such an approach?

In one way the answer is yes. Training and innovation were certainly key terms in the policy papers of these years. Furthermore for the first few years of the new 1997 administration there was careful and sustained attention to productivity issues, especially in the competitiveness indicator reports. The second report (DTI 2001) began by attributing 'disappointing' productivity levels to a 'skills gap, low spending on R&D and innovation, a legacy of underinvestment and a culture that does not sufficiently encourage risk-taking and enterprise' (p.5). An underlying problem of macroeconomic instability was diagnosed with volatility in output growth, inflation and exchange rates all higher than for European competitors over a twenty year period.

The problems may have been diagnosed but the remedies were fitful, mainly consisting of minor changes to the tax system.[5] Nor was the problem of stability resolved. There was an essential contradiction between the open markets agenda and the objective of macroeconomic stability, supposed to ensure investment and growth. New instruments (Central Bank Independence and Fiscal Rules) may have helped to keep interest rates stable, but the corollary was that the burden of flexibility fell on individuals and undiversified firms. The academic literature on the

---

[5] Corry (2011) adds other measures that he says produced a 'profound set of changes to the way that capitalism worked' including labour market measures to stop a race to the bottom, infrastructure investment, regional development agencies, while admitting that many will see these steps as lacking ambition.

merits of inflation targeting is conflicting and does not support a notion that it is a magic bullet for growth. But how were the Department of Trade and Industry (DTI) policymakers to know this when the pervasive ideology was relentlessly insisting that markets would always deliver? This pressure led the DTI (2001) to proclaim that: 'Macroeconomic stability and lower long-term interest rates are the most important contribution that the Government can make to encourage investment' (p.37). This statement came without references or argument. Nor was there ever a post-audit of the accompanying statement that macroeconomic stability was 'beginning to feed through to the levels of investment' (p.37). Shortly afterwards, the emphasis shifted away from promoting capital investment which was seen as an intractable problem.

Stability by itself may facilitate growth when there is no need for big changes. But that was not the case for the UK, as the policymakers came to learn. The DTI drafted in competitiveness experts from Harvard Business School to give an overview of the UK international position. These experts, led by the world's leading strategy academic Michael Porter, indicated the need for a change of strategy (Porter and Ketels 2003). In their view 'the UK currently faces a transition to a new phase of economic development ... from ... competing on relatively low costs of doing business to ... competing on unique value and innovation' (p.5). This view was broadly correct and at this stage the Porter analysis was that low productivity, particularly in UK manufacturing, was 'consistent with lower spending on capital investment and R&D relative to other locations' (p.38). The DTI was also won over to these arguments, noting that 'market-based reforms ... are now running into diminishing returns' (Pryce and Cairncross 2003).

This analysis was however to shift significantly within a year. In a talk to the Smith Institute, Porter's collaborator Ketels (2004) downplayed the importance of capital investment, suggesting that some studies had shown that France and Germany with their bank-based systems and artificially low interest rates 'had extensively over-invested in the capital stock ... creating intense pressure on employment' (p.53). Clearly the Harvard contingent had gone native, influenced by their hosts' antipathy to capital investment. But there was no basis for their view which indeed reflected a profound ignorance of the facts. Capital intensity had also, from the mid-1990s, stalled in France (Cette et al 2009) and to some extent in Germany (Aiginger 2003a).[6]

---

[6] In Europe at the time, as James Tobin (1997) explained, policy was 'more dedicated to price stability to the exclusion of high output and employment' (p.18).

Despite being hostile or indifferent to a policy of raising capital accumulation, UK policymakers nevertheless accepted that a new phase of reform was needed. Roughly speaking the view was that privatization, labour market reform and so on had worked to halt Britain's relative decline but that new positive approaches were needed to generate growth. The difficulty was how to square the need for intervention with an overarching philosophy that the market would deliver. As Corry (2011) remarks, there was 'limited room for manoeuvre, not least given the strength of prevailing orthodoxy' (p.S130). Refuge was sought in the idea that government could set an agenda but that 'culture takes a long time to change' (Pryce 2004). The scene was set but the actors were missing. Leadership is a hands-on affair and not much was likely to happen without it.

The UK policy perspective from the late 1990s was that financialization offered the chance of a grand bargain between nation states and global capital in which everyone could prosper. As recorded by the former secretary of state for innovation (Denham 2011), a 'precept' of the Blair-Brown government was that globalization was 'a benign and challenging opportunity if only we responded to it appropriately [through a] pro-business stance, lax regulation, flexible labour markets and being positive towards legal migration' (p.S47).[7]

The experience of the US, particularly in the late 1990s in the run-up to the dot-com crash, was constantly envied, as was the ensuing productivity growth in IT using industries such as retail. But the real debate over the role of labour flexibility in the US model, versus its higher rate of capital and R&D investment, remained under-researched (Aiginger 2003b).[8] Griffith and Harrison (2003) argued that business funded R&D explained all of the UK's poor productivity performance compared with the US.

Denham (2011) argues that the failure, early on, to establish an industrial strategy made the country vulnerable to the financial crisis at the

---

[7] A variant of this view, held by some, was that perfunctory adherence to market principles was a requirement for evading them in practice. The more one advertises the market view, the more room there is for autonomous deviation (Corry 2011; Usher 2011). The latter view however ignores the inevitable dischord and inefficiency of a system where culture and practice are divergent. One result was the astonishing failure to insist that companies paid their fair share of tax. The charity Action Aid has calculated that of the FTSE 100's 34,216 subsidiaries, about a quarter – 8492 – are in tax havens.

[8] Griffith (2007) suggests that some differences in productivity between the UK and US can be explained by consumer behaviour.

end of the administration in which he served. In that he is surely right. The reliance on capital mobility to allocate resources had left the UK with an uncoordinated set of supply chains and isolated islands of specialism. The most important growth sector – that of business services – was heavily orientated towards the reckless banking sector. Neither state nor market was going to find it easy to 'rebalance the economy' given the choices that had been made over previous decades.

The globalization agenda of the Blair-Brown years thus continued the trends of the previous administration including a focus on finance, a neglect of production and a redistribution from labour to capital. It seems fair to say that throughout the whole period starting in the early 1980s, industrial planning and policy was seen as a relic of the past. There were eleven different ministerial occupants at the department of industry/enterprise in the Thatcher-Major years from 1979 to 1997 and eight more changes in the Blair-Brown years up to 2010. There were several changes of nomenclature and status for the organization itself, none of which seemed essential. The reality was that it scarcely mattered who the minister was or how the organization was constituted; industrial policy had become a sideshow oriented to the simple task of building and maintaining a 'level playing field'. Only in the last five years of the Blair-Brown administration was there any critical mass of research reports on the future of industry and the need for a competition policy. But these reports merely documented the daunting task that has been inherited by decades of inaction.

6.3   Financialization and the corporation

The ways in which financialization has affected the UK economy and constrained its sustainable growth are not limited to macroeconomic and industrial policy. Even more significant, in our view, is the changed (and still changing) balance of power between the 'providers' of finance on the one hand and company executives on the other. The tension between owners and managers has been a perennial theme in finance since the owner-managed firms gave way as the dominant form of enterprise – first to joint stock companies in which families and individuals continued to play an important executive role and later to today's shareholder owned firms with external ownership. Once the provision of finance is split from the executive function there is a problem of alignment of interests. Under some conditions that split is efficient, as attested to by Irving Fisher's 'separation theorem' of finance. In fact the separation theorem is no more than an example of the well-known economic principle of comparative advantage. In international trade for example countries should choose their output mix so as to specialize in what can give them greatest value in international exchange rather than producing for their own consumption. So also, in corporate finance, it is not individual firm's preferences in terms of time horizons or risk that matters but the financial market's revealed preferences as expressed in the price of these attributes.[9] The theory tells us nothing about why firms possess a comparative advantage in the first place.

The simple point of the separation theorem is that the firm itself is not a useful level at which objectives should be formulated. Rather firms (or their owner-managers) should be looking to arrange financial strategy to maximize returns as they would be valued by the stock market. An overlooked question here perhaps is whether firms may have a comparative advantage not only in seeing existing investment projects through to a conclusion, but also in searching for and generating new investment projects and hence their role in the overall balance between consumption and investment.

The major stumbling block in implementing the separation theory is information. In managerial firms with external finance, there is a question as to whether a delegated agent (the manager of the firm) can be expected to act in the interests of dispersed owners (the principals) when managers' performances cannot easily be assessed. In the absence of transparency, agents have to be incentivized by schemes such as sharecropping or profit sharing (Stiglitz 1974). Such incentives involve various costs (agency costs) so that owners may prefer instead to actively monitor their managers using the 'voice option' (Hirschman 1970). Contrariwise

---

[9] In his *Theory of Interest*, Fisher (1930) considered the decisions involved when a landowner faces three alternative uses of a given piece of land – in farming, forestry or mining. Farming produces constant prospective returns, while mining tends to produce a declining, and forestry a rising (at least initially), set of prospective returns. In Fisher's example, the mining prospect produces the highest present value. In the absence of capital markets, the choice will however depend upon the *subjective* valuation of the alternative consumption streams that the different prospects allow. If for example, the landowner has a strong preference for a steady flow of consumption over time (or a less risky activity) then farming may well be chosen over mining. However in the presence of a perfect capital market that allows the landowner to lend or borrow at a constant 'market' rate of interest (and to compensate properly for risk), the production and consumption decisions can be separated. Modern portfolio theory fills in the picture by showing for example how the price of risk is determined.

where shareholding is highly dispersed, and 'voice' not usually viable, liquid equity markets provide an 'exit' option for owners dissatisfied with corporate management. Inefficiency is resolved through buying and selling of companies in whole or in part, though that also has its own difficulties, as any history of takeover effects will affirm. In general, all these ideas for aligning the interests of investors and managers (principals and agents) have had mixed success in practice but they are seen as inescapable features of the system of external finance for firms. Indeed the notion of alignment features so centrally in modern finance theory and corporate governance that it is easy to forget that it was not at all central to managerial practice until the financialization period.

Managerial capitalism

In the 1950s and 1960s, there were considerable possibilities for managerial discretionary control. This stemmed from the dynamism of US large firms at the time that were operating at the end of the era of managerial capitalism as described by economic historians such as Chandler (1977, 1990). Permanence, power and continued growth are the characteristics that Chandler identified in managerial capitalism.

> Stock was often widely owned, and stock-holders did not have the influence, knowledge, experience or commitment to take part in the high command. Salaried managers determined long-term policy as well as short-term operating activities. They dominated top as well as lower and middle management.
>
> (Chandler 1977, p.10)[10]

In the era of managerial capitalism the (principal–agent) split between ownership and control as analysed by Berle and Means (1932), had in effect been resolved in favour of agents. By the time that Berle (1965) again surveyed the issue, he had come to regard owners as close to irrelevant, possessing wealth in a form that was 'supine and passive'

---

[10] Patterns among the big corporations did of course vary according to financial structure. In the US some banks provided significant amounts of 'outside capital' and where they often placed part-time representatives on the board (financial capitalism). Earlier, before the Glass-Steagall Act of 1933, banks were important in the US not just in finance provision, but also in promoting consolidation and concentration.

(p.52). Power lay with the executive managers. As Reich (2006) reminds us: 'The CEO of the 1950s and 1960s had no particular need to meet with shareholders ... their jobs were secure' (p.75).

In the UK, the system was different, but arguably only in degree. Chandler held that, for the UK, a less dynamic system of 'personal capitalism' ruled, dominated by family firms who could not match the concentration of resources of their US counterparts. In reality, as Franks et al (2004) show, family control was challenged quite early by the institutional investors – the latter could control a third of firms as early as 1960, with professional management of firms increasing in importance. These firms tended to be growth-oriented rather than profit maximizers, as described in the theories of Marris (1964, 1972). British managers were more constrained than their US counterparts in that they faced the early emergence of a market for corporate control that foreshadowed financialization. Nevertheless the UK system was similar in kind to that of the US in that it allowed for far more autonomy by professional managers than they were to have from the 1980s onwards. In Marris' 1998 revised edition of his 1964 *The Economic Theory Managerial Capitalism*, he argued that the growth orientation of managerial capitalism was – via its favourable influence on the macro growth rate:

A Good Thing. It was responsible for, at least closely associated with, the historically unique period of economic growth that occurred in North America, Australasia, Western Europe and Japan over the twentieth century as a whole. I dare anyone to claim seriously that if there had been all kinds of laws and other constraints compelling firms to be always small or, if large, always exceptionally owner-orientated, the level of social welfare, in the economists' sense of the word, would have been better.

(2nd edition 1998, p.ix)

Financialization and corporate control

Financialization changed the balance of power. The tensions between owner and manager appeared again on the agenda, particularly as the proportion of shares held by large institutions increased rapidly. The new tendency from the 1980s onwards was towards eliminating that tension in favour of owners, at least in liberal market economies. Shareholder power increased and the results were felt in a retreat from capacity building and firm-centred organic growth that had earlier been regarded as the essence of management and the *raison-d'etre* of business.

Financialization as applied to the corporate arena advertises itself as restraining the privileges of executive management, such as a quiet life or private benefits. The basic proposition is that the discipline exerted by capital mobility and takeover threats ensures a superior allocation of resources that should raise owners' wealth. Other forms of discipline are facilitated by the rise of particular institutional investors such as private equity or hedge funds who may exert influence through direct oversight or representation at board level. The set of principles by which the interests of owners and managers are aligned has come to be known as *corporate governance*.

Corporate governance is really a set of theories and debates that divides the academic community. But in practical terms it is now commonly understood as a process of safeguarding measured shareholder value (Deakin 2008; Holmstrom and Kaplan 2001; Reberioux 2007). Senior managers of public corporations have come to internalize the perceived views of their shareholder investors and are increasingly accountable. The tenure of senior managers such as the Chief Executive Officer (CEO) has fallen, and the performance-related turnover of the CEO has increased, in all geographical regions (Kaplan and Minton 2006; Booz Allen 2007). The numbers are striking with a tripling of performance-related CEO turnover in the five years to 2000 in the US (Gracia 2004). There has also been a greater use of shareholder-friendly metrics such as Economic Value Added (Krafft and Ravix 2005); more active shareholders (ICR 2006; Rogers 2008); and more pressure on managers to distribute rather than retain profits (Lazonick 2008). The implications of this pressure on executive management are captured in the study by Roberts et al (2006) on the routines followed by executives in preparing for board meetings. The executives:

> [C]ome to transform themselves, their understanding and their actions in the images of the investor's desires ... Autonomy is realised not against but through meeting the demand for shareholder value
>
> (Roberts et al 2006, p.287)

Corporate governance rules are predicated on a one-size-fits-all philosophy. By reducing firms to spread-sheets with tick-boxes showing which features of corporate governance codes have been satisfied, the firms themselves become commodities that are more easily assessed or at least valued by the investment institutions that are the main players in the 'market for corporate control' (Lysandrou and Parker 2011). It is in this sense that corporate governance is an inherent feature of financialization. It operates to limit manager's freedom in the corporate arena, just as government freedom is curtailed in macroeconomic and industrial policy. In liberal market economies, the result is a set of formulaic performance rules that threaten managers' autonomy to allocate resources within the firm.

In theory, the effects of financialization in the corporate sphere should be as beneficial as in that of the macroeconomy. Increased attention to the interests of financial investors should ensure their willingness to provide funds at lower cost. Insofar as firms may be unwilling to access external funds because of a perceived cost premium, that constraint should at least be reduced under a more shareholder friendly system. However as with the macroeconomic issues reviewed in section 6.2, there is a plausible story that financialization may in fact exert a negative effect on firms' capital investment and other forward commitments.

The effects on capital investment

How does the firm make shareholder-oriented investment decisions? Without any distortions the firm is supposed to maximize the present value (V) of a one-period investment project (I) discounted by the cost of capital (r). Managers, however, may behave in ways that imply over-investment or under-investment. With such biases to decision-making, the usual net target $[V(I)/(1+r) - I]$ may be shifted by a multiplier $(1 + \lambda)$ where λ is positive in the case of 'empire building' (over-investment) and negative for over-cautious managers (under-investment). Additionally, the presence of asymmetric information between managers and investors may worsen the terms on which external finance is available by a shift factor θ so that the firm's problem becomes one of maximizing:

$$[1+\lambda]\left[\frac{V(I)}{1+r}\right] - I - \theta C(e) \qquad (1)$$

where $C(e)$ is the cost of (outside) equity capital and financial frictions are indexed by θ. The combination of the two effects leads to an indeterminate bias in investment (Stein 2003).

Over-investment is expressed by positive values of λ, reflecting irrational exuberance or confidence in the ability to make quick gains before shifting the loss and risk to a third party. Examples here are technology bubbles and empire building projects, often of the form of acquisitions and often fuelled by unexpected cash windfalls. Under-investment is likely where managerial career concerns are such as to encourage the avoidance of risk or where executives do not feel their contribution would be rewarded. In addition, where communication with shareholders is imperfect, the premium θ on the cost of external capital will depress investment.

Short-termism and risk-aversion

Financialization can claim to have a beneficial effect on future commitments like capital investment and R&D where it corrects managerial over-investment and enhances communication between shareholders and companies. Nevertheless it is reasonable to argue that much of 'managerial over-investment' was simply countering an endemic tendency of shareholder capitalism to demand short-term results and to forego projects with a good but lengthy return. Under financialization, this short-termism is embraced by executive managers who are forced to respond more readily to investor demands.

Where short-termism applies, firms systematically only take account of near-term projected earnings when authorizing investment and thus turn down valuable opportunities that the firms' managers might wish to pursue but are not attractive to investors whose time horizons are shorter.[11] The pervasive use of payback as an investment criterion, documented in Chapter 4, is clearly compatible with this practice.

The issue of short-termism in the UK was recently revisited by Haldane and Davies (2011) of the Bank of England who surveyed impressive historical evidence for short-termism in case studies and interviews. Their concern was that 'for some of the jury, however it [the evidence] remains inconclusive', prompting them first rigorously to test and subsequently confirm that excessive target returns were used by UK firms. Within a week, the *Financial Times* Lex column had brushed the findings aside with the dictum that 'directors generally invest for the future and shareholders generally go along' (Lex 30 May). It is easy for commentators to dismiss seemingly rigorous tests of short-termism because the latter often miss the complex contextual and behavioural points of

---

[11] There is a historic debate over whether short-termism is due to managers or investors (Nickell 1995). Under financialization the distinction is blurred.

the issue.[12] In our view, the best way of demonstrating short-termism is to show how broad and deep is the *informal* weight of evidence which has accumulated over several decades. We report here a set of additional material beyond that cited in Haldane and Davies and that focuses on the R&D decision where short-termism will be most damaging.

One early study related to city attitudes to R&D (NEDO 1986). Interviews with senior analysts in the most important stockbroker houses made clear that although R&D was valued in the share price it was also likely to have distorting effects. A problem was perceived both in regard to firms (who preferred acquisitions over organic growth) and investors who preferred to attach valuation only when results were coming through as earnings or at least the project was in the development (D) of the R&D phase. Furthermore because analysts 'were not Nobel prize winners', market reaction could be crude; firms would find it hard to break out of the norms for their industry or their market power class. Bank finance was more likely to be available for process or cost-cutting R&D where downside risk avoidance would benefit the debt-holder; product R&D would need to rely on equity but there was a perceived problem here with raising cash specifically for R&D being a very rare event; as one respondent put it 'it would be instantly dilutive of earnings ... an extremely good way of making the share price go down ... investors only look one year ahead'. Even large blue chip companies that needed large and lumpy cash for R&D faced stock market pressure because of the resultant instability in earnings. Very similar observations were made in the Innovation Advisory Report 1990 that recommended the setting up of the R&D scoreboard of top spending companies. This report also argued that increasing institutional ownership had strengthened pressure on UK companies to trim R&D spending

---

[12] Haldane and Davies are in fact testing joint hypotheses of rational expectations, market efficiency, lack of myopia and the CAPM model in a way that makes their results difficult to interpret. The *Investors Chronicle* notes: 'But is a constant risk premium really rational? Think about the sort of things that might cause a firm to collapse – and such collapses, remember, are more common than you might think. It might get a bad or unlucky chief executive. It might adopt the wrong strategy. It might be supplanted by new technology. In the short-term, these risks are small, because we have a fair idea who the chief executive will be next year, or what technology will be. But in the long term, we don't have a clue. It's reasonable, then, to apply a more than constant risk premium to future cash-flows – more precisely speaking, an uncertainty premium. And if we do this, what looks like irrational excessive discounting becomes quite reasonable', (Irrationally short-termist? By Chris Dillow, 16 May 2011). The logic here is correct even if standard discounting does penalize later risk more.

due largely to the high proportion of pension funds that were under external management and judged on short-term criteria.

A comprehensive set of studies reported in the *European Journal of Finance* (1998) on the attitudes of investors and the way they were perceived by industrial managers showed a complex picture. Analysts working for institutions such as pension funds companies were *not* seen as short-termist by the largest companies, while sell-side analysts researching companies for stockbrokers did appear to be so (Marston and Craven 1998). Short-termism in relation to R&D was confirmed with finance directors observed to act under a belief that capital markets were short-termist (Demirag 1998; see also separate confirmatory research reported in Grinyer et al 1998). In the same issue of the journal other papers reported that British companies were relatively more short-termist than Dutch ones and that performance management contributed to the short-term orientation of fund managers.

The weight of the evidence is that at least some institutions are endemically short-termist. Managerialism may thus be argued to have offered some form of second-best counterweight to this effect. Seen in this light, the effect of financialization will be to reduce the demand (by firms) for new capital investment while simultaneously reducing the financial constraint that may have been experienced under managerial capitalism for those firms relying on external finance. But the net effect may well have been to reduce overall capital investment. Almost everyone agrees that some form of short-termism exists or at any rate there is very little evidence against it (Nickell 1995). But the more difficult question, as Nickell notes is its overall importance. That depends on whether there is a tradition of underinvestment that would be aggravated by shareholder primacy. Even those who argue that shareholder governance is optimal tend to suggest that managers (at least of non-financial firms) have developed a preference for the 'quiet life' rather than empire building (Bertrand and Mullainathan 2003). True believers in shareholder control want to correct such under-investment by even more direct control by owners (Bebchuk and Fried 2004). This view echoes those who argue for a form of stakeholding predicated on ownership, or the idea of the universal owner with institutions engaging directly in strategy at company board level (Aglietta 2007; Myners 2001). Our argument, developed in the next chapter, is that shareholder primacy is an unsuitable framework for correcting under-investment in innovative projects because the information asymmetry is insoluble. In our view, financialization has magnified the impact of short-termism by removing the counterweight of managerial autonomy that had existed formerly and which was conducive to growth in the era of managerialism. If short-termism was damaging before (as many thought) it is more so now that the counterweight has been removed.

How shareholder pressure affects investment

The good and bad effects of financialization on capital investment and R&D can be illustrated together with the aid of a standard diagram in the supply and demand of investment finance (Hubbard 1998). In principle, financialization should increase the availability of finance and lower the cost of external funds insofar as it involves pressure to conform to the 'good governance' or pro-shareholder agenda. The question however is whether the same pressures that increase the supply of finance simultaneously lower the demand for it so that growth suffers.

According to a well-known theory, in finance there is a 'pecking order' in managers' choices of finance for investment projects such as that in R&D being considered here. Internal finance is preferred before accessing external finance (Myers 2003; Frank and Goyal 2008). This preference ordering corresponds to a kink in the supply curve where the cost of finance rises as the firm expands beyond the point that can be met from internal sources, that is retained earnings. The idea is shown in Figure 6.1. The slope of the supply curve to the right of the kink depends among other things on the degree and quality of information and oversight possessed by investors. As transparency and control increase under 'good governance', the slope will rotate clockwise to become near horizontal so that firms will not experience financial constraints; in other words the external market more closely resembles the perfect capital market in which the firm can access the external capital market at rates equal to internal sources.

For illustrative purposes suppose that the demand curve initially cuts through the supply curve close to the kink point and the equilibrium is at point A (upper panel). If at this point internal finance were to fall short of expectations (a translation to the left of the kinked supply curve as indicated), the firm might find itself finance constrained in that finance would now only be available at a rate that could not justify the previous level of investment. In the upper panel the equilibrium moves from A to B so that investment drops from R_0 to R_1. In a perfect capital market there would have been no change to the level of investment. The sensitivity of the fall in investment depends upon the slope of the supply schedule beyond the kink, which in a 'better' corporate governance regime falls only to R_2.

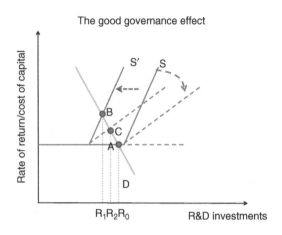

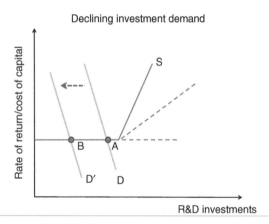

Figure 6.1 Governance Effects vs Cautious Investment on the Demand and Supply for Finance

A large body of empirical work has attempted to identify and estimate the presence of such financial constraints. Much of this has taken the form of testing the sensitivity of investment to internal funds (free cash flow). While the results remain controversial it has been argued that a positive coefficient on free cash flow demonstrates that firms are indeed constrained by finance (Angelopoulou and Gibson 2009). Recent empirical work however shows that the coefficient of investment on cash flow has been decreasing over time in liberal market economies such as the US (Brown et al 2009). One interpretation is that financialization has led to better governance and transparency and a deeper capital market lessening the extent of imperfections in the supply of finance as indicated in the upper panel.

There is, however, an alternative explanation that fits better with the history of capital investment and its relationship to profitability. As shown in the lower panel, this is that the *demand curve* has shifted inward under financialization rather than the supply curve rotating down. Put differently, financialization can be argued to have reduced the appetite of firms for investment by reducing the autonomy of managers and enforcing excessive target rates of return. The decline in demand for funds shown in the lower panel results in many more firms resembling that depicted, operating further away from the kink, so whether or not the kink has flattened becomes secondary to the fact that more firms are operating well below any kink in the supply of funds schedule.

For some, such conclusions would neither be surprising nor unwelcome. From the perspective of those who see the main problem of managerial empire building, excessive diversification and wasteful investment, the reduction in investment spending that accompanied tighter corporate governance and a more shareholder oriented approach is presumably a positive development (Jensen 1993). However a notable member of an earlier generation who took managerial motivation seriously, Marris (1996), noted the contradiction in all this:

> [A]ble economists ... publish elegant mathematical theories supporting financial incentives designed to reduce management incentives to growth. When I argue with them about this they reply that their theory is not supposed to have macroeconomic implications. (p.108)

Put differently, there are fallacies of composition at work – as everyone tries to invest less in the name of efficiency, there is less macro-level growth. A reduction in forward commitments by companies under shareholder pressure is only welcome if one believes an unproven assertion that over-investment is the main distortion in modern corporations. In the era of the growth of huge conglomerates, that argument may have had more force. But, there is virtually no evidence for this as a general proposition, especially in the current context. The main danger is the reverse – that executive managers will exercise excessive caution in respect of long-run projects especially where they are incentivized in relation to current earnings and disbursements.[13] Far easier to return money to shareholders in the form of share buy-backs for example than to oversee the search for long-run strategic investments. The effect of financialization shareholder-oriented corporate governance in particular is to tilt the balance away from reinvestment and indeed from capital investment and forward commitments generally (Lazonick and O'Sullivan 2000; Stockhammer 2006; Bauer et al 2008). Concrete evidence that this is happening for the case of UK R&D is given in Driver and Guedes (2012) where panel data estimates show that firms with a higher corporate governance score are conducting less R&D than their peers.

Internal and external finance

Shareholder primacy is a philosophy rooted in the concept of the 'dispossessed shareholder' (Reberioux 2007). It owes its modern legitimacy to the assumed opportunism of executives and employees in putting private benefits before delivering value for owners. Whereas national markets of the era before financialization had offered some sphere of influence to executives even in countries like the UK, this space shrank under the competitive race to protect returns. Shareholder value became 'the only intellectually respectable theory of corporate purpose' (Stout 2005). This agenda tends to play out conservatively because investors often have no way of being reliably informed about complex opportunities. They are thus led to attempt to pursue maximum current extraction of value and pressurize executive managers to achieve this.

The first approach to implementing shareholder value – pursued between the mid-1970s and late 1980s – involved an increase in managerial ownership through debt-financed buy-outs of businesses. The benign view of debt reflected its supposed role as a discipline on opportunistic managers, that is, that contractual interest payments rather than discretionary dividend payments would constrain managers from squandering shareholder cash (Jensen 1993). One observer noted that the 'ultimate purpose' of the restructuring of the 1980s was to improve performance by 'reducing investment' (Donaldson and Preston 1995, p.90). It certainly seems to have checked expansionary investment in the UK with a tightening of the trend capacity utilization ratio so that less capacity

---

[13] See Hennessy and Levy (2002). Popular perception may be different because of the experience in the financial crash of Financial CEOs recklessly gambling with shareholder money. But banks are a special case due to the 'too big to fail' phenomenon. Managers of cash-rich resources firms in the 1970s also overspent (Chirinko and Schaller 2006). But this too is a special case.

was held in relation to expected output (Driver and Shepherd 2005).[14] The subsequent ratcheting up of leverage and recourse to low quality bond finance eventually led to instability and company failures in the US and UK culminating in the 1990s recessions.[15] Subsequently, the methods changed, though the objective of disciplining managers remained.

A modified approach to shareholder value was pursued from the 1990s where the intention was to align the interests of managers and owners through compensation packages. The idea was to convert managers into part-owners by increasing top-level executive pay and making it dependent on shareholder performance. The process was made possible by 'delayering' – shedding layers of middle managers and concentrating power in the hands of a smaller managerial elite. Not only were positive incentives increased but managers' tenure was increasingly conditional on performance (Gracia 2004). It goes without saying that if these performance measures are tied to stock market valuations, managers have a direct incentive to drive stock prices higher through manipulating results and skimping on long-term investments (Bresnahan et al 1992).

What unites these approaches to disciplining managers is the aim of disgorging the surplus back to its owners rather than creatively looking for ways to grow the business. The assumption that managers cannot be trusted despite (or maybe because of) their vast compensation now dictates that surpluses be recycled – insofar as possible – through the stock market so that internal finance is only grudgingly sanctioned.

This bias against internal finance deserves to be questioned. Despite a comprehensive ideological win for shareholder theory in recent decades, it is now harder to make the case that this is the only viable variety of capitalism. It is no longer clear that 'British and American firms' have outperformed 'the manager-oriented model that evolved in the U.S. in the 1950's and 60's, the labor-oriented model that reached its apogee in German codetermination, and the state-oriented model that until

---

[14] In the UK, management buy-outs focused on cost-cutting, though with increases in efficiency investment (Wright et al 1992; Thompson and Wright 1995).

[15] US Treasury Secretary Brady remarked that the takeover phenomenon had produced the opposite result to that intended by stoking a preoccupation with the short term (*Financial Times* 14 May 1990). Subsequent to a spate of bankruptcies that ended this period, there followed a set of legal judgments and reform of US corporate law that made hostile takeovers more difficult, arguably amounting to a partial retreat from shareholder orientation (Blair 1995).

recently was dominant in France and much of Asia' (Hansmann and Kraakman 2000, p.i). For example, while the Dow Jones experienced only three years of falls in the two decades from 1980, it suffered five years of falls in the single decade that followed. Using a different time-scale for comparison, Martin (2010) notes 'Shareholders of the S&P 500 earned less overall returns during the "shareholder value" era than during the "managerial era"'.[16] In terms of productivity comparisons, the ratio of EU to US countries' GDP per hour was, at 90 per cent, the same figure in 2005 as in 1985 (Van Ark et al 2008). Although the problems of the Euro area have yet to play themselves out there is no sound basis for the case that EU productivity would benefit from less internal use of funds, except perhaps in industries where new entry is severely restricted by funding.

An important advantage of internal capital markets is the high quality information available within the firm that enables a CEO to pick winners across divisions so as to restructure effectively (Allen and Gale 2000; Stein 2003). Internal capital markets have been argued to work well not only in stable industries but under changing technologies as well, given that much new technology is secret and difficult to transmit across firm boundaries (Liebeskind 2000; Arrow 1983; Osterloh and Frey 2006). An influential counter argument has been put by Holmstrom and Kaplan (2001) and echoed in Pagano and Volpin (2008). Under unusually fast structural or technical change the potential for relatedness diminishes to the point where any advantage of internal allocation is cancelled by the need for resource building in new industries and firms. This then becomes an explanation for increased shareholder orientation: 'When it comes to moving capital long distances from declining industries to emerging industries', markets do it more effectively than managers (Holmstrom and Kaplan 2001, p.137). The focus thus shifts to the ability of firms with growth prospects to attract external capital and to the role of governance in facilitating that task.

The Holmstrom and Kaplan argument seemed at the time to have some merit in that new start-up and finance for high technology was more readily available in the US in the 1990s. However the provision of such venture capital was never more than a tiny percentage of the

---

[16] Careful cross-firm econometric analyses yield a more complex picture but there are only a handful of papers that confirm a robust relation between shareholder value orientation and corporate success, while others find null or weak results; for conflicting studies see, for example, Gugler (2001); Bhagat and Black (2002); Brown and Caylor (2009).

total capital investment; it was only significant for a few years before the dot-com crash and it was arguably partly responsible for that crash. With hindsight too, it is difficult to accept the argument that the stock market allocation of finance to industries has been particularly efficient in the US and UK with its huge channelling of resources into the financial intermediation industry. Nor is there strong evidence that the US system of external finance has allowed more transfer of resources across (heterogeneous) sectors than in Europe. A shift-share analysis of the productivity data shows that US productivity advantage lies *within* sectors and in whatever starting composition it had before the 1990s (Maudos et al 2008).

6.4 Conclusions

From the shareholder primacy perspective, the firm is a machine to produce dividends more than a project to ensure organic growth.[17] This contrasts with a vision of the firm as an integrated body in which managers play the central task of coordinating innovation (Chandler 1992; O'Sullivan 2000; Lazonick 2010; Pitelis and Teece 2010). Shareholder orientation runs the risk of excessive disgorgement of resources away from companies – share buy-backs; high and special dividends – that constrain finance for internal expansion and probably fit the 'easy-life' for executives rather better than getting on with the business of using and developing capabilities. Lazonick (2008) has analysed such a process for the US and it seems also to have characterized the UK corporate sector (Hill and Taylor 2001). A critical question is whether 'strategic managers possess the cognitive capabilities to allocate resources to the innovation process' (Lazonick 2010, p.335). The answer would appear to be negative under the governance norms dictated by financialization. Strategy is focused not on company growth but on share holder returns. This is either saying that shareholders are the only stake holders that matter or that what is good for UK plc is good for the country. In the next chapter we will engage further with these views.

---

[17] From this perspective, deep knowledge of the firm is unimportant and can be controlled by outside directors who may know little of relevance for the industry or technology of the firm. For example, in keeping with the combined code on corporate governance in the UK, all of the FTSE100 companies have a majority of outsiders on the board.

7
Reforms to Corporate Governance

7.1 Introduction

Macroeconomic and industrial policies are not the only – and maybe not even the most important – ingredients for economic success. Company boards set decisions that can unleash or constrain growth and when these individual decisions are closely correlated they may even be decisive for the macroeconomic growth rate. Company boards, in turn, are conditioned and constrained by custom and law and in particular by the duties of directors. Whether the duties of directors are defined narrowly as primarily to shareholders, or are more pluralist, extending to other stakeholders, is one of the great issues of *corporate governance*.[1]

Corporate governance is often presented as no more than a set of principles or codes that ensure accountability and the alignment of company strategy with the demands of shareholders. The rationale for this is sometimes explained in terms of the natural rights of owners. By and large the academic literature does not accept this rationale, even if it does mostly accept the more general framework of shareholder primacy. Most academic discourse now accepts that ownership rights are never absolute; they vary by asset and are always circumscribed in law. For over a century it has been accepted that the public company is a social institution and is not simply a piece of private property (Dean

---

[1] Some scholars see corporate law as casual in a different sense in that it is supposed to explain the form in which external finance is provided (debt or equity for example). Others view countries' voting systems as determining both the system of labour law and the form of finance provision. These debates are largely unresolved and we do not enter into them here.

2001). It is circular reasoning to infer decision rights from the legal status of those who own the shares in a company since the legal status requires a treatment of decision rights (Stout 2005; Deakin 2008).

Specialists in corporate governance theory have searched for definitions of governance that recognize the social nature of public companies, often arriving at a broadly sensible view irrespective of whether they advocate shareholder primacy or not. Thus Tirole (2001) argues for a broad definition of governance as the 'design of institutions that induce or force management to internalize the welfare of stakeholders' (p.4). Zingales (2000b) defines corporate governance as 'the complex set of constraints that shape the ex post bargaining over the quasi rents generated by a firm' (p.498). Both of these authors recognize that shareholder primacy can only be defended by showing that it is the best system for achieving a fair distribution of benefits. This opens up a space for discussion. Tirole for example suggests that control rights should be concentrated in the hands of the party whose incentives are such that they will not otherwise supply the most valuable input. Inevitably, there is a need for prior judgement in such a theory. The most controversial assumption here is that access to finance is the crucial problem for the firm, an assumption that in turn provides a more solid basis for shareholder primacy.

Often finance may be an issue, though we have queried the generality of this in Chapter 6. Others have pointed to human resources being of equal if not greater importance to the performance of firms, at least those firms that might be termed part of the innovation economy where highly creative and skilled people account for much of the added value. The centrality of human resources may seem uncontroversial given that many companies proclaim how their people constitute their greatest asset. Theoretically, however, this is difficult to analyse within the standard view of corporate governance which relies heavily on 'principal–agency' theory (Jensen and Meckling 1976). According to this theory, shareholder return, or profit, is the only 'residual' or non-contractual claim, that is, the only form of income not subject to contract.[2] This directs attention away from the contribution of other stakeholders such as employees and suppliers who are seen as fairly rewarded for their contracted inputs. The principal–agency view is thus uniquely concerned with incentives to deliver profit and in particular with the idea that

---

[2] Simply put, this means that maximizing profit is the same as maximizing total firm income; if total income (T) is then sum of contractual income (C) and non-contractual income (NC), maximizing NC is the same as maximizing T if C is fixed.

profit may partly be misappropriated by managers or other agents. Good governance measures are seen as an antidote to this threat, providing the security necessary if investors are to provide finance.

The agency approach has been challenged as overly narrow by academics in several fields including those working on transaction costs.[3] The criticism here is that contracts are rarely, and generally cannot be, fully specified so that we need a theory of *incomplete contracts*. An even more serious question has been posed by economic and legal theorists in respect of the combination of principal–agent and shareholder value theories. If contracts are incomplete, how can contracts with all parties other than the shareholder contain no residual risk? (Blair 1995; Stout and Blair 2001; Hart 1995; Mitchell 2004; Boot and Macey 2004; Deakin 2008). Under incomplete contracts the supplier of specific inputs that cannot be easily re-allocated to another use also faces risk. Such agents need to rely on ex-post bargaining (after commitment) to guarantee a return and indeed to provide an incentive for the initial investment or effort. But ex-post bargaining power may be weak unless agents have taken care not to over-specialize. On the other hand if they are wary of specialization this can destroy growth opportunities. Principal–agent governance rules may thus be inappropriate if they conflict with maximizing incentives for non-contractible inputs. In this case a new basis for corporate governance must be found, for example for those sectors of the economy where managers and workers are called upon to sink their own risky human capital. This perspective is known as the 'property rights theory' in recognition that human resources are the property of the bearer and it lends support to a stakeholder model of governance.

7.2   Varieties of governance

The logic of the property rights approach is that all those supplying inputs with risky return require control rights over the firms' decisions as they are subject to 'hold-up' in the sense that they have to apply unrecoverable effort or resources to the firm. Without control rights there will be under-investment in these commitments.

The principal–agent view can also deal with agents taking risk, but it does so differently. Here, control rights remain with the principal

---

[3] See Williamson (1985). The agency perspective was also challenged by those working on the theory of the firm and firm-based competitive advantage (Demsetz 1997).

but part of the profits may be used to incentivize agents. This is only necessary where agents work in an environment where their effort is not able to be directly observed or inferred from their output. A classic example is sharecropping where the weather may introduce a random shock to output so that pay based on output would only incentivize farmers optimally if the risk attitude of owners and farmers were similar. Generally the assumption is of risk-averse agents, so that a profit sharing arrangement with the farmer's share large enough to encourage risk-taking is the best solution available given the inability to achieve what would be best under perfect information. The results of this model have been used widely to infer appropriate pay structures for employees and managers.

Despite the enormous increase in compensation of top managers in recent years, there is little direct evidence supporting the view that higher pay–performance sensitivities generally lead to better long-run performance even as measured by market criteria. Criticism of existing practices originates in part from those who argue for more direct share-holder control of the corporation. The argument here is that the board of directors is captive to managers who may manipulate accounting indicators, adjust the performance standards and so on in order to influence compensation committees' decisions concerning executive pay (Bebchuk and Fried, 2004). On this view the failure of pay for perform-ance systems is due merely to its design. Other critics have responded differently, noting the drawbacks of any system of high-powered incen-tives within the firm (Osterloh and Frey 2000). Such incentives are problematic in the presence of 'multi-tasking' so that anything that is not prescribed as a target tends to be neglected (Roberts et al 2004).[4]

7.3 Active investors

The difficulty of aligning interests of owners and managers through executive compensation schemes suggests using an alternative which relies on direct monitoring instead. In practice this is extremely difficult because of information asymmetries and the free-rider problem

---

[4] Others argue that pay-for-performance not only does not solve the incentive problem in a team but also discourages workers' 'pro-social intrinsic' motivations. In effect, it sends a signal to managers that effort without pecuniary reward is 'socially inappropriate'. Consequently there is insufficient investment in firm-specific common goods (Frey and Osterloh 2005).

where ownership is diffused and there are significant costs attached to monitoring. Widely held shares may enhance the liquidity of a firm's holdings but the downside is that dispersed shareholders may be unable or unwilling to monitor firms appropriately; control is then exercised through 'exit' rather than 'voice', putting the burden of discipline on the share price and the takeover mechanism.

It is of course true that institutions account for a large proportion of company shares in the UK. It might be thought that these institutions could perform the role of monitor on behalf of investors. However at present many of these funds are managed passively and many subcontract investment business to specialist fund managers. There is a separate principal–agency problem here, making it difficult to incentivize the agents engaged in the buying and selling of shares. The effect of this is that they tend to focus on the current share price and, as discussed in Chapter 6, where the share price is subject to systematic mis-valuation, this results in the diversified corporation having to pay attention to short-run success, because they know that fund managers themselves are rewarded on this basis.[5] It leads to insecurity amongst managers in the invested firms who are constantly anticipating market reactions that are based on imperfect knowledge of the firm.

One approach to overcoming the collective action of dispersed shareholders is to encourage block-holding (where at least one shareholder has 5–10 per cent of shares) or even concentrated private ownership (Black 1997; Elson 2007),[6] a pattern which is common in some countries even among the largest corporations. The idea here is that concentrated ownership can more easily facilitate monitoring, while it also becomes more worthwhile for investors to access information on the company. Finance should be more readily available where financial analysts are better able to understand the technicalities underlying the companies in which their clients are trading (Tylecote and Visintin 2008).

---

[5] Far from being resolved, the problem of short-termism is arguably gaining importance in Anglo American economies, as suggested in recent comments and reports by the president of the UK employers' organization (CBI) and two US business groups: the Aspen group and the Donaldson group. See various issues of the *Financial Times* dated 18 June; 27 June and additional comments in Stefan Stern's column, *Financial Times* 28 March 2007.

[6] It is however important not to equate block-holding with long-term proactive investment strategies. At present these tend to be the preserve of individual contrarian investors, a small number of pension funds that emulate them and possibly some sovereign funds.

There is some support for policy initiatives to persuade institutional investors – pension funds, life insurance companies and mutual funds – to participate more in the firms in which they invest and to engage in direct oversight of board strategy and actions. The unit cost of monitoring is lower for these organizations and they need to hold specific shares for long periods if they engage in index tracking. Tylecote et al (2002) identify different current modes of institutional investor activity including a proactive mode that involves boards taking a strategic view before outsiders are in a position to do so.

In the UK active institutional investment has been cautiously encouraged in a series of government reports (Myners 2001; see also Aguilera et al 2006; Mallin et al 2005). However this would be a large cultural change for these organizations. Many of them are internationally focused and may not wish to pursue a separate policy for the UK. Even those organizations such as Blackstone or the Norwegian Government Pension Fund that adopt interventionist strategies have to ration their involvement given the large number of investments that they have.[7] Furthermore, company law prevents companies that are in receipt of privileged information through insider monitoring from trading these shares so that they have to create 'Chinese walls' within their organizations. There is thus a conflict between liquidity and oversight and indeed efficiency within these enterprises.

In assessing the role of institutional investors, it should not be forgotten that it was the rise of this class of investor that initially sparked concern with short-termism in the UK in the 1980s (Walker 1985); nor that they pioneered stock option incentives in the US. Furthermore, the average holding period for institutional funds has been falling, perhaps as they have become more internationally focused (Christenson et al 2008). All this suggests that it may not be possible to expect the institutions to internalize externalities and play the long game. It is hard to accept the view that, as 'owners of small parts of global capital' they have a need to 'induce efficiency in the real economy' (Aglietta 2007, p.14).

What of the evidence? There is as yet no convincing evidence that activism by institutional investors, even where it occurs spontaneously makes a difference either to the economy or to private investors. One area where it should be possible to discern a difference, if it exists, is the provision of finance for forward commitments like R&D. The usual assumption in the literature is that managers are not taking on enough

---

[7] Tomorrow's Company (2011) accept that it will be difficult to engage all companies but argues that it is sufficient to attract a 'critical mass' (p.24) to the task. But there is no discussion of what this might comprise.

risk so that profitable R&D projects may be passed over or money will be allocated to projects with a worse risk–return profile than the owners would prefer (Eisenhardt 1998; Hall 1990). Good governance would aim to prevent this underinvestment. But the evidence for an ownership effect is not consistent. It is true that some work points to a positive effect on R&D of concentrated or institutional holdings. For example, Aghion et al (2009) find a (weak) effect of institutional ownership on R&D. But the variety of other results in the literature makes it difficult to draw robust conclusions (Driver 2012).

Enlightened shareholder value

Enlightened shareholder value recognizes that shareholders may be led to behave in a manner contrary to their own long-term interests. By focusing too much on measured shareholder value they perhaps lose sight of the loss of reputation and trust that feeds back negatively on the system of value creation as a whole, if not to the specific company responsible. Enlightened shareholder value is closely related to the idea of stewardship where companies are envisaged to have a common purpose (Tomorrow's Company 2011). It encourages inclusive decision-making on grounds of efficiency and commitment (Driver and Thompson 2002). It can thus be seen as a sort of hybrid between stakeholding and shareholding in which directors, managers, employees, customers and suppliers are seen as cooperating in a form of ownership structure but without the need for shared control rights: 'Expanded ownership will foster commonality of interest and help make investors more aware of the value of investment spillovers' (Porter 1997, p.14). Similar arguments for co-ownership have informed the ESOPS subsidy programme in the US and the cooperative movement. Such ideas are also central to the corporate social responsibility (CSR) agenda. CSR is a field in which stakeholder pressure groups and companies test each other to arrive at a balance of concessions on issues such as fair trade, resource depletion, climate change, working conditions or human rights.[8]

Enlightened shareholder value commanded much attention in recent reviews of UK company law that investigated the duties of directors

---

[8] CSR assumes that companies care about their image and the trust that it conveys. From a company-centred point of view trust is a strategic asset, not an end in itself. The extent to which trust is maintained will depend partly on relative costs and on a calculation of how to discount the stored value of trust (Baker et al 1997). The CSR agenda thus tends to be gamed by companies.

and the question of in whose interests should companies be run. Introducing the report on the 2006 Companies Act, Industry Minister Margaret Hodge wrote that the new legal framework 'marks a radical departure in articulating the connection between what is good for a company and what is good for society at large' (DTI 2007a).

In fact, the 2006 Act was much less radical than Hodge stated. Although preceded by considerable debate on fundamental reform, the eventual Act continued to accept the principle of shareholder primacy – simply adding that companies should 'have regard to factors ... such as the interests of the company's employees and the impact of the company's operations on the community and the environment'.[9] This was not a substantive advance on previous company law and many commentators saw it as simply trying to change culture without legislation. Certainly there is no enforcement mechanism for any enlightened action. Hodge herself concluded that 'the best way to achieve lasting cultural change is to go with the tide and the broad consensus of opinion' (p.3). None of this signalled any understanding that there could be a conflict between the objectives of attracting finance and incentivizing other stakeholders (Wen and Zhao 2011).

7.4 Stakeholding and shared control rights

One argument for employee control rights is that work commitment in some workplaces is an issue of equal if not greater significance than access to finance. The balance of the two objectives of governance may vary between sectors, but at least in creative and science-based industries, the willingness of workers to identify with the company will be crucial for success. Stakeholding is a form of guarantee to those who are required to sink their knowledge and expertise in the firm and thus put these assets at risk.[10]

Knowledge workers in particular may require special governance mechanisms to counter hold-up problems and encourage commitment to firm-specific learning and routines. Indeed some have argued that the intelligent pursuit of shareholder value would lead owners to share power within the firm to achieve this end (Hart 1996). The argument

---

[9] Section 172: Duty to promote the success of the company.

[10] The approach to stakeholding here is a narrowly functional one based on the concept of 'hold-up', familiar in the literature since work on bilateral monopoly (Williamson 2002).

here is that stakeholders are not fully protected by contract, so that they may need control rights in order to commit (Grant 1996; Blair 1995). The stakeholding approach has been formally rationalized in a model due to Roberts and Van den Steen (2000). Workers choose a level of skills investment that is not subject to enforceable contract. Anticipated ex-post bargaining over the surplus then determines the incentives to invest in this human capital. Where training is financed by workers but is entirely firm specific, worker representation on the board confers control rights and increases their incentive to invest in skills. A shareholder-oriented approach is biased as it takes into account only the contribution to measured profit (total profit should include returns to all risky inputs) so that human capital may be undersupplied.[11]

Although the shareholder may have a private incentive to grant some bargaining power to workers so as to encourage human capital formation, this process has clear limits. For example, a stakeholder tradable veto over changing a specific technology involves a trade-off between increased incentives for human capital and a fall in profitability. Given that stakeholder control potentially lessens shareholder protection it may result in restricted access to external finance (Tirole 2001, 2006). The types of insider governance that characterizes Germany and some of Northern Europe may, on this perspective, be more conducive to innovation as long as it is not too dependent on new equity finance.

The ability of the board or top management to generate workforce commitment is certainly a challenge. The key question for stakeholding is whether it is either necessary or sufficient to resolve this. Traditionally commitment has been thought to be an issue for management rather than governance. Holmstrom (1999a) lists among the most important management instruments: delegation; control of information; and corporate culture. The managerial labour market can also play a role, as long as productivity indicators are not too noisy (Fama 1980; Holmstrom 1999b). An organizational solution to motivating employees, suggested by Rajan and Zinglales (2000a) argues for power to be dispersed towards middle managers who can then offer 'access' to incentivize a team.

---

[11] The model differentiates between specific technology (where specific skill is totally devalued on arrival of a new vintage) and general technology where that is not the case. Under the specific technology, if the new vintage is adopted (probability $= p$) workers bargained wage is zero; otherwise (with probability $1-p$) the wage depends on the bargaining power of workers in a Nash game to divide the surplus. General technology is advantageous to employees because it involves a skills switching option in the event that a new vintage is adopted.

Other approaches see *informal* delegation of control to subordinates as necessary to obtain commitment (Aghion and Tirole 1999).

For a variety of theoretical and practical reasons these managerial approaches to securing trust and commitment do not appear to have worked. The downsizing of the 1980s and 1990s resulted in rising insecurity and lower trust particularly for middle management (DiMaggio 1997). In the UK, there 'is little evidence of middle managers gaining autonomy' (Morris et al 2008, p.705). Even senior managers who report directly to the CEO appear to lose their own professional voice (Jacoby 2005). Empirical work using the British Skills Survey (Felstead et al 2007, p.xxi) notes that:

> [T]he rise in skills among employees over the last two decades has not been accompanied by a corresponding rise in the control they can exercise over their jobs. For example the proportions reporting a great deal of influence over how to do tasks at work fell from 57 per cent in 1992 to 43 per cent in 2001, where it remained in 2006.

The comparative UK–French study reported in Conway et al (2008) – while confirming that firms may be interested in motivating and training employees – noted that 'they are less willing to give them a voice in the way work is organised' (p.663).

In brief, organizational change within the firm has not provided a solution to the potential underinvestment in inputs that are hard to contract for, such as committed effort. It is hard to believe that much progress is possible without fundamental reform of company law. At a minimum provision should be made to enable those firms who wish to do so to opt for this form of governance, perhaps as part of a broader negotiation with the state of their role in the economy.

In our view it is essential to maintain a sphere of autonomy for management in respect of *strategic* decisions.[12] The theoretical case for this has been made by those who argue from a 'property rights' position that stakeholders need protection before they will be willing to

---

[12] To be sure, some of these arguments are self-serving on behalf of power-hungry or maverick managers. Some of the criticism of the controls placed on managers in the Sarbanes Oxley legislation in the US seem to be so motivated. It is not our intention to deny an important role to boards to set standards of propriety and to monitor for fraud and aggrandizing actions on the part of top management. Much of this by necessity has to be done after the fact but the establishment of a framework of accountability is important.

commit. Managerial solutions such as 'golden handshakes' may insulate key personnel from failure but it is not just top managers that matter. In our view the granting by law of control rights is a necessary step to ensure commitment of workers at all levels to an innovative trajectory. *Informal* control rights have been analysed in models where asymmetry of information makes it difficult for managers to obtain commitment of innovators (Aghion and Tirole 1997). But such informal control only works where the top manager can guarantee not to renege on previous assurances, that is not to over-ride the granted autonomy. In the context of tight governance at board level it is not possible to give that assurance, and in any case it is inconsistent where takeovers are frequent events. Our preference therefore is for strong *internal governance*, where there is scope for a mutual monitoring by management below the top layer. Research shows that firms perform better when they have a higher proportion of top management not appointed by the current CEO that is with more independent positions in the hierarchy (Landier et al 2005).

The discussion above on an innovative growth path for firms connects with much work that has been carried out on the low skill nature of much of British industry, that seems somehow to be co-determined with the low investment climate (Feingold and Soskice 1988; Mayhew and Keep 1999). Several studies have confirmed the idea that the problem of skills is largely one of *low demand by employers* who see no reason to upgrade their product mix: 'Rather than seeking to break into new markets and technologies, British employers have tended to adjust to, and reinforce, the existing skill situation by relying heavily on technical continuity, long production runs, and heavy use of semi-skilled rather than skilled labour' (Glynn and Gospel 2007, p.112). Similar points are made in and Mason (2004) where it is shown that production 'tends to be concentrated towards the more standardised and less complicated end of the quality spectrum' especially in companies oriented to local and regional markets (p.3). Such research illustrates both the potential for change and the challenge in getting the necessary initial commitment.

The debate on an appropriate form of stakeholding to restore trust and commitment in organizations is far from over. There is concern that shared control might lead to 'rent dissipation' in a struggle between various factions. Some have therefore argued for a greater autonomy of the board of directors to hold the ring and decide on trade-offs (Blair and Stout 2001; Asher et al 2005). Others worry that the board is too far removed from real information to do more than have an ex-post monitoring role. Here the role of executive managers is stressed along with their need to be insulated from financial market pressure. Executive stakeholding is supported in Lazonick (1992) and O'Sullivan (2000) because it is said to facilitate innovation by 'strategic decision makers who are and remain integrated into the processes of organizational learning' (Lazonick 1992, p.41). A similar case for the manager, as steward or trustee, has been made by proponents of the resource view of management. What these accounts bring to the table is a characterization of the firm as a repository of knowledge, both technical and strategic, which is not always codifiable or communicable beyond an inside group of involved agents management.

It remains to be seen whether there is a conflict between a stakeholder model of employee control rights and a governance approach that privileges executive managers. To our mind these approaches are complementary because of the need for peer control at executive level. This is what formal control rights achieve in the German model whose success has often been attributed to harnessing the key information at lower executive level to act as a check on senior management.

Of course different problems require different solutions and there is no single prescription for governance style. There may be sectors where finance is crucial – start-ups, small companies and buy-outs for example. But it is a mistake to focus all the energy of governance reform on the issue of finance because the problem is more generally one of trust and commitment by both stakeholders and investors alike. In one sense the problem can be considered as a coordination game. If governance is approached as one of extracting the maximum surplus and minimizing retentions it will provoke the distrust and lack of commitment that it fears. The excessive compensation for senior managers is only necessary because norms of trust and commitment have broken down. On the other hand, given that we are where we are in terms of trust, any relaxation of tight accountability of management by the board is feared as leading to slack, paralysis and even a coalition for a quiet life between stakeholders and managers. The stable equilibria in this game appear to be either the present one of tight governance with disaffected workers, grudgingly low capital investment and overpaid managers; or a more functional state where trust has been established so that commitments of effort and funds can be made under an assumption of fair division of the surplus. Anglo-American capitalism was catapulted into the first state by the advent of global competition (Reich 2006). No doubt the result has neither been wholly good nor wholly bad. But the limits of downsizing and win–win coalitions were reached fairly quickly. To establish a growth path based on unleashing human creativity will require something equally forceful. We see a legislated change in corporate governance to give powers to stakeholders as central to that task.

7.5 Conclusion

Reforms to corporate governance are vital to unlock the creative power of employees especially in organizations that rely on complex interactive and hard-to-monitor jobs where commitment is a key element. Principal–agent theory offers little help in understanding the role of governance in such settings. While some problems of governance can be dealt with from a purely shareholder perspective, this role reaches its limits once basic compliance can be taken for granted and once investors are assured that they have reasonable protection for the risks that they take. Enlightened stakeholder value is an attempt to change the language of power while leaving to purely voluntary action any provision to mitigate the problems caused by the absence of collective action under dispersed share ownership. While ownership concentration and institutional investor involvement has been seen as a solution to collective action, there is neither strong evidence for its effectiveness nor certainty that such reforms are practical. Moreover these proposed reforms are one-sided in that by enforcing the idea of owner primacy they fail to engage with the theoretical rationale for stakeholding as shared control rights. In that respect any system of shareholder value whether enlightened or not risks missing the goal of incentivizing the commitment of human actors that is necessary if complementary investments in capital and R&D are to be justified. Such a goal is unlikely to be met without legislating for formal stakeholder rights and supplanting the idea of the corporation as a commodity.

8
A Look Ahead

8.1 Swimming with the tide

The UK is an exemplar of a free market economy; reforms pursued by all governments since the 1980s have resulted in 'one of the most market-friendly economies in the world' (Card et al 2004, p.13). The UK has tended to lead France and Germany and even the US on the degree of flexibility in hiring and firing and related matters (Card and Freeman 2004). Extensive labour inflows, particularly from Eastern Europe, have increased labour market competition. Despite the welcome introduction of a minimum wage, throughout the period, labour laws discouraged industrial action and employment protection was limited; one result of this was the fall in labour share depicted in Figure 2.3, particularly for the bottom half of workers (Atkinson 2009).

Open and deep capital markets have kept investors assured, and have made governments responsive to their needs on issues such as low taxation. Extensive foreign direct ownership of firms has checked the influence of labour unions. No policy has checked the reallocation of resources from capital intensive industries to those based on intangibles such as business and finance. Takeovers, buy-outs, short-selling and corporate tax-avoidance have been regarded not so much as potentially harmful, but as inevitable quirks of the modern way of doing business and generating wealth. Personal taxation policy has generally been favourable to those on the highest incomes, with a higher tax band only imposed as the curtain was coming down on the pre-crash era.

Yet the paradox remains that the UK growth rate continued to disappoint during these years, the rate of inactivity stayed continuously high, and productivity growth in important sectors of the economy showed little or no improvement on earlier periods. One of our contentions is that these long-run adverse trends have been disguised and ignored because they are not amenable to unaided market solutions but rather require a robust policy regime that pressures the corporate sector to commit resources for the long term. The permanent uplift to growth that had been promised since the first Thatcher administration was always elusive. It is now hard to detect any such break in the trend of productivity growth, as we have shown in Chapter 1. While some progress has been noted on relative productivity growth against some comparator countries up to the financial crash, it has now been brought into question by the deeper recession and slower recovery of the UK, amplified by a loss of capacity in high productivity sectors.

In a remarkable demonstration of the effects of cognitive dissonance, a belief in the success and inevitability of the Thatcher reforms strengthened, even as the evidence for its success of waned.[1] As time went on it seemed more difficult to question the road that the UK had embarked on. Perhaps this was a natural behavioural reaction to the sunk cost element of the reforms. Perhaps also it reflected broader international trends in which a convergence on US style capitalism seemed inevitable. The Soviet Union had collapsed, which was seen in popular – if not academic – circles as evidence for free market superiority.[2] The liberalization of the US and UK banking sectors required a new respect for the power of global finance. Additionally perhaps, the landscape changed after 1992 with the ejection of the UK from the exchange rate mechanism in a single day of speculative activity during which a 5 per cent rise in interest rates and the complete reserves of the Bank of England proved powerless to move markets.[3] Coordinated

---

[1] While privatization, deregulation and competition were central to the original Thatcher worldview, the pendulum had not yet swung so far as to reject price-fixing and intervention. For one thing, despite an atavistic dislike of Europe by much of the cabinet, the Thatcher government pragmatically signed up for the fixed-price ERM to contain inflation. Even more remarkably, Thatcher herself was persuaded to write that 'some other countries do seem able to identify the promising new areas with industrial potential sooner than we do and act on them more quickly' (ACARD 1985).

[2] Stiglitz (1994) in his Wicksell lectures makes a case that the demise of the Soviet Union, where central planners set prices corresponding to conjectured market prices, demonstrated that markets cannot function without institutional supports.

[3] In a retrospective on ERM exit for the BBC programme 'Money Changers', Kenneth Clarke, the then Home Secretary, remarked that he had always believed theoretically in the power of markets but had never until then believed that states could be so powerless.

market economies in Europe at this time were groaning under the twin burdens of German reunification and budget cutting in preparation for economic and monetary union (Modigliani et al 1998). The promise of Japan and its coordinated markets (Jacoby 2005) seemed to evaporate in the 1990s with the collapse of its own asset price bubble. And in the US, productivity grew strongly from 1995 in IT related industries and services.

Buoyed by these comparisons, it was still possible to be optimistic about the UK even if the evidence was mixed. Oulton (1995) asked the question 'what happened to the miracle?' and remained hopeful despite what he regarded as poor macroeconomic policies, arguing that higher profitability from labour market reforms 'should eventually lead to an increase in investment of all types [and a higher] rate of growth permanently'. Others also thought the corner had been turned. The historian Nicholas Crafts (1997) reviewing the productivity performance thought that it 'might be enough over the medium term to end and even slowly reverse economic decline relative to Europe' (p.52). Card et al (2004) agreed that, at some cost in the form of a less equal income distribution, 'the market oriented reforms of the UK seem to have accomplished their broad goal of improving UK economic performance after a long period of relative decline'. But they also note that the reforms did not bring UK productivity up to the level of the US or to the level of its major EU partners in France or Germany (see our discussion in Chapter 1). And the main quantitative exercise in their edited volume could not confirm a relationship between market-friendly regimes and productivity growth.[4] This is not surprising. There is a noticeable absence in this list of any direct instruments for the stated target of productivity.

Why should firms invest for the future if the aim of public policy is to enable them to make profits by containing wages and working conditions? Why should firms re-skill their workforce when the thrust of policy was market-led industrial training? In an extraordinary frank commentary, the consultancy firm McKinsey explained the situation

---

[4] The reforms said to illustrate supply side progress include eleven steps: employee protection, product market competition, foreign ownership, stock options, welfare reforms, youth subsidies, pension reform, curbing union power, national minimum wage, rent reform and general benefit reform. Some of the areas covered, such as pension reform, stock options, competition policy and housing policy are universally seen as having been highly problematic while many others have faded from memory due to lack of impact.

thus: 'because of flexible labour markets, economic underperformance does not necessarily translate into considerably lower unemployment. Rather employers simply tolerate lower productivity, rewarding it with lower wages' (The McKinsey Global Institute 1999, p.6). Of course there was some increase in skills content over the subsequent years and higher education was expanded. But by 2010, 22 per cent of UK adults had the lowest level of skill compared to 17 per cent for comparator countries (Toynbee and Walker 2011).

The limits of an economic strategy based largely on labour market issues increasingly became hard to ignore. But the incoming labour administration of 1997 was just as accepting of market principles as the one they replaced. Although the senior policymakers of the DTI came to realize that labour market reforms were experiencing diminishing returns (Porter and Kettels 2003), the politicians felt that they had to prove their pro-market credentials. That, and perhaps because they could not figure out a way to generate broad support for anything different, explains the continuity in policy.

8.2   Is the tide turning?

There has always been a contradiction at the heart of the market-knows-best approach as practised in the UK. This is that the economists most supportive of that general thrust in policy were generally well-disposed towards institutional explanations. The NAIRU model that underpinned labour market policy sets itself up as a counterweight to neoclassical labour models. The idea of an independent central bank is supported by the institutionalist notion of tying one's hands. Nevertheless solutions were only acceptable if they involved a conservative agenda, usually one of mimicking of the market. Institutional approaches that challenged markets were labelled 'corporatist' – a spectre that alarmed a whole generation of thinkers. Bean and Symons (1989) asked whether successful corporatist policies in the 1980s would have allowed more gain and less pain but concluded that 'the basic structure of the British Economy was not conducive to Scandinavian-style solutions' (p.54). And while Oulton (1995) accepted that low investment and R&D were problematic, so that 'the UK might have fared better with German or Swedish trade unions or with Japanese managers', he thought labour market reform the only practical remedy for the UK. For New Labour too, institutional reform was to be narrowly interpreted, since it believed that there 'was no point in trying to redesign the architecture of British capitalism'.[5] The question now is whether the tide has turned in favour of an interventionist institutional framework?

Some might argue that the perspective that we have adopted in this book already has broad appeal and that related reform measures can be carried through with immediate popular support. For example the banking crisis has produced anxiety and distrust at the extent to which business appears unaccountable; there is considerable support for reining in a culture of overpaid executives who are seen as uninterested in orienting their companies to the public good. While such a standpoint may appear a natural one for parties of the left or centre, it seems increasingly to be shared by those on the right. The uneven distributions of income and wealth in liberal market economies have been coming under attack from some surprising quarters, especially in the US. *Businessweek* magazine and similar commentators have criticized excessive inequality for encouraging rent dissipation, for obstructing access for the less privileged to enterprise and for fostering a culture of consumption based on debt rather than income.[6] Not only that, but the very contention that free market capitalism will automatically deliver for ordinary people is disputed by conservative commentators who recall a pre-globalization period where capitalism was more embedded in the nation and community. Thus for example a leading 'Red Tory', Jesse Norman MP urges an approach where 'markets are used but not venerated' and where free-market conservatism replaces free-market neo-liberalism. He complains that the type of financial capitalism that has grown up in the UK and the US in the last twenty years is 'a species of financial crony capitalism that has disguised economic reality, shielded underperformance, cosseted poor management and leached away value' (Norman 2011, p.4). Whereas leading UK banks had been founded on Quaker principles, now there is little connection to the wider community 'only one-tenth of UK bank lending goes directly to real, productive companies' (p.10) while the corporate compensation culture encourages 'takeovers and mergers, rather than organic growth' (p.12). The argument is made for 'reshaping the laws and institutions in which markets are embedded' (p.19).

---

[5] The quotation is from a critical work by David Marquand cited in Corry (2011, p.S125).
[6] See 'How inequality hurts the economy', *Businessweek* 16 November 2011 and comments by notable free-market protagonists such as Paul Volcker, Warren Buffett and Raghuram Rajan.

What these types of interventions have in common is a partial retreat from globalization and ambivalence towards the power of unregulated markets to enforce solutions across states and economies. They represent an attempt to juggle with what Rodrik (2011) calls the 'trilemma' of globalization. This is the idea that you can have any pair (but only a pair) of the three entities: state power, people power and global power. The hyper-globalization that Rodrik sees as on the ascendant since the end of Bretton Woods represents a cutting-out of people power with state and global market power hand in glove. The earlier Bretton Woods agenda that clipped the wings of global power with regulation was more defined along the axis of people and state. The third possibility of global and people power requires intergovernmental organizations that are only incipient and whose foremost example (the EU) is under threat. Red Tories – and indeed Blue Labour – among others – see a retreat from globalization as necessary to sustain a moral climate with community values and social cohesion.

But while Norman and others may hanker after a different type of capitalism, neither the economic agenda nor the political basis for action is explained. The arguments are overwhelmingly negative with a heavy emphasis on a critique of financial capital; indeed the word 'bank' or 'banking' appears over sixty times in little more than twenty pages with only six references to companies. Oddly the nineteenth century trading companies such as the East India Company are linked to 'public interest' in Norman's account whereas they are much more similar to today's banks as an example of mercantilist expansion with state aid. Increased regulation is welcomed one minute by Norman to enforce values, but the next it is said to be a characteristic of fake capitalism. The message is garbled perhaps because in search of a constituency that would back a morals-based capitalism, a supportive narrative has to be invented. Thus it is argued that the idolizing of markets emerged only in the 1990s. The contrast is with a golden age of conservatism where a more pragmatic view of markets ruled. In this book we have tried to show that the reverse is true. The Labour administrations after 1997 took on board the exaggerated view of infallible markets that had been in the ascendant from the early 1980s. When Norman tries to date the onset of neo-liberal capitalism from the late 1990s the intention is to suggest that conservative governments were always ambivalent about market power. The facts speak differently however. While the market may not have completed its transition to shibboleth in the 1980s, public interest capitalism was hardly the watchword either. The administration did not see it as part of governing to predict, second-guess or direct the market-led economy, but trusted in the 'self-directing power of unrestricted free-enterprise' (Dow 1999, p.359).

The difficulty that Norman and others like him have in constructing a positive case for 'public interest capitalism' is at root the same difficulty they have in engaging a constituency to support it. The kinds of actions that would be necessary to challenge the excesses of markets and globalization, to mediate fairly the interests of capital and labour and to ensure that rent-seeking is contained while enterprise and risk-bearing is encouraged requires a rewriting of the neo-liberal agenda in favour of an interventionist approach by the state. But a distrust of the state has been endemic in conservative policies at least since the end of the Macmillan period.

To be sure, if the arguments for a new capitalism are missing on the right it is not clear that they exist on the left either. The problem here is the same – how to create a constituency that will support radical changes that might be both risky and with benefits loaded towards the long term, particularly if the UK economy becomes more of a rentier one, as unequal wealth is inherited and as the population ages. Some associated interest groups may come to distrust state intervention and prefer the 'democracy of the markets ... professional investors acting on behalf of you and me and our pension funds'.[7] Nor does economic decline inevitably augment the reform constituency; indeed the experience in the US reveals a strong correlation between a decline in income for white males and increased support for Republican candidates. For some such as the Blue Left equivalents of Norman, this pattern necessitates a turn towards non-economic concerns – perhaps thinking that issues of growth are secondary to issues of identity and community. All of this explains why there is a vacuum of clear ideas for organically building up a sustainable domestic economy in a way that can command a popular mandate.

8.3   Dangerous currents

The case for a moral capitalism intersects with a claim that liberal market economies have become too dependent on debt and that there should be a return to a responsible economy where thrift is a virtue. Like many simple ideas this is an attractive but also a dangerous reading of the situation. First, it is premised on a view of excessive public debt and state expenditure which are not the fundamental problems. Public debt

---

[7] Former Chancellor Norman Lamont, *Today Programme*, BBC 4, Wednesday 26 October 2011.

in some countries may now be a central issue but it was not the origin of the great crash of 2008, prior to which only a handful of countries such as Greece were a cause for concern. In the UK, the level of public net indebtedness in 2007 as a ratio of GDP was lower than for Germany or the US.[8] To be sure, we can now see that some of that GDP was fictitious. But that simply confirms that the broader issue of the economic growth and its direction is the primary issue rather than the secondary one of the absolute level of public debt. Private indebtedness is another matter, with very high relative levels in some countries including the UK, partly reflecting the disproportionate size of its banking sector. But here again there is a need for caution because the issue is often presented as simply one of consumer debt. As we noted in Chapter 1, UK consumer debt, now accounting for about 100 per cent of GDP, was a response to falling living standards in the UK as the neo-liberal market agenda pushed down real incomes and maintained huge disparities in income and wealth.[9] As former Labor Secretary Robert Reich (2010) said of the similar situation in the US:

> [T]he problem is not that [middle] Americans spent beyond their means but that their means had not kept up with what the larger economy could and should have been able to provide them (p.3).

To focus on consumer debt as a fundamental cause of an unbalanced economy is to miss the larger picture that explains the emergence of that debt. Furthermore arguing for lower private indebtedness in the short run without allowing for compensating public indebtedness is a recipe for a deeper slump. Only those who believe in the arcane and generally discredited economics of 'Ricardian equivalence' believe otherwise.[10]

But what about the longer-term rebalancing of the economy towards a higher investment rate that is surely necessary? Does this not require a long-run move towards a higher savings ratio? Here we meet a similar confusion. Debt is normally expressed as a ratio of the amount owed to GDP or some other income level. Long-run policies to reduce private

---

[8] IMF Fiscal Monitor, April 2011 and June 2011 Update: http://www.brookings.edu/articles/2011/0731_debt_burden_prasad.aspx

[9] Ben Broadbent of the Monetary Policy Committee has argued that household debt largely responded to house prices. It remains to be seen whether such debt looks sustainable under future paths of prices and mortgage rates.

[10] Those who disagree might like to check the effect of country episodes of fiscal contraction in the EU with indicators of business confidence, which are clearly insignificant.

debt as a ratio of income can either involve a rise in income or a rise in savings. The former is welcome but the latter is only useful if savings are invested. To believe that investment automatically follows saving requires a pre-Keynesian notion of markets that adjust through prices rather than quantities, employment and incomes. More savings as a mechanism for restoring the savings ratio is not a long-run but a short-run idea, involving the danger of exacerbating the lack of growth through demand contraction. Some economic commentators have either never known or have forgotten this. In his entertaining book *Made in Britain*, which makes some sensible arguments for the importance of manufacturing, the BBC economics reporter Evan Davis (2011) attributes the current economic difficulties to consumer behaviour. His argument is that with low consumer savings, banks have had less to lend: 'the companies themselves are not to blame. Nor are the Bank of England or the Treasury ... Our collective behaviour has made life difficult for manufacturers, not someone else's' (p.125). But this rather misses the point that companies are awash with unspent cash. Davis goes on to argue that the UK saves and invests a lower proportion of disposable income than a number of advanced countries, without apparently noting the lack of correlation between the household savings ratios and the investment ratios in his table. Put differently he wrongly assumes that higher consumer savings leads directly to higher investment and even argues that as a result of a savings shortage, the economy has tended to gravitate towards sectors 'where capital requirements are lower'. These views are all the more astonishing because Davis claims in the introduction that his book does not offer 'unambiguous assertions where issues are fuzzy or complicated' (p.10). Of course economic rebalancing is necessary but it needs to be addressed by hard choices in devising a growth plan, rather than in complacent notions that if we all saved as much as our parents our growth rates would be restored. This takes us back again to the question: which independent steps are necessary for growth and how can a constituency be found to support them?[11]

8.4   Ideas for growth

The great consensus on the British economy for more than three decades has been one of containing inflationary pressure by labour market reform and letting investment and the rest of the supply side look after

---

[11] Schmidt (2003) shows that investment is exogenous to savings rather than the converse.

itself. Only occasionally have questions been raised as to the dangers of a depleted manufacturing sector (Kenway 1996; Kitson and Michie 1996; Hutton 1996; Rose 2009); the social value of the financial sector (Bresnahan et al 1992; Glyn 2006) or the downside of flexible labour markets (Taylor 2003). But these voices – and those of the current authors – were rowing against the mainstream. To renew the process we suggest the creation of an institutional bargaining framework among national partners. This should be seen to complement the reforms of company law and corporate governance that were discussed in Chapter 7.

The remit of this institutional framework would be to undertake active intervention. This goes under different names – indicative planning, industrial strategy, coordination, focal point solutions – but they have a common meaning in seeking to deal with an uncertain world where cooperation can be fruitful. The intention must be to correct an underlying policy failure of recent years of an exaggerated view of the importance of market forces (King 2010).

It will not be easy to construct a multipartite framework for discussion and bargaining. The old National Economic Development Council and Office worked well for its time. However the decision to deplete union power made the institution less viable (Bean and Symons 1989). Today, too, weak unions may still be a problem. Corry (2011) in a retrospective view of New Labour says that a return to NEDO was not possible then due to weakness in both union and employer organizations, with the former 'becoming less able to engage in serious strategy discussions' (p.S132). Ultimately however, competent trade union representation is a product not just of the prevailing environment but of government policy and in particular a respect for bargaining that will encourage social partners to engage.

Increased cooperation between industrial partners and coordination within and across industries does not substitute for macroeconomic policy but is a useful complement to this. As a former industrialist and economic director of NEDO explained, 'the detail of industrial deficiencies is intricate and the necessity for cooperative solutions paramount so that policies have to be discovered and agreed upon by those actively engaged in each industry' (Stout 1979, p.190). Even previous cheerleaders for the free market such as Lord Mandelson talked in the closing months of the Brown administration of the need to learn from the 'interventionist approach of countries such as Germany, France, Korea and Singapore', though of course the rhetoric did not quite match the reality.[12]

---

[12] *Financial Times* 18 March 2010 'Industrial activism to boost manufacturing', p.4.

One example of the need for active industrial policy concerns supply relationships. This has been recognized as a problem particularly for manufacturing for many years. The economist Paul Geroski built on studies carried out at the National Institute for Economic and Social Research to show how it affected the poor performance of industries such as kitchen furniture relative to Germany where there was extensive interaction between machine tool suppliers and the downstream manufacturers; this contrasted with the UK where the result was a clustering in the low quality end of the market (Geroski and Knight 1991). More recently the issue has arisen in respect of parts suppliers for vehicles and construction equipment with comments from both Vauxhall and JCB about the shrinking supply base in their UK industries with adverse effects on their domestic performance. Such issues have not always been on the radar of policy makers, whose idea of planning has tended to start and stop with inflation targeting. In the first instance therefore industrial policy must concern itself with industrial structure and relationships.

Secondly, it is not possible to combine industrial activism with an ultra-loose policy towards takeovers, particularly where this involves foreign takeovers that result in a loss in industrial coherence. It is one thing where there are demonstrable efficiency reasons for a change of ownership. However it is now generally accepted that the takeover code allows short-run financial gain to dominate ownership change – especially where hedge funds dominate the share register. Even the former CEO who sold Cadbury plc argues that the takeover code should be tightened.[13] While individual deals may be good or bad for investors or indeed the company, there seems increasing support (including from the CBI) for the idea that the loss of domestic control for so many UK firms including infrastructure utilities such as BAA or energy companies and industrials innovators such as Pilkington and many high-tech niche manufacturers is damaging for the economy. Overseas control makes the decisions taken by these companies less regarding of domestic concerns while making any industrial policy that relies on coordinating national enterprises more difficult.

Britain is an open economy with increasingly low correlation between domestic production and ownership of firms. No amount of takeover control can remove the need for an international dimension to any planning framework. This is particularly true of technology where trends in science and business have interacted with globalization

---

[13] *Financial Times* Weekend 13/14 March 2010 'Eat or be eaten', Jenny Wiggins pp.31–5.

to call into question the national innovation systems of even the largest countries. It is no longer possible to rely on national technological champions because today's technologies are increasingly complex, inter-linked and too expensive to be confined within a single firm. National technological specializations will increasingly be the result of deals that combine public centres of advanced knowledge with the development capabilities of foreign based firms (Patel and Pavitt 2000). This does not mean the end of national planning but it may mean the end of national technological champions.

Planning does not always work. There are trade-offs between coordi-nation and competition. But any reading of the output of government departments over recent years will be struck by the uncertain and timid tone and a lack of confidence in intervention – even when it is recognized as useful. A number of issues require collective thought, cooperation and bargaining between interest groups. These include energy policy, infrastructure, regional policy, industry support and finance, immigration policy, skills training and child care. As noted by the consultant Diana Coyle, there are huge challenges in predicting and preparing for economic changes such as an ageing population that requires a 'shared strategic vision for economic growth' but where no individual employer was the incentive or capacity to provide this.[14] It is not just the scale of the issue that is relevant but whether bargains need to be struck. For example, in health care, the business model of most pharmaceutical companies has shifted from exploration to exploitation with attempts to offload risk to small firms and public research bodies, a process which may not be sustainable and which requires a policy steer. National planning forums allow controlled bargaining between interest groups, including the state, to prevent a disorderly and unnecessary resolution through disputes or unilateral action. An ambitious bargaining framework would see the merging of institutions such as competition authorities within an overarching multi-party planning body with a trade off between profit controls and a commitment to growth or other targets such as skills training, investment and R&D. Competition and new entry are not ends in themselves but can be important for growth when companies are close to the technological frontier (Aghion et al 2005). The appropriate level of competition needs a strategic rather than a rules-based approach.

---

[14] *Financial Times* 'Time to end the taboo and have an industrial policy again' by Diana Coyle and Paola Subacchi, 27 November 2011.

The issue of skills and education is central to a fairness agenda, with some arguing that it determines, with a lag, the distribution of income (Goldin and Katz 2008). UK policy has wrestled with the adequacy of educational and skills standards for decades and the indicators still reveal startling inadequacies in reading skills and numeracy with the latter problem extending to teacher education as well. The CEO of the UK Commission for Employment and Skills recently warned that skills shortages were imminent and would last for years.[15] The reasons for seeing this as an industrial planning issue are first that cooperative arrangements are needed horizontally within sectors to limit poaching or internalize the training cost externality. Secondly and perhaps of even more importance is the fact that skills and human capital are not independent of the way in which work is organized. Increasingly there is polarization between 'good' and 'bad' jobs as computers displace routine work and enhance the requirements of non-routine work. Crucially, the choice between routine and non-routine work is not just given exogenously but is determined by the manner of work organization and the management culture of firms (Green 2010).[16] In a report to the Economic and Social Research Council, drawing on a large research programme on the future of work, Taylor (2003) concluded that there should be a greater integration of industrial strategy with workplace development programmes, that is, the integration of skill programmes with work-place reorganization. Philpott (2009) suggests that only one in five UK organizations are implementing people management processes consistently. Efficiency and productivity will be elusive targets without the work-place commitment that such reorganization can secure. The flexible labour markets of the UK have tended to increase productivity in a one-sided way by enforcing managerial discipline rather than obtaining cooperation.[17] That is a process with diminishing returns and stores up future problems.

One merit of a forum such as that of the National Economic Development Council is that it allows different sectors of industry

---

[15] *Financial Times* 22.11.11 'Skills training is "turning corner" says top advisor', Brian Groom, p.4.

[16] Earlier versions of this argument suggesting that human capital and physical/knowledge capital are strategic complements may be found in Finegold and Soskice (1988).

[17] A disturbing example of this was recently documented for the privatized company Network Rail where two-thirds of accidents were not notified to the company because of a climate of fear experienced by operators and section managers: http://www.bbc.co.uk/news/business-12278569

to prioritize projects for public support. Even more importantly, it facilitates discussion of projects that combine sectors horizontally or vertically. A key issue here in regard to the vertical supply framework is the role that equipment suppliers play in the spread of advanced skills necessary to operate the installed systems. Skills shortages are less in evidence where the equipment manufacturers provide them; this appears to be much more the case in the US because of its larger economies of scale and where education institutions partner with equipment suppliers. Programmes to encourage combined capital and skills packages are therefore important.

Retraining for future skills needs is important in recessions when companies may be hoarding labour and where time slack could be used productively. This could be implemented by government financing of option payments on behalf of purchasing firms expiring at a variety of future dates chosen by the purchasing firm. These payments would be conditional on the equipment suppliers providing advance training programmes in-house for the purchasing firms. Firms that do not exercise the options would be obliged to pay back a portion of the subsidy at a rate depending on the state of the economy when the option expired, so that firms with no prospects of realistic return on the investment at the point of expiry (due to poor macroeconomic or industry conditions) would not be heavily penalized or would be allowed to roll the options over. A merit of the scheme is that it makes heavy use of the information stock of both buyers and sellers of capital goods with the latter acting as monitors in the allocation of the fund.

Active industrial strategy has to ensure that growth strategies are adequately financed. There are a number of separate issues here. Finance for industrial infrastructure, finance for start-ups and finance for growth. The first of these links with the macroeconomy. The Treasury's own estimate of infrastructure requirements (due to many years of low public spending in this area) is close to £40 billion a year but there is no firm indication that even this is going to be forthcoming. Yet, as *Financial Times* correspondent Martin Wolf has repeatedly pointed out, financing costs are low now and likely to get higher, so that there is a free lunch in simultaneous creation of supply and demand. Furthermore respected economists – such as Nobel prize winner Michael Spence – have warned that the era of cheap capital is over and that expensive projects will become harder to finance in the long run as emerging countries build up their domestic consumption industries. A national infrastructure bank, such as that proposed in the US by Felix Rohatyn, would provide direct funds from government and have the option of borrowing with state guarantees. In the UK that could be combined with the mooted tapping of pension funds. Such a bank would have the added advantage of choosing projects on merit and avoiding the horse-trading associated with politically expedient investments.

Risk finance is important in other areas as well. The majority of finance provided for private firms is not venture capital but private equity, where the model is to increase the profitability of businesses in a short period of time so that they can be returned to the market. This model has run out of easy pickings largely because it was based on high borrowing. Current research does not appear to be able to demonstrate increased profitability for this model in recent years. The alternative vehicle is true venture capital for businesses that are not asset backed to the same degree. However the money raised in this way is much less than what is claimed as venture capital. There is a financing gap here if not for other sizes or sectors of the economy, particularly since the dot-com crash of 2000. Funds here may need to be provided publicly, perhaps on a local or regional basis in cooperation with universities. The risks of start-ups are much greater than established business expansion or buy-outs and it has proved difficult to get financial institutions interested.[18]

Start-up finance is most important for technological firms where potential growth is rapid. From the mid 1970s the UK government operated a National Enterprise Board (NEB) that invested in such companies. Recent retrospective study has concluded that it obtained a 'decent success rate of between 25% to 32%' for its high technology start-ups and that nearly half of the firms supported survived which is high by the standards of venture capital funds (Yong 2002). The NEB became part of the privatized British Technology Group (BTG) in 1991, along with a book of public patents from the National Research Development Corporation (NRDC). As a private corporation, BTG will subsequently have sought to develop its technology interests for its own gain. But the loss of this public function will have reduced the opportunities for locating synergies for a national technology strategy. It seems reasonable

---

[18] The recent formation of the Business Growth Fund is said to emulate the Finance Corporation for Industry set up by the Bank of England and major clearing banks to aid post-war reconstruction, which eventually ended up as the private equity firm, 3i. However it appears that the fund is simply competing with existing private equity houses in the same (mostly non-technology) sectors and with the same turnover bracket that excludes the smaller companies with sales of less than £10 million.

to think that there may be a case for the recreation of a NEB with the objective of technological scanning to provide a steer for an active new-technology industrial policy.

Apart from technology start-ups, more simple start-ups can act as a medium term solution to sustain employment. While there has been some recognition of financial constraints here (Wren 2001) perhaps there has been too little attention to the *non-financial* obstacles to growth such as easy imitation. One answer here may be regional or local knowledge exchanges where new ideas (not necessarily technological) can be registered and receive privileged access to public information channels or publicity sources for a limited period.

Start-ups are unlikely to constitute more than a small fraction of new business. Most of that will come from established firms and here the challenge is to deal with cases where firms shelve projects with good prospect often for reasons more to do with the firm than the economy. There are cases where good ideas are produced internally but are rejected because they constitute a poor strategic fit; they cannibalize existing sales; or they simply fall victim to managerial game playing. Some effort should be made to resolve these issues because it is far from certain that a good idea that is rejected will quickly be adopted by alternative producers. Some of the corporate governance reforms discussed in Chapter 7 may help. In addition it may be necessary to legislate for the right of company managers to bid to spin out divisions where intellectual property is being suppressed internally. There is a precedent for this in compulsory licensing of patents and in the provision for the patent office to de-register patents that are not used within a given timeframe. Such a policy would need to be framed sensitively however – and perhaps involve the competition authorities – so as not to penalize companies holding appropriate strategic options for future exploration.

Several of the proposals above will find support from employers' organizations, trade associations and trade unions. One more contentious issue is of taxation of capital and the uses of tax income. The employers' body – the CBI – is pressing for reductions in the rate of corporate tax to 18 per cent. Here again a forum for bargaining is important. We have shown throughout this book that profits have risen faster than investment and R&D and that income distribution has widened considerably in favour of profits and top income earners. Reduction in the corporate tax take seems unreasonable in such circumstances and in any event, the headline rate seems to have little correlation with the amount collected from the major companies. There can however be a bargain over relating the *use* of profit to its taxation. More investment is one of the few ways of balancing the economy as it reduces supply constraints. To encourage this without further pressure on the public purse, companies will have to tilt their use of funds toward investment and away from disbursements. This can be done in a tax-neutral way by raising the rate of corporation tax simultaneously with increasing capital allowances. Alternatively if it is judged appropriate, interest tax relief for large companies can be substituted by higher investment allowances.[19] The latter step might well have the added benefit of increasing the role of internal capital markets and putting executive managers back in the driving seat for company expansion, as discussed in the proposals for 'bottom up governance' in Chapter 7.

No active industrial policy is likely to succeed without being able to tap a substantial initial pool of funds that can perhaps be leveraged through the banking arm of the strategic authority. Finance is often scarce when, as now, it is most needed; thus new ideas have to be found to generate revenue without damaging a recovery. Here we suggest a possible free lunch. We propose to tax inputs to the productive process where the associated productivity on the input depends largely on a rival's input. Put differently we seek to contain a 'business arms race' that tends to develop without any overall gain. The chief example of such a process is consumer advertising. Much of this advertising is not informative, particularly where it is not targeted. There is little correlation between heavy advertising sectors (washing powder, cereals, bottled water and so on) and the provision of, or need for, information. Insofar as it is helpful, academic theory supports advertising for its signalling aspect – the notion that the producer is signalling quality because otherwise it would not risk a large amount of advertising expenditure. But in this case it does no damage to the company or industry if the advertising is more expensive (due to higher taxation) as the quality is inferred by the *relative* expenditure. We thus expect that an additional 'vice' tax on advertising would reduce the overall volume without damaging the message content of informative advertising. At the same time it would yield valuable tax yield to the revenue. It would potentially tilt the balance of activity towards innovation and technical progress rather than uninformative advertising (where the pay-off tends

---

[19] If such steps sound radical it should be recalled that something similar was proposed by Martin Feldstein, Chairman of President Reagan's Council of Economic Advisers (*Financial Times* 2 August 2006 'Europe has to face the threat of America's trade deficit').

to be quicker).[20] Any adverse effect on industry employment could be compensated by redirecting part of the proceeds internally, for example towards expansion of the film and other media industries.

The exact design, remit and activities of an active industrial strategy are not issues that can be settled here. We have sought here to give some possible ideas and illustrations because the memory of industrial activism has faded over the years to the point where many regard any such steps as impractical or contradictory. No doubt there are difficulties in producing clear lines of attack, with instruments found for each objective. But as we have shown in this book the alternative has also been a process of relying on luck and muddling through, that is now adrift. The years of the fast buck are coming to an end and with that the need arises for fresh thinking on progressive alternatives.

---

[20] The media executive Martin Sorrell complains of western companies' 'Willingness to invest in the brand and maintaining or increasing market share rather than increasing capacity and fixed expenses' BBC website 4 March 2011 Robert Peston, 'Sorrell: the UK is a league of one team'.

References

Abbott, L.F. (ed.) (2003) *Manufacturing in Britain: A Survey of Factors Affecting Growth and Performance* (ISR Business, Finance & Investment Reports) (Manchester: Industrial Systems Research).

Abdel-Kader, M.G. and D. Dugdale (1998) 'Investment in advanced manufacturing technology: A study of practice in large UK companies', *Management Accounting Research*, 9, 261–284.

Abel, A.B., A.K. Dixit, J.C. Eberly and R.S. Pindyck (1996) 'Options, the value of capital, and investment', *Quarterly Journal of Economics*, 111, 753–777.

Abramovsky, L., R. Griffith and R. Harrison (2005) 'Background facts and comments on "Supporting growth in innovation: Enhancing the R&D tax credit"', Technical report, IFS Briefing Notes (BN68) Institute for Fiscal Studies.

ACARD (1985) 'Exploitable Areas of Science', Advisory Council for Research and Development.

Aggarwal, R.K. and A.A. Samwick (2006) 'Empire-builders and shirkers: Investment, firm performance and managerial incentives', *Journal of Corporate Finance*, 12, 489–515.

Aghion, P. (2006) 'A Primer on Innovation and Growth', Bruegel Policy Brief, Brussels.

Aghion, P., N. Bloom, R. Blundell, R. Griffith and P. Howitt (2005) 'Competition and Innovation: An inverted-U relationship', *Quarterly Journal of Economics*, 120(2), 701–728.

Aghion, P. and R. Griffiths (2005) *Competition and Growth: Reconciling Theory and Evidence* (Cambridge (MA): MIT Press).

Aghion, P. and J. Tirole (1997) 'Formal and real authority in organizations', *Journal of Political Economy*, 105(1), 1–29.

Aghion, P., J. Van Reenan and L. Zingales (2009) 'Innovation and Institutional Ownership', NBER Working Paper No. 14769.

Aglietta, M. (2007) 'New Trends in Corporate Governance: The Prominent Role of the Long-Run Investor', IGWF workshop, London 12–13 February.

Aguilera, R.V., C.A. Williams, J.M. Conley and D.E. Rupp (2006) 'Corporate governance and social responsibility: A comparative analysis of the UK and the US', *Corporate Governance*, 14(3), 147–158.

Aiginger, K. (2003a) 'Insufficient Investment into Future Growth: The Forgotten Cause of Low Growth in Germany', Department of Economics, Johannes Kepler University Linz, Austria WP 2003–14 http://ideas.repec.org/p/jku/econwp/2003_14.html accessed 13 April 2012.

Aiginger, K. (2003b) 'The Relative Importance of Labour Market Reforms to Economic Growth', WIFO Working Papers, No. 208, Vienna.

Akerlof, G., W. Dickers and G. Perry (1996) 'The macroeconomics of low inflation', *Brookings Papers on Economic Activity*.

Akerlof, G.A. and R.J. Shiller (2009) *Animal Spirits: How Human Psychology Drives the Economy, and why it Matters for Global Capitalism* (Princeton (NJ): Princeton University Press).

Akkermans, D., C. Castaldi and B. Los (2009) 'Do "Liberal Market Economies" really innovate more radically than "Coordinated Market Economies"? Hall and Soskice reconsidered', *Research Policy*, 38, 181–191.

Alkaraan, F. and D. Northcott (2006) 'Strategic capital investment decision-making: A role for emergent analysis tools? A study of practice in large UK manufacturing companies', *The British Accounting Review* 38(2), 149–173.

Allen, F. (2005) 'Corporate governance in emerging economies', *Oxford Review of Economic Policy*, vol. 21, No. 2, 164–177.

Allen, F. and D. Gale (2000) 'Corporate governance and competition', in X. Vives (ed.) *Corporate Governance: Theoretical and Empirical Perspectives* (Cambridge: Cambridge University Press) pp. 23–94.

Angelopoulou, E. and H.D. Gibson (2009) 'The balance sheet channel of monetary policy transmission: Evidence from the United Kingdom', *Economica* 76, 675–703.

Arestis, P. and I. Biefang-Frisancho (2000) 'Capital stock, unemployment and wages in the UK and Germany', *Scottish Journal of Political Economy*, 47(5), 487–503.

Arestis, P. and M. Sawyer (2005) 'Aggregate demand, conflict and capacity in the inflationary process', *Cambridge Journal of Economics* 29(6), 959–974.

Argyris, C. (1998) 'Empowerment: The emperor's new clothes', *Harvard Business Review*, May–June, 98–105.

Arnold, G.C. and P.D. Hatzopoulos (2000) 'The theory-practice gap in capital budgeting: Evidence from the United Kingdom', *Journal of Business Finance & Accounting*, 27, 603–626.

Arrow, K.J. (1962) 'The economic implications of learning by doing', *Review of Economic Studies*, 29, 155–173.

Arrow, K. J. (1983) 'Innovation in large and small firms', in R. Swedberg (ed.) (2000) *Entrepreneurship: The Social Science View* (Oxford: Oxford University Press).

Asher, C.C., J.M. Mahoney and J.T. Mahoney (2005) 'Towards a property rights foundation for a stakeholder theory of the firm', *Journal of Management and Governance* 9, 5–32.

Ashworth, P. and E.P. Davis (2001) 'Some evidence on financial factors in the determination of aggregate business investment for the G7 countries', Discussion Paper No. 187, National Institute of Economic and Social Research.

Asplund, M. (2000) 'What fraction of a capital investment is sunk costs?', *Journal of Industrial Economics*, 48(3), 287–304.

Atkinson, A.B. (2009) 'Factor shares: The principal problem of political economy?', *Oxford Review of Economic Policy*, 25(1), 3–16.

Atkinson D. and L. Elliott (2007) *Fantasy Island: Waking Up to the Incredible Economic, Political and Social Illusions of the Blair Legacy* (London: Constable and Robinson Ltd).

Autor, D.H., L.F. Katz and M.S. Kearney (2008) 'Trends in US wage inequality: Revising the revisionists', *Review of Economics and Statistics* 90(2), 300–323.

Autor, D.H., F. Levy and R.J. Murnane (2003) 'The skill content of recent technological change: An empirical exploration', *Quarterly Journal of Economics* 118(4), 1279–1333.

Awano, G., M. Franklin, J. Haskel and Z. Kastrinaki (2010) 'Measuring investment in intangible assets in the UK: Results from a new survey', *Economic and Labour Market Review* (4)7, 66–71.

Baker, G., R. Gibbons and K.J. Murphy (1997) 'Implicit Contracts and the Theory of the Firm', NBER Working Paper No. 6177.

Ball, L. and R. Moffitt (2001) 'Productivity Growth and the Phillips Curve', NBER Working Paper No. 8421.

Balogh, T. (1979) 'Comment on: Stout, D.K. (1979) De-industrialisation and industrial policy', in F. Blackaby (ed.) *De-industrialisation* (London: National Institute of Economic and Social Research), pp. 196–201.

Baltagi, B.H., P.O. Demetriades and S.H. Law (2009) 'Financial development and openness: Evidence from panel data', *Journal of Development Economics* 89(2), 285–296.

Barker, K. (1999) 'Investment policy and the employers perspective', in C. Driver and P. Temple (eds.) *Investment Growth and Employment* (London: Routledge) pp. 301–308.

Barney, J.B. and D.N. Clark (2007) *Resource Based Theory: Creating and Sustaining Competitive Advantage* (Oxford: Oxford University Press).

Barrell, R., E.P. Davis, D. Karim and I. Liadze (2010) 'The impact of global imbalances: Does the current account balance help to predict banking crises in OECD countries?' National Institute of Economic and Social Research Discussion Paper, April.

Barrell, R. and O. Pomerantz (2007) 'Globalization and Technology Intensity as Determinants of Exports' National Institute of Economic and Social Research Discussion Paper.

Basu, S. (1996) 'Procyclical productivity: Increasing returns or cyclical utilization?', *Quarterly Journal of Economics*, August, 719–751.

Bator, F. (1958) 'The anatomy of market failure', *Quarterly Journal of Economics*, 72(3), 351–379.

Bauer, R., R. Braun and G.L. Clark (2008) 'The emerging market for European corporate governance: The relationship between governance and capital expenditures, 1997–2005', *Journal of Economic Geography*, 8(4), 441–469.

Baum, C.F., M. Caglayan and O. Talavera (2008) 'Uncertainty determinants of firm investment', *Economics Letters*, Elsevier, 98(3), 282–287.

Baumol, W. (1967) 'The macroeconomics of unbalanced growth: The anatomy of urban crisis', *American Economic Review* 57(3), 415–426.

Baysinger, B., R. Kosnik, and T. Turk (1991) 'Effects of board and ownership structure on corporate strategy', *Academy of Management Journal* 34, 205–214.

Bean, C. (1989) 'Capital shortage', *Economic Policy* April, 11–54.

Bean, C. (1994) 'European unemployment: A survey', *Journal of Economic Literature*, 573–619.

Bean, C., R. Layard and S. Nickell (eds.) (1986) *The Rise in Unemployment* (Oxford: Blackwell).

Bean, C. and J. Symons (1989) 'Ten years of Mrs T', *NBER Macroeconomics Annual* 1989, vol. 4 (Cambridge (MA): MIT Press) 13–72.

Bebchuk, L.A. and J.M. Fried (2004) *Pay without Performance: The Unfullfilled Promise of Executive Compensation* (Cambridge and London: Harvard University Press).

Becht, M., P. Bolton and A. Roell (2003) 'Corporate governance and control', in G.M. Constantinides, M. Harris and R.M. Stulz, *Handbook of the Economics of Finance*, vol. 1A Corporate Finance (Amsterdam: Elsevier).

Benito, A., K. Neiss, S. Price and L. Rachel (2010) 'The impact of the financial crisis on supply', *Bank of England Quarterly Bulletin*, Q2, 104–114.

Berle, A.A. (1965) The Impact of the Corporation on Classical Economic Theory, *Quarterly Journal of Economics* 79, 25–40, reprinted in T. Clark (ed.) (2004) *Theories of Corporate Governance: The Philosophical Foundations of Corporate Governance* (London: Routledge).

Berle, A.A. and G.C. Means (1932) *The Modern Corporation and Private Property* (2nd edition, 1967) (New York: Harcourt, Brace and World).

Bernanke, B.S. 'The Great Moderation' Remarks by Governor Ben S. Bernanke at the meetings of the Eastern Economic Association, Washington, DC 20 February, 2004.

Bernanke, B.S. and R.S. Gurkaynak (2001) 'Is growth exogenous? Taking Mankiw, Romer and Weil seriously', *NBER Annual*, vol. 16, pp. 1–72.

BERR (2008) 'BERR's role in raising productivity: New evidence', BERR Economics Paper No. 1 2008 February.

Bertrand, M. and S. Mullainathan (2003) 'Enjoying the quiet life? Corporate governance and managerial preferences', *Journal of Political Economy* 111(5), 1043–1075.

Bhagat, S. and B. Black (2002) 'The non-correlation between board independence and long-term firm performance', *Journal of Corporation Law* 27(2), 231–272.

Bhagwati, J. (2010) 'The manufacturing fallacy' http://www.project-syndicate. org/commentary/bhagwati3/English accessed 26 April 2012.

Bhaskar, V. and A. Glyn (1995) 'Investment and profitability: The evidence from the advanced capitalist countries', in G. Epstein and H. Gintis (eds.) *Macroeconomic Policy after the Conservative Era* (Cambridge: Cambridge University Press) pp. 175–196.

BIS (2010) 'UK Innovation Survey 2009 Statistical Annex' (London: Department for Business Innovation and Skills).

BIS (2010a) 'Learning From some of Britain's Successful Sectors: An Historical Analysis of the Role of Government', BIS Economics Paper No. 6, March 2010 (London: Department for Business Innovation and Skills).

BIS (2010b) 'UK Trade Performance: Patterns in UK and Global Trade Growth', BIS Economics Paper No. 8, November 2010 (London: Department for Business Innovation and Skills).

Black, B. (1997) 'Institutional investors and corporate governance: The case for institutional voice', in D.H. Chew (ed.) *Studies in International Corporate Finance and Governance Systems: A Comparison of the U.S, Japan & Europe* (Oxford: Oxford University Press) pp. 160–173.

Blair, M. (1995) *Ownership and Control: Rethinking Corporate Governance for the Twenty-First Century* (Washington, DC: The Brookings Institution).

Blanchard, O.J. (1986) 'The wage-price spiral', *Quarterly Journal of Economics* 101, 543–566.

Blanchard, O.J. (1986) 'Comments and discussion', *Brookings Papers on Economic Activity*, 1, 153–156.

Blanchard, O.J. (1997) 'The Medium Run', *Brookings Papers on Economic Activity* 2, 89–158.

Blanchard, O.J. and J. Wolfers (2000) 'The role of shocks and institutions in the rise of European unemployment: The aggregate evidence', *Economic Journal* 110, C1–C33.

Blanden, J. and S. Machin (2007) *Recent Changes in Intergenerational Mobility*, Report for the Sutton Trust (London: Sutton Trust).

Blaug, R. and R. Lekhi (2009) 'Accounting for intangibles: Financial reporting and value creation in the knowledge economy', The Work Foundation http://www.theworkfoundation.com/assets/docs/publications/223_ intangibles_final.pdf accessed 13 April 2012.

Boisot, M. (1998) *Knowledge Assets: Securing Competitive Advantage in the Information Economy* (Oxford: Oxford University Press).

Bombach, G. (1985) 'Post-war economic growth revisited' *Professor Dr. F. De Vries Lectures in Economic Theory, Institutions, Policy*, vol. 6 (Amsterdam: Elsevier).

Bond, S. and T. Jenkinson (1996) 'The assessment: Investment-performance and policy', *Oxford Review of Economic Policy* 12(2), 1–29.

Boone, J. (2000) 'Technological progress, downsizing and unemployment', *The Economic Journal* 110, 581–600.

Boot, A. and J. Macey (2004) 'Monitoring corporate performance: The role of objectivity, proximity and adaptability in corporate governance', *Cornell Law Review* 89, 356–393.

Booz, A. (2007) 'CEO succession 2006: The era of the inclusive leader', Summary of research in Strategy+Business, June; Boozallen.com/news/3660808.

Boston Consulting Group (2006) 'Global delayering for competitive advantage', BCG.

Bosworth, B.P. and J.E. Triplett (2000) 'What's new about the new economy? ICT, economic growth and productivity' (Mimeo, Washington (DC): Brookings Institute).

Brech, M.J. and D.K. Stout (1981) 'The exchange rate and non-price competitiveness: A provisional study within UK manufacturing exports', *Oxford Economic Papers*, 33, 268–81.

Bresnahan, T., P. Milgrom and J. Paul (1992) 'The real output of the stock exchange', in Z. Griliches (ed.) *Output Measurement in the Service Sectors* (Chicago: University of Chicago Press).

Brinkley, I. (2008) 'The Knowledge Economy: How Knowledge is Reshaping the Economic Life of Nations', The Work Foundation, March.

Brown, J.R., S.M. Fazzari and B.C. Petersen (2009) 'Financing innovation and growth: Cash flow, external equity, and the 1990s R&D boom', *Journal of Finance*, 64 (1), 151–185.

Brown, L.D. and M.L. Caylor (2009) 'Corporate governance and firm operating performance', *Review of Quantitative Finance and Accounting*, 32(2), 1573–7179.

Brown, J.R. and B.C. Petersen (2009) 'Why has the investment-cash flow sensitivity declined so sharply? Rising R&D and equity market developments', *Journal of Banking & Finance* 33, 971–984.

Bulli, S. (2008) 'Business innovation investment in the UK'. Science and Innovation Analysis Department of Innovation, Universities and Skills, London.

Burnside, C. (1996) 'Production function regressions, returns to scale, and externalities', *Journal of Monetary Economics*, 37, 177–201.

Burton-Jones, A. (1999) *Knowledge Capitalism: Business, Work and Learning in the New Economy* (New York: Oxford University Press).

Busby, J.S. and C.G.C. Pitts (1997) 'Real options in practice: An exploratory survey of how finance officers deal with flexibility in capital appraisal', *Management Accounting Research*, vol. 8, No. 2, June 1997, 169–186(18).

Buxton, T., D. Mayes and A. Murfin (1991) 'UK trade performance and R&D', *Economics of innovation and New Technology*, 1, 243–56.

Caballero, R. (1999) 'Aggregate investment', in J.B. Taylor and M. Woodford (eds.) *Handbook of Macroeconomics*, vol. 1B (Amsterdam: Elsevier).

Campello, M., J.R. Graham and C.R. Harvey (2010) 'The real effects of financial constraints: Evidence from a financial crisis', *Journal of Financial Economics*, 97(3), 470–487.

Cantwell, J. (2005) 'Innovation and competitiveness', in J. Fagerberg, D.C. Mowery and R. Nelson (eds.) *Oxford Handbook of Industrial Innovation* (Oxford: Oxford University Press).

Card, D., R. Blundell and R. Freeman (2004) *Seeking a Premier Economy: The Economic Effects of British Economic Reforms 1980–2000*, NBER.

Card, D. and R. Freeman (2004) 'What have two decades of British economic reform delivered?', in Card, D., R. Blundell and R. Freeman (eds.) *Seeking a Premier Economy: The Economic Effects of British Economic Reforms 1980–2000* (Chicago: University of Chicago Press) pp. 9–62.

Carlin, W., A. Glyn and J. Van Reenan (2001) 'Export market performance of OECD countries: An empirical examination of the role of cost competitiveness', *The Economic Journal*, 111, 128–62.

Carlin, W. and C. Mayer (2000) 'How do financial systems affect economic performance?', in X. Vives (ed.) *Corporate Governance: Theoretical and Empirical Perspectives* (Cambridge: Cambridge University Press) pp. 137–159.

CBI (1992) 'Making it in Britain', National Manufacturing Council, Autumn.

CBI (2001) 'Realistic Returns: How do Manufacturers Assess New Investment?', CBI special survey, London.

Cette, G., Y. Kocoglu and J. Mairesse (2009) 'Productivity growth and levels in France, Japan, the United Kingdom and the United States in the twentieth century', NBER Working Paper No. 15577.

Chan, A., D. Savage and R. Whittaker (1995) 'The new Treasury model', Government Economic Service Working Paper No. 128 (Treasury Working Paper No. 70), London, HM Treasury., p. 181.

Chandler, A.D. (1977) *The Visible Hand: The Managerial Revolution in American Business* (Cambridge (MA): Harvard University Press).

Chandler, A.D. (1990) *Scale and Scope: The Dynamics of Industrial Capitalism* (Cambridge (MA): Harvard University Press).

Chandler, A.D. (1992) 'Organizational capabilities and the economic history of the industrial enterprise', *Journal of Economic Perspectives* 6(3), 79–100.

Child, J. and S.B. Rodriguez (2004) 'Repairing the breach of trust in corporate governance', *Corporate Governance* 12(2), 143–151.

Chirinko, R.S. (1993) 'Business Fixed Investment Spending: Modelling Strategies, Empirical Results, and Policy Implications', *Journal of Economic Literature*, 31, 1875–1911.

Chirinko, R.S. and H. Schaller (2004) 'A revealed preference approach to understanding corporate governance problems: Evidence from Canada', *Journal of Financial Economics*, 74, 181–206.

Choudhary, M.A., P. Temple and L. Zhao (2012) 'Taking the measure of things: The role of measurement in EU trade', *Empirica*, DOI: 10.1007/s10663-011-9178-z.

Christensen, C.M., S.P. Kaufman and W.C. Shih (2008) 'Innovation killers: How financial tools destroy your capacity to do new things', *Harvard Business Review* January, 98–105.

Clarke, T. (2007) *International Corporate Governance: A Comparative Approach* (Abingdon: Routledge).

Coakley, J. and A. Wood (1999) 'Components of investment and growth' in C. Driver, P. Temple (eds.) *Investment, Employment and Growth: Perspectives For Policy* (London: Routledge).

Coase, R. (1937) 'The Nature of the Firm', *Economica* 4(16), 386–405.

Coates, J. C. IV (2007) 'The goals and promise of the Sarbanes-Oxley Act', *Journal of Economic Perspectives* 21(1), 91–116.

Coffee, J. (2004) 'What caused Enron? A capsule social and economic history of the 1990s', in T. Clark (2004) *Theories of Corporate Governance: The Philosophical Foundations of Corporate Governance* (London: Routledge).

Cohen, W. and D. Levinthal (1989) 'Innovation and learning: The two faces of R&D', *The Economic Journal* 99, September, 569–596.

Conway, N., S. Deakin, S. Konzelmann, H. Petit, A. Rebérioux and F. Wilkinson (2008) 'The influence of stock market listing on human resource management: Evidence for France and Britain', *British Journal of Industrial Relations*, 46(4), 631–673.

Conyon, M.J. and R.B. Freeman (2004) 'Shared Modes of Compensation and Firm Performance U.K. Evidence', in D. Card, R. Blundell and R.B. Freeman (eds.) *Seeking a Premier Economy: The Economic Effects of British Economic Reforms, 1980–2000* (Chicago: University of Chicago Press and NBER) pp. 109–146 <http://ideas.repec.org/h/nbr/nberch/6744.html> accessed 13 April 2012.

Cornelius, M. and K. Wright (1995) 'Company profitability and finance', *Bank of England Quarterly Bulletin* 1995.3, 270–79.

Corrado, C.A., C.R. Hulten and D. Sichel (2006) 'Intangible Capital and Economic Growth,' NBER Working Papers No. 11948, National Bureau of Economic Research, Inc.

Corry, D. (2011) 'Labour and the economy, 1997–2010: More than a Faustian pact', in P. Diamond and M. Kenny (eds.) *Reassessing New Labour: Market, State and Society under Blair and Brown* Special issue of *Political Quarterly* (Oxford: Wiley-Blackwell) pp. S123–139.

Corry, D. and A. Glyn (1994) 'The macroeconomics of equality, stability and growth', in A. Glyn and D. Miliband (eds.) *Paying for Inequality* (London: London Institute of Public Policy Research).

Cottrell, T. and G. Sick (2001) 'First mover (dis) advantage and real options', *Journal of Applied Corporate Finance*, 14, 41–51.

Coutts, K., A. Glyn and R. Rowthorn (2007) 'Structural change under New Labour', *Cambridge Journal of Economics* 2007, 31, 845–861.

Crafts, N. (1997) 'Britain's relative economic decline: A quantitative perspective', Social Market Foundation Paper No. 29, cited in L. Hessleman (1999) 'Perspectives on the productivity debate', *The Business Economist* 30(2), 11.

Crafts, N. (1991) 'Reversing Relative Economic Decline? The 1980s in Historical Perspective,' *Oxford Review of Economic Policy*, 7(3), Autumn, 81–98.

Crespi, C. and P. Patel (2003) 'Engineering and Physical Science in the UK', Report to the EPRSC, SPRU, University of Sussex.

Criscuolo, C. and J. Haskel (2002) 'Innovations and Productivity Growth in the UK', ONS Productivity Workshop.

Crotty, J.R. (1996) 'Is New Keynesian investment theory really "Keynesian"? Reflections on Fazzari and Variato', *Journal of Post Keynesian Economics* 18(3), Spring, 333–357.

Crouch, C. (2011) 'Markets power and politics: Is there a liberalism beyond social democracy?', in *Policy Network Priorities for a New Political Economy: Memos to the Left* (Policy Network London) http://www.policy-network.net/ publications/4002/Priorities-for-a-new-political-economy-Memos-to-the-left accessed 13 April 2012.

Cummins, J. (2005) 'A new approach to the valuation of intangible capital', in C. Corrado, J. Haltiwanger and D. Sichel (eds.) *Measuring Capital in the New Economy* (Chicago: University of Chicago Press).

Darby, J. et al, (1999) 'The impact of exchange rate uncertainty on the level of investment', *Economic Journal, Royal Economic Society*, 109(454), C55–67.

Davis, E. (2011) *Made in Britain: How the Nation Earns its Living* (London: Little, Brown).

Deakin, S. (2003), 'Corporate Governance after Enron: The Return of History, Issue 14, The Edge Economic and Social Council.

Deakin, S. (2008) 'The corporation and society in historical perspective' and 'The diversity of contemporary corporate governance', Tanner lectures delivered at the Said Business School and Brasenose College, University of Oxford, February.

Dean, J. (2001) 'Stakeholding and company law', *The Company Lawyer*, 22(3), 66–74.

DeLong, J. B. and L.H. Summers (1991) 'Equipment investment and economic growth', *Quarterly Journal of Economics*, 106, 445–502.

Demirag, I.S. (1998) 'Boards of Directors' short-term perceptions and evidence of managerial short-termism in the UK', *European Journal of Corporate Finance* 4, 195–211.

Demsetz, H. (1993) 'The theory of the firm revisited', in O.E. Williamson and S.G. Winter (eds. 1993) *The Nature of the Firm: Origins, Evolution and Development* (New York: Oxford University Press) pp. 159–178.

Demsetz, H. (1997) 'The firm in economic theory: A quiet revolution', *American Economic Review*, May, 87 (2), 426–429.

Denham, J. (2011) 'Reappraising New Labour's political economy', in P. Diamond and M. Kenny (eds.) *Reassessing New Labour: Market, State and Society under Blair and Brown*, Special Issue of Political Quarterly (Oxford: Wiley-Blackwell) pp. S46–52.

Dillow, C. (2011) Irrationally short-termist? <http://www.investorschronicle. co.uk/2011/05/12/comment/chris-dillow/irrationally-short-termist-WjCeSdvw0UCyQ1YEp9WH6M/article.html> accessed 26 April 2012.

DiMaggio, P. (ed. 1997) *The Twenty-First Century Firm* (Princeton (NJ): Princeton University Press).

Donaldson, T. and L.E. Preston (1995) 'The Stakeholder Theory of the Corporation: Concepts, Evidence and Implications', *Academy of Management Review* 20(1), 65–91.

Dore, R. (2000) *Stock Market Capitalism: Welfare Capitalism: Japan and Germany Versus the Anglo-Saxons* (New York: Oxford University Press).

Dougherty, D. and E.H. Bowman (1995) 'The effects of organizational downsizing on product innovation', *California Management Review*, 37(4), 28–44.

Dow, C. (1999) *Major Recessions: Britain and the World, 1920–1995* (Oxford: Oxford University Press).

Dreze, J.H. and C. Bean (eds.) (1990) *Europe's Unemployment Problem* (Cambridge (MA): MIT Press).

Drèze, J.H. and H. Sneessens (1995) 'Technological development, competition from low-wage economies and low-skilled unemployment', in D.J. Snower and G. de la Dehesa *Unemployment Policy: Government Options for the Labour Market* (Cambridge: Cambridge University Press) p.250.

Driffield N., J.H. Love and K. Taylor (2009) 'Productivity and labour demand effects of inward and outward foreign direct investment on UK industry', *The Manchester School* 77(2), 171–203.

Driver, C. (2007) 'Business optimism for Small, Medium and Large Firms: Does It Explain Investment' *Fiscal Studies*, 8(2), 205–255.

Driver, C. (2012) 'Governance, Innovation and Finance' in T. Clarke and D. Branson (eds. 2012) *The Sage Handbook of Corporate Governance* (London: Sage Publications).

Driver, C. and M. Guedes (2012) Research and development, cash flow, agency and governance: UK large companies. Research Policy (2012), http://dx.doi.org/10.1016/j.respol.2012.04.003

Driver, C. and S.G. Hall (2007) 'Production constraints and the NAIRU', *Economics: The open-access, open-assessment e-journal*, 2.

Driver, C. and N. Meade, (2001) 'Persistence of capacity shortage and the role of adjustment costs', *Scottish Journal of Political Economy*, Scottish Economic Society, 48(1), 27–47.

Driver, C. and J. Muñoz-Bugarin (2010) 'Capital investment and unemployment in Europe: Neutrality or not?', *Journal of Macroeconomics*, 32 (1), 492–496.

Driver, C. and D. Shepherd (1999) 'Supply constraints and inflation', in C. Driver and P. Temple (eds.) *Investment Growth and Employment* (London: Routledge).

Driver, C. and D. Shepherd (2005) 'Capacity utilisation and corporate restructuring: A comparative study of the US, UK and other EU countries', *Cambridge Journal of Economics*, 29, 119–140.

Driver, C. and P. Temple 'Why do hurdle rates differ from the cost of capital?', *Cambridge Journal of Economics*, 34(3), 501–523.

Driver, C., P. Temple and G. Urga (2006) 'Identifying externalities in UK manufacturing using direct estimation of an average cost function', *Economics Letters*, Elsevier, 92, 228–233.

Driver, C., P. Temple and G. Urga (2006) 'Contrasts between types of assets in fixed investment equations as a way of testing real options theory', *Journal of Business & Economic Statistics*, American Statistical Association, 24, 432–443.

Driver, C., P. Temple and G. Urga (2005) 'Profitability, capacity and uncertainty: A model of UK manufacturing investment', *Oxford Economic Papers*, 57, 120–141.

Driver, C. and G.F. Thompson (2002) 'Corporate governance and democracy: The stakeholder debate revisited', *Journal of Management and Governance*, 6, 111–130.

Driver, C. and B. Whelan (2001) 'The effect of business risk on manufacturing investment: Sectoral survey evidence from Ireland', *Journal of Economic Behavior & Organization*, 44(4), 403–412.

DTI (1996) 'UK Investment performance: Fact and Fallacy', Department of Trade and Industry and Cabinet Office.

DTI (2001) 'UK Competitiveness Indicators: Second edition', Department of Trade and Industry.

DTI (2005) 'The Empirical Economics of Standards', DTI Economics Paper No. 12, London: Department of Trade and Industry.

DTI (2005a) 'R&D intensive Businesses in the UK', DTI Economics Paper No. 11, March.

DTI (2007a) 'Companies Act 2006: Duties of Company Directors', Ministerial Statement: Introduction, Rt. Hon Margaret Hodge <http://www.bis.gov.uk/files/file40139.pdf> accessed 13 April 2012.

DTI (2007b) 'Business Services and Globalisation', DTI Economics, Paper No. 19, Department of Trade and Industry, January.

Eccleshall, R. and G.S. Walker (1998) *Biographical Dictionary of British Prime Ministers* (London: Routledge).

Eisenhardt, K.M. (1989) Agency theory: An assessment and review, *Academy of Management Review*, 14(1), 57–74.

Elliott, L. and D. Atkinson (2008) *The Gods that Failed: How Blind Faith in Markets has Cost us our Future* (New York: Nation Books).

Elson, C. (2007) 'The state of US corporate governance: An interview with Charles Elson', *Journal of Applied Corporate Finance*, 19(1), 74–80.

Eltis, W. (1996) 'How low profitability and weak innovativeness undermined UK industrial growth', *Economic Journal*, 106, 434, 184–95.

Enriques, L. and P. Volpin (2007) 'Corporate governance reforms in continental Europe', *Journal of Economic Perspectives*, 21, 117–140.

Evangelista, R. (1999) *Knowledge and Investment: The Sources of Innovation in Industry* (Cheltenham: Edward Elgar).

Fagerberg, J. (1988) 'International competitiveness', *The Economic Journal*, 98(391), 355–374.

Fagerberg, J. (1996) 'Technology and competitiveness', *Oxford Review of Economic Policy*, 12(3), 39–51.

Fagernäs, S., P. Sarkar and A. Singh (2008) 'Legal origin, shareholder protection and the stock market: New challenges from time series analysis', in K. Gugler and B. Yurtoglu (eds.) *The Economics of Corporate Governance and Mergers* (Cheltenham: Edward Elgar).

Fair, R.C. (2000) 'Testing the NAIRU model for the United States', *Review of Economics and Statistics* 82(1), 64–71.

Fama, E.F. (1980) 'Agency problems and the theory of the firm', *The Journal of Political Economy*, 88(2), 288–307.

Fama, E.F. and K.R. French (1997) 'Industry costs of equity', *Journal of Financial Economics*, 43, 153–193.

Favaro, K., P.O. Karlsson, and G.L. Neilson (2010) 'CEO Succession 2000–2009: A Decade of Convergence and Compression' *strategy+business* 59, Summer, Booz&Co, reprint 10208, 1–14.

Fazzari, S. (2009) 'Modern business behavior: The theory of the active firm', in J.P. Goldstein and M.G. Hillard (eds.) *Heterodox Macroeconomics: Keynes, Marx and Globalization* (Abingdon: Routledge) Chapter 7.

Fazzari, S., Ferri P. and E. Greenberg (2008) 'Cash flow, investment, and Keynes–Minsky cycles', *Journal of Economic Behavior & Organization* 65(3–4), 555–572.

Fazzari, S. and A.M. Variato (1994) 'Asymmetric information and Keynesian theories of investment', *Journal of Post Keynesian Economics*, 6(3), 351–370.

Filatotchev I., J. Jona and R. Jensinson (2011) 'Cass-Junction RDS Project: Shareholder Patterns of FTSE 100 Companies', Cass Business School

Conference on 'Management, Governance and Regulation in the Changing Investor Landscape', Cass Business School, London, September.

Felstead, A., D. Gallie, F. Green and Y. Zhou (2007) 'Skills at work, 1986–2006' ESRC Centre on Skills, Knowledge and Organisational Performance Universities of Oxford and Cardiff.

Finegold, D. and D. Soskice (1988) 'The failure of training in Britain: Analysis and prescription', *Oxford Review of Economic Policy*, 4(3), 21–53.

Fisher, I. (1930) *The Theory of Interest* (New York: Macmillan).

Forth J. and N. Millward (2002) 'Union effects on pay levels in Britain', *Labour Economics*, 9, 547–61.

Foss, N.J., H. Lando and S. Thomsen (2000) 'The theory of the firm', in B. Bouckaert and G. De Geest (eds.) *Encyclopedia of Law and Economics* vol. III. (Edward Elgar: Cheltenham) pp. 631–658.

Frank, M.Z. and V.K. Goyal (2008) 'Trade off and pecking order theories of debt', in E. Eckbo (ed.) *Handbook of Corporate Finance: Empirical Corporate Finance*, vol. 2, Handbooks in Finance Series (Elsevier) Chapter 12.

Franks, J.R., C. Mayer and S. Rossi (2004) 'spending less time with the family: the decline of family ownership in the UK', ECGI - Finance Working Paper No. 35/2004.

Frey, B.S. and M. Osterloh (2005) 'Yes, managers should be paid like bureaucrats', *Journal of Management Inquiry*, 14(1), 96–111.

Froud J., A. Leaver, G. Tampubolon and K. Williams (2008) 'Everything for Sale: How Non-executive Directors Make a Difference', CRESC Working Paper No. 46, University of Manchester.

Froud J., J. Sukhdev, J. Law, A. Leaver and K. Williams (2011) 'Rebalancing the Economy (or Buyer's Remorse)' CRESC Working Paper series WP No. 87, University of Manchester.

Fumas, V.S. (2007) 'Governance of the knowledge-intensive firm' Documentos de trabajo 26 Fundacion BBVA, University of Zaragoza.

Gaeremynck, A., P. Sercu and A. Renders (2010) 'Corporate governance ratings and company performance: A cross-European study', *Corporate Governance – An International Review*, 18(2), 87–106.

Geroski, P.A. (1991) 'Innovation and the sectoral sources of productivity growth', *Economic Journal* 101, 1431–1451.

Geroski, P.A. (1994) *Market Structure, Corporate Performance and Innovative Activity* (Oxford: Oxford University Press).

Gieve, Sir John (2006) 'The puzzle of UK business investment' Bank of England Quarterly Bulletin Q4, 442–446.

Gilchrist, S. and E. Zakrajsek (2007) 'Investment and the Cost of Capital: New Evidence from the Corporate Bond Market', NBER Working Paper No. 13174.

Girma, S. and K. Wakelin (2002) 'Are there regional spillovers from FDI in the UK?', in D. Greenaway, R. Upward and K. Wakelin (eds.) *Trade, Investment, Migration and Labour Markets* (Basingstoke: Macmillan).

Glyn, A. (1997) 'Does aggregate profitability really matter?', *Cambridge Journal of Economics*, 21, 593–619.

Glyn, A. (1998) 'Employment growth, structural change and capital accumulation', Centre for Business Research, University of Cambridge, WP 97.

Glyn, A. (2006) *Capitalism Unleashed: Finance, Globalization, and Welfare* (Oxford: Oxford University Press).

Glyn, A. and B. Sutcliffe (1972) *British Capitalism, Workers and the Profit Squeeze* (Harmondsworth: Penguin).

Glynn, S. and H. Gospel (2007) 'Britain's low skill equilibrium: A problem of demand?', *Industrial Relations Journal*, 24(2), 112–125.

Goldin, C. and L. Katz (2008) *The Race Between Education and Technology* (Cambridge MA: Harvard University Press).

Goolsbee, A. (1998) 'Investment tax incentives, prices, and the supply of capital goods', *Quarterly Journal of Economics*, 113(1), 121–148.

Goos, M. and A. Manning (2007) 'Lousy and lovely jobs: The rising polarisation of work in Britain', *Review of Economics and Statistics* 89(1), 118–133.

Gordon, D. (1995) 'Putting the horse (back) before the cart: Disentangling the macro relationship between investment and saving', in G.A. Epstein and H.M. Gintis (eds.) *Macroeconomic Policy after the Conservative Era: Studies in Investment, Saving and Finance* (New York: Cambridge University Press) pp. 57–108.

Gorg, H. and D. Greenaway (2003) 'Much Ado About Nothing? Do Domestic Firms Really Benefit from Foreign Direct Investment?', Discussion Paper No. 944, IZA.

Gracia, E. (2004) 'Corporate short-term thinking and the winner take all market', <http://www.westga.edu/~bquest/2004/thinking.htm> accessed 13 April 2012.

Graham, J. R., and C.R. Harvey (2001) 'The theory and practice of corporate finance: Evidence from the field', *Journal of Financial Economics*, 60, 187–243.

Graham, J.R., C.R. Harvey and S. Rajgopal (2005) 'The economic implications of corporate financial reporting', *Journal of Accounting and Economics*, 40, 3–73.

Grant, R.M. (1996) 'Towards a knowledge-based theory of the firm', *Strategic Management Journal*, 17, 109–122.

Grant, R.M. (2003) 'The knowledge-based view of the firm', in D.O. Faulkner and A. Campbell, *The Oxford Handbook of Strategy* (New York: Oxford University Press) Chapter 8, pp. 203–230.

Green, F. (2009) 'Employee Involvement, Technology and Job Tasks,' NIESR Discussion Papers 326, National Institute of Economic and Social Research.

Greenhalgh, C. (1990) 'Innovation and trade performance in the United Kingdom', *Economic Journal*, 100(400), 105–118.

Greenhalgh, C., P. Taylor and R. Wilson (1994) 'Innovation and export volumes and prices: A disaggregated study', *Oxford Economic Papers*, New Series, 46(1), 102–135.

Greenhalgh, C. and M. Rogers (2010) *Innovation, Intellectual Property and Economic Growth* (Woodstock: Princeton University Press).

Gregg, P., S. Jewell and I. Tonks (2005) 'Executive pay and performance in the UK 1994–2002', WP05/122, Centre for Market and Public Organization, University of Bristol.

Gregory, A. and M. Michou (2009), 'Industry cost of capital: UK evidence', *Journal of Business Finance and Accounting*, June/July, 679–704.

Griffith, R. and R. Harrison (2003) 'Understanding the UK's poor technological performance', IFS Briefing Note 37, Institute of Fiscal Studies, London.

Griffiths, R. (2007) 'Technology, productivity and public policy', *Fiscal Studies*, 28(3), 273–291.

Griliches, Z. (1992) 'The search for productivity spillovers', *Scandinavian Journal of Economics*, 94, 29–47.

Grinyer, J., A. Russell and D. Collison (1998) 'Evidence of managerial short-termism in the UK', *British Journal of Management*, 9, 13–22.

Gugler, K. (2001) *Corporate Governance and Economic Performance* (New York: Oxford University Press).

Haldane, A.G. and R. Davies (2011) 'The short long', <http://www.bankof england.co.uk/publications/Documents/speeches/2011/speech495.pdf> accessed 26 April 2012.

Hall, B.H. (1990) 'The impact of corporate restructuring on industrial research and development', *Brookings Papers on Economic Activity: Microeconomics* (Washington, DC: Brookings Institution).

Hall, P. and D. Soskice (eds.) (2001) *Varieties of Capitalism: The Institutional Foundations of Comparative Advantage* (New York: Oxford University Press).

Hall, R.E. (2000) 'E-Capital: The Link between the Stock Market and the Labor Market in the 1990s', *Brookings Papers on Economic Activity*, 2, 73–118.

Hansmann, H. (1996) *The Ownership of Enterprise* (Cambridge MA: Bellknapp Press).

Hansmann, H. and R. Kraakman (2000) 'The end of history for Corporate Law', ISSN 1045–6333 Discussion Paper 280, Harvard Law School, <http://www.law. harvard.edu/programs/olin_center> accessed 13 April 2012.

Hart, O. (1995) *Firms, Contracts and Financial Structure* (Oxford: Oxford University Press).

Hart, O. (1996) 'The Meaning of "Ownership"', a discussion, in Margaret M. Blair, *Wealth Creation and Wealth Sharing* (Washington (DC): The Brookings Institution).

Haskel, J. et al (2009) 'Innovation, Knowledge Spending and Productivity Growth in the UK: Interim Report for NESTA Innovation Index Project' NESTA.

Hatton, T.J. (2007) 'Can productivity growth explain the NAIRU? Long-run evidence from Britain, 1871–1999', *Economica*, 74, 475–491.

Hennessy, C.A. and A. Levy (2002) 'A unified model of distorted investment: Theory and evidence', Working Paper, Haas School of Business, U.C. Berkeley.

Hermalin, B.E. and M.S. Weisbach (2003) 'Boards of Directors as an Endogenously Determined Institution: A Survey of the Economic Literature' FRBNY Economic Policy Review / April.

Higgs, D. (2003) *Review of the role and effectiveness of Non-Executive Directors*, DTI London.

Hill, C. and S. Snell (1988) 'External control, corporate strategy and firm performance in research-intensive industries', *Strategic Management Journal*, 9, 577–590.

Hill, I. and R. Taylor (2001) 'Recent trends in dividends payments and share buybacks' *Economic Trends* 567, 41–43 (London: Office of National Statistics).

Hirschman. A.O. (1970) *Exit, Voice, and Loyalty: Responses to Decline in Firms, Organizations, and States* (Cambridge, MA: Harvard University Press).

HMSO (1985) 'Employment, the Challenge for the Nation', Cmd 9474 (London: HMSO).

Hodgson, G. (ed. 2007) *The Evolution of Economic Institutions: A Critical Reader* (Bheltenham: Edward Elgar).

Holmstrom, B. (1999a) 'Future of cooperatives: A corporate perspective', *The Finnish Journal of Business Economics*, 4, 404–417.

Holmstrom, B. (1999b) 'The firm as a sub-economy' *Journal of Law, Economics & Organization*, 15(1), 74–102.

Holmstrom, B. (2005) 'Pay without performance and the managerial power hypothesis: a comment', *Journal of Corporation Law*, 30(4), 1–13.

Holmstrom, B. and S.N. Kaplan (2001) 'Corporate governance and merger activity in the U.S.: Making sense of the 1980s and 1990s', *Journal of Economic Perspectives*, 15 (2), 121–144.

Holmstrom, B. and J. Roberts (1998) 'The Boundaries of the firm revisited', *Journal of Economic Perspectives* 12(4), 73–94.

Holopainen, H. (2007) 'Essays on corporate governance, stakeholders, and restructuring', University of Helsinki, Helsinki.

Hooper, P., K. Johnson and J. Marquez (2000) 'Trade elasticities for the G-7 countries', *Princeton Studies in International Economics*, No. 87.

Hopner, M. and G. Jackson (2001) 'An emerging market for corporate control? The Mannesmann takeover and German corporate governance' MPIFG Discussion Paper 01.4 ISSN 0944–2073, Max Planck Institut.

Hoskisson, R.E., M.A. Hitt, R.A Johnson and W. Grossman (2002) 'Conflicting voices: The effects of institutional ownership heterogeneity and internal governance on corporate innovation strategies', *Academy of Management Journal*, 45(4), 697–716.

Houseman, S.N. (1995) 'Job growth and the quality of jobs in the U.S. economy', *Labour*: Special issue, s93–124.

Houthakker, H.S. and S.P. Magee (1969) 'Income and price elasticities in world trade', *Review of Economics and Statistics*, 51(2), 111–125.

Hubbard, R.G. (1998) 'Capital-market imperfections and investment', *Journal of Economic Literature*, 36, 193–225.

Hubbard, R.G. and D. Palia (1999) 'A re-examination of the conglomerate merger wave in the 1960s: An internal capital markets view', *Journal of Finance*, 54, 1131–1152.

Hughes, A. (2008) 'Innovation policy as cargo cult: Myth and reality in knowledge-led productivity growth' in Bessand, J and Venables, T (eds.) *Creating Wealth from Knowledge: Meeting the Innovation challenge* (Cheltenham: Edward Elgar).

Hutton, W. (1996) *The State We're In* (revised edition) (London: Vintage).

ICR (2006) 'The growing trend of activist investing and its implications for corporate communications & investor relations', Integrated Corporate Relations, June.

IMF (2003) United Kingdom: Selected Issues: Section III 'UK Investment: Is there a Puzzle?', IMF Country Report, February.

Innovation Advisory Board (1990) *Innovation: City Attitudes and Practices* (London: Department of Trade and Industry).

Jacoby, S.M. (2005) *The Embedded Corporation: Corporate Governance and Employment Relations in Japan and the United States* (Princeton (NJ): Princeton University Press).

Jagannathan, R., I. Meier and V. Tarhan (2011) 'The Cross-Section of Hurdle Rates for Capital Budgeting: An Empirical Analysis of Survey Data NBER Working Paper Series', vol. w16770, Available at SSRN: <http://ssrn.com/abstract=1754921> accessed 13 April 2012.

Jensen, M.C. and W.H. Meckling (1976) 'Theory of the firm: Managerial behavior, agency costs and ownership structure', *Journal of Financial Economics*, 3(4), 305–360.

Jong, S. (2009) 'The development of Munich and Cambridge therapeutic biotech firms: A case study of institutional adaptation', in C. Crouch and H. Voelzkow

Innovation in Local Economies: Germany in Comparative Context (New York: Oxford University Press) pp. 121–138.

Joyce, R., A. Muriel, D. Phillips and L. Sibieta (2010) 'Poverty and Inequality in the UK 2010', *IFS Commentary C116* (London: Institute for Fiscal Studies).

Kaldor, N. (1961) 'Capital accumulation and economic growth', in D.C. Hague (ed.) *The Theory of Capital* (London: Macmillan) pp. 177–222.

Kaldor, N. (1978) 'The effects of devaluations on trade in manufactures' in N. Kaldor, *Further Essays on Applied Economics* (London: Duckworth).

Kanter, R.M. (1999) 'Change is everyone's job: Managing the extended enterprise in a globally connected world', *Organizational Dynamics* 28(1), 7–22.

Kaplan, S.N. and B. Minton (2006) 'How has CEO Turnover Changed? Increasingly Performance Sensitive Boards and Increasingly Uneasy CEOs,' NBER Working Papers No. 12465, National Bureau of Economic Research, Inc.

Katz, L. and D. Autor (1999) 'Changes in the wage structure and earnings inequality', *Handbook of Labor Economics*, vol. 3, part 1, pp. 1463–1555.

Kay, J. and A. Silberston (1995) 'Corporate governance', *National Institute Economic Review*, August, pp. 84–95, reprinted in G. Kelly, D. Kelly and A. Gamble: 1997, *Stakeholder Capitalism* (London: Macmillan).

Kenway, P. (1996) 'Too little investment: Why investment is low and why that matters and what a new Labour government could do about it', Institute of Public Policy Research.

Kenway, P. (1998) 'Stimulating Investment: A role for policy', Institute for Public Policy Research.

Ketels, C. Co-author, *UK Competitiveness: Moving to the next stage*, DTI and ESRC and principal associate, Institute for Strategy and Competitiveness, Harvard Business School, The Smith Institute Seminars on Improving Competiveness 16 March, 2004.

Keynes, J.M. (1937) 'The general theory of employment', *Quarterly Journal of Economics*, February. [Pagination from The Collected Writings of John Maynard Keynes, vol. XIV, pp. 109–123].

King, S. (2010) *Losing Control: The Emerging Threats to Western Prosperity* (New Haven: Yale University Press).

Kitson, M. and J. Michie (1996) 'Britain's industrial performance since 1960: Underinvestment and relative decline', *The Economic Journal*, 106(434) (January), 196–212.

Kneller, R. and G. Young (2000) 'The new British economy', paper given to the NIESR conference 'Technical progress economic growth and the new economy', 29 September 2000. London.

Krafft, J. and J.L. Ravix (2005) 'The governance of innovative firms: An evolutionary perspective', *Economics of Innovation and New Technology*, 14(3), 125–147.

Krafft, J., F. Quatraro and P. Saviotti (2008) 'Evolution of the knowledge base in knowledge intensive sectors,' Working Papers hal-00264261_v1, HAL Université de Nice Sophia-Antipolis.

Krafft, J. and J.L. Ravix (2008) 'Corporate Governance in Advanced Economies: Lessons in a Post Financial Crash Era. Introduction to the Special Issue' *Recherches Economiques de Louvain/Louvain Economic Review*, 74(4).

Kristensen, P.H. and J. Zeitlin (2005) *Local Players in Global Games: The Strategic Constitution of a Multinational Corporation* (Oxford: Oxford University Press).

Krugman, P. (1989) 'Differences in income elasticities and trends in real exchange rates', *European Economic Review*, 33, 1031–1049.

La Porta, R., F. Lopez-de-Silanes, A. Shleifer and R. Vishny (2000) 'Investor protection and corporate governance', *Journal of Financial Economics*, 58(1–2), 3–27.

Landes, E.M. and A.M. Rosenfield (1994) 'The durability of advertising revisited', *Journal of Industrial Economics*, 42(3), 263–276.

Landier, A., D. Sraer and D. Thesmar (March 15, 2005) 'Bottom-Up Corporate Governance', AFA 2006 Boston Meetings Paper. Available at SSRN: <http://ssrn.com/abstract=687542> accessed 13 April 2012.

Layard, R. and S. Nickell (1987) 'The labour market' in R. Dornbusch and R. Layard (eds.) *The Performance of the British Economy* (Oxford: Oxford University Press).

Layard, R., S. Nickell and R. Jackman (1991) *Unemployment: Macroeconomic Performance and the Labour Market* (Oxford: Oxford University Press).

Lazonick, W. (1992) 'Controlling the market for control: The historical significance of management capitalism', *Industrial and Corporate Change*, 1(3), 445–488.

Lazonick, W. (2007) 'The US Stock market and the governance of innovative enterprise', *Industrial and Corporate Change*, 16(6), 983–1035.

Lazonick, W. (2008) 'The quest for shareholder value: Stock repurchases in the US economy', *Recherches économiques de Louvain*: 74(4), 479–540.

Lazonick, W. (2010) 'The Chandlerian corporation and the theory of innovative enterprise', *Ind Corp Change*, 19 (2), 317–349.

Lazonick, W. and M. O'Sullivan (2000) 'Maximising shareholder value: A new ideology of corporate governance', *Economy and Society*, 2000, 29(1), 13–35.

Lev, B. (2001) *Intangibles: Management, Measurement, and Reporting* (Washington (DC): The Brookings Institute).

Levin, R.C., A. Klevorick, R. Nelson and S. Winter (1987) 'Appropriating the returns from industrial research and development', *Brookings Papers on Economic Activity*, 3, 783–831.

Lieberman, M. (1987) 'Strategies for capacity expansion', *Sloan Management Review*, Summer, 19–27.

Liebeskind, J.P. (2000) 'Internal capital markets: Benefits, costs, and organizational arrangements', *Organization Science*, 11(1), 58–76.

Littler, C.R. and P. Innes (2004) 'The paradox of managerial downsizing' *Organization Studies* 25; 1159.

Lomax, R.H. (1990) 'Implementing endgame strategies: Comment', in C. Baden-Fuller (edn 1990) *Managing Excess Capacity* (Wiley-Blackwell) pp. 212–13.

Love, J.H. and S. Roper (2005) 'Economists' perceptions versus managers' decisions: An experiment in transaction-cost analysis', *Cambridge Journal of Economics*, 29, 19–36.

Lysandrou, P. and D. Parker (2010) 'Commercial Corporate Governance Ratings: An Alternative View of Their Use and Impact' 8th International conference on Corporate Governance, University of Birmingham, 23 June.

Machin, S. (1996) 'Wage inequality in the UK', *Oxford Review of Economic Policy*, 7, 49–62.

Machin, S. and J. Van Reenen (1998) 'Technology and skill structure: Evidence from seven OECD countries', *Quarterly Journal of Economics*, 113(4), 1215–1244.

Maddison, A. (1982) *Phases of Capitalist Development* (Oxford: Oxford University Press).

Mairesse, J., B.H. Hall and B. Mulkay (1999), 'Firm-Level Investment in France and the United States: An Exploration of What We Have Learned in Twenty Years', Working Paper No. 7437, National Bureau of Economic Research.

Malley, J. and T. Moutsos (2001) 'Capital accumulation and unemployment: A tale of two "continents"', *Scandinavian Journal of Economics*, 103(1), 79–99.

Mallin, C., A. Mullineux and C. Wihlborg (2005) 'The financial sector and corporate governance: The UK case', *Corporate Governance: An International Review*, 13, 532–541.

Manacorda, M. and B. Petrongolo (1999) 'Skills mismatch and unemployment in OECD countries', *Economica*, 66 (262), 181–207.

Mansfield, E. (1984) Chapter 6 in Z. Grilliches and A. Pakes, *Patents, R&D and Productivity* (Chicago: University of Chicago Press).

Mansfield, E. (1987) 'How rapidly does new industrial technology leak out?', *Journal of Industrial Economics*, 19(2).

Marglin, S. and A. Bhaduri (1990) 'Unemployment and the real wage: The economic basis for contesting political ideologies', *Cambridge Journal of Economics*, 14, 375–93.

Marrano, M.G., J. Haskel and G. Wallis (2007)' Intangible Investment and Britain's Productivity: Treasury Economic', Working Paper No. 1, London, HM Treasury.

Marris, R.L. (1964) *The Economic Theory of Managerial Capitalism* (London: Macmillan).

Marris, R.L. (1972) 'Why economics needs a theory of the firm', *Economic Journal*, 82 (325), 321–52.

Marris, R. (1996) *How to Save the Underclass?* (London: Macmillan).

Marston, C.L. and B.M. Craven (1998) 'A survey of corporate perceptions of short-termism among analysts and fund managers', *European Journal of Corporate Finance* 4, 233–256.

Martin, R. (2010) 'The age of consumer capitalism', *Harvard Business Review* January-February reprint #: R1001B-PDF-ENG, pp.1–10.

Mason, G. (2004) 'Enterprise product strategies and employer demand for skills in Britain: Evidence from the Employers Skill Survey SKOPE Working Paper # 50, ESRC Centre on Skills, Knowledge and Organizational Performance, Oxford and Warwick Universities.

Matthews, R.C.O. (1968) 'Why has Britain had full employment since the war?', *Economic Journal*, 78.

Maudos, J., J.M. Pastor and L. Serrano (2008) 'Explaining the US-EU productivity growth gap: Structural change vs. intra-sectoral effect', *Economics Letters*, 100(2), 311–313.

Mayer, C. (1988) 'New issues in corporate finance', *European Economic Review*, 32, 1167–88.

Mayhew, K. and E. Keep (1999) 'The Assessment: Knowledge, skills and competitiveness', *Oxford Review of Economic Policy*, 15(1), 1–15.

McAdam, B.P. and K. McMorrow (1999) 'The Nairu concept – measurement uncertainties, hysterisis and economic policy role', *Economic Papers* No. 136 (Brussels: European Commission).

McDonald, I.M. and R. Solow (1981) 'Wage Bargaining and Employment', *American Economic Review*, 71(5), 896–908.

McKinsey & Co (1988) 'Performance and competitive success: Strengthening competitiveness in UK electronics', NEDO books.

McKinsey Global Institute (1998) Driving productivity and growth in the UK economy, McKinsey and Company <http://ww1.mckinsey.com/mgi/reports/pdfs/ukprod/ukprod.pdf> accessed 13 April 2012.

Mellahi, K. and A. Wilkinson (2008) 'A study of the association between downsizing and innovation determinants', *International Journal of Innovation Management*, 12(4), 677–698.

Melliss, C. and A.E. Webb (1997) 'The United Kingdom NAIRU: Concepts, measurement and policy implications', Economic Working Paper No. 182. H.M. Treasury.

Michie, J. and M. Sheehan-Quinn (2001) 'Labour market flexibility, human resource management and corporate performance', *British Journal of Management*, 12 (4), 287–306.

Mitchell, L.E., The Legitimate Rights of Public Shareholders (March 2, 2009). GWU Legal Studies Research Paper No. 461; GWU Law School Public Law Research Paper No. 461. Available at SSRN: <http://ssrn.com/abstract=1352025> accessed 13 April 2012.

Modigliani, F., J.P. Fitoussi, B. Moro, D. Snower, R. Solow, A. Steinherr and P. Sylos Labini (1998), 'An economists' manifesto on unemployment in the European Union', *Journal of Income Distribution*, 8, 163–187.

Morris, J., J. Hassard and L. McCann (2008) 'The resilience of institutionalised capitalism: Managing managers under shareholder capitalism and managerial capitalism', *Human Relations*, 61: 687–710.

Myers, S.C. (2003) 'Financing of corporations', in G.M. Constantinides, M. Harris and R.M. Stulz (eds.) *Handbook of the Economics of Finance*, edition 1, volume 1, chapter 4 (Amsterdam: Elsevier) pp. 215–253.

Myners, P. (2001) Institutional Investment in the UK: A Review (the Myners Report) HM Treasury National Manufacturing Council.

National Equality Panel (2010) 'An Anatomy of Inequality in the UK: Report of the National Equality Panel' (London: Government Equalities Office).

NEDO 1996 R&D and Financial Markets, Summary of Interview Responses, National Economic and Development Office UK.

NESTA (2006) The innovation gap: Why policy needs to reflect the reality of innovation in the UK.

NESTA (2009a) The innovation index: Measuring the UK's investment in innovation and its effects.

NESTA (2009b) Innovation, knowledge spending and productivity growth in the UK: Interim report for NESTA Innovation Index project.

NESTA (2011) Driving economic growth: Innovation, knowledge spending and productivity growth in the UK.

Nickell, S., L. Nunziata and W. Ochel (2005) 'Unemployment in the OECD since the 1960s: What do we know?', *The Economic Journal*, 115(1), 1–27.

Nickell, S.J. (1995) *The Performance of Companies* (Oxford: Blackwell).

Nickell, S. and D. Nicolitsas (1996) *Does innovation encourage investment in fixed capital?* CEPDP, 309. Centre for Economic Performance, London School of Economics and Political Science, London, UK.

Nickerson, J.A. and T.R. Zenger (2004) 'A Knowledge-Based Theory of the Firm: The Problem-Solving Perspective', *Organization Science*, 15(6), 617–632.

Norman, J. (2011) 'Conservative Free Markets, and the Case for Real Capitalism', House of Commons, December.

O'Shaughnessy, T. (2001) 'Unemployment, hysteresis and capacity', mimeo, University of Oxford.

O'Sullivan, M. (2000) 'The innovative enterprise and corporate governance', *Cambridge Journal of Economics*, 2000, 24(4), 393–416.

OECD (1992) *Technology and the Economy: The Key Relationships* (Paris: Organisation for Economic Cooperation and Development).

OECD (2002) *Frascati Manual 2002: Proposed standard practice for surveys on Research and Development* (Paris: Organisation for Economic Cooperation and Development).

OECD (2010) *STAN Database for Structural Analysis 2009 edition, ESDS International*, University of Manchester. DOI: 10.5257/oecd/stan/2010

Oliner, S.D., D.E. Sichel, K.J. Stiroh (2008) 'Explaining a productive decade', *Journal of Policy Modeling*, 30, 633–673.

O'Mahony, M. and M. Vecchi (2003) 'Is there an ICT impact on TFP? A heterogeneous dynamic panel approach,' NIESR Discussion Papers 219, National Institute of Economic and Social Research.

Osterloh, M. and B.S. Frey (2000) 'Motivation, knowledge transfer and organizational forms', *Organization Science*, 11(5), 538–50.

Osterloh, M. and B.S. Frey (2006) 'Shareholders should welcome knowledge workers as directors', *Journal of Management and Governance*, 10, 325–345.

Osterloh, M. and W.W. Powell (1997) 'The capitalist firm in the twenty-first century: Emerging patterns in western enterprise' in P. DiMaggio (ed. 1997) *The Twenty-First Century Firm* (Princeton (NJ): Princeton University Press).

Oughton, C. (1997) 'Competitiveness policies in the 1990s', *The Economic Journal*, 107, 1486–1503.

Oulton, N. (1995) 'Supply side reform and UK economic growth: What happened to the miracle?', National Institute Economic Review, November.

Oulton, N. (1996) 'Increasing returns and externalities in UK manufacturing: Myth or reality?', *Journal of Industrial Economics*, 99–114.

Oulton, N. and Young, G. (1996) 'How high is the social rate of return to investment?', *Oxford Review of Economic Policy*, 12(2), 48–69.

Oxford Economic Forecasting (2005) *Economic Outlook*, Winter.

Pagano, M. and P. Volpin (2005) 'The political economy of corporate governance', *The American Economic Review*, 95(4), 1005–1030(26).

Pagano, M. and P. Volpin (2008) 'Labor and Finance' Draft paper prepared for the conference on 'Labor, Law, Politics and Finance' organized by the Korea Money and Finance Association (KMFA) 20 June.

Patel, D.P. and K. Pavitt (2000) 'National systems of innovation under strain', in R. Barrell, G. Mason and M. O'Mahony (eds.) *Productivity, Innovation and Economic Performance* (Cambridge: Cambridge University Press) pp. 217–235.

Paul, C.J. and D. Siegel (1999) 'Scale economies and industry agglomeration externalities: A dynamic cost function approach', *American Economic Review*, 89(1), 272–290.

Philpott, J. 'Managing Manufacturing', in R. Lea (ed) *Nations Choose Prosperity*, Civitas, pp. 42–46.

Pichelmann, K. and A.U. Schuh (1997) 'The NAIRU – Concept: A few remarks', OECD Working Paper OCDE/GE(97)89.

Pitelis, C.N. and Teece, D.J. (2010) 'Cross-border market co-creation, dynamic capabilities and the entrepreneurial theory of the multinational enterprise', *Industrial and Corporate Change*, 19(4) (DOI: 10.1093/icc/dtq030)

Porter, M. (1983) 'The technological dimension of competitive strategy,' in R. Rosenbloom, *Research on Technological Innovation, Management and Policy* vol. 1 (Greenwich, Conn: J.A.I. Press).

Porter, M. (1997) 'Changing the way America invests in industry', in D.H. Chew (ed.), *Studies in International Finance and Governance Systems: A Comparison of the U.S., Japan, and Europe* (Oxford: Oxford University Press).

Porter, M. and A.M. Spence (1982) 'The capacity expansion decision in a growing oligopoly: The case of corn wet milling' in J.J. McCall (ed.) *The Economics of Information and Uncertainty* (Chicago: University of Chicago Press) pp. 259–316.

Porter, M.E. and C.H.M. Kettels (2003) DTI economics paper No. 3 'UK Competitiveness moving to the next stage' DTI and ESRC 2003.

Poterba, M. and L.H. Summers (1995) 'A CEO survey of companies' time horizons and hurdle 610 rates', *Sloan Management Review*, 37(1), 43–53.

Pryce, V. (2004) 'Response' to the discussion on Monopolies, competition and efficiency, January p.69.

Pryce, V. and F. Cairncross (2003) 'Foreword' to Porter and Kettels (2003).

Pryor, F.L. (2001) New trends in U.S. industrial concentration? *Review of Industrial Organization*, 18, 301–326.

Rajan, R.G and J. Wulf (2003) 'The Flattening Firm: Evidence on the Changing Nature of Corporate Hierarchies', NBER Working Paper No. 9663.

Rajan, R.G and J. Wulf (2006) 'The flattening firm: Evidence on the changing nature of firm hierarchies from panel data', *The Review of Economics and Statistics*, November, 88(4), 759–773.

Rajan, R.G. and L. Zingales (1998) 'Power in a theory of the firm', *Quarterly Journal of Economics*, May, 387–432.

Rajan, R.G. and L. Zingales (2000) 'The governance of the new enterprise' WP 7958 NBER <http://www.nber.org/papers/w7958> accessed 13 April 2012, in X. Vives (ed. 2000) *Corporate Governance: Theoretical and Empirical Perspectives* (Cambridge: Cambridge University Press) p. 201.

Rajan, R.G. and L. Zingales (2003) 'The great reversals: The politics of financial development in the twentieth century', *Journal of Financial Economics*, 69, 5–50.

Rapachi, D.E. and M.E. Wohar (2007) 'Forecasting the recent behavior of US business fixed investment spending: An analysis of competing models', *Journal of Forecasting*, 26, 33–51.

Rappaport, A. (1992) CFOs and Strategists: Forging a common framework, HBR Reprint #92309–PDF–ENG, pp.1–7.

Reberioux, A. (2007) 'Does shareholder primacy lead to a decline in managerial accountability?', *Cambridge Journal of Economics*, 31, 507–524.

Reich, R. (2008) *Supercapitalism: The Battle for Democracy in an Age of Big Business* (Cambridge: ICON books).

Reich, R. (2010) *Aftershock: The Next Economy and America's Future* (New York: Vintage).

Roberts, J. and E. van den Steen (2000) 'Shareholder interests, human capital investment and corporate governance', Research paper 1631 Graduate School of Business, Stanford University.

Roberts, J., P. Sanderson, R. Barker and J. Hendry (2006) 'In the mirror of the market: The disciplinary effects of company/fund manager meetings', *Accounting, Organizations and Society*, 31, 277–294.

Robson, M., J. Townsend and K. Pavitt (1988) 'Sectoral patterns of production and use of innovations in the UK: 1945–83', *Research Policy*, 17, 1–14.

Rodrik, D. (2011) *The Globalization Paradox: Why Global Markets, States and Democracy can't Coexist* (Oxford: Oxford University Press).

Rogers, B. (2008) 'Complexities of shareholder primacy: A response to Sanford Jacoby', *Comparative Labour Law and Policy Journal*, 30, 95–109.

Romer, D. (2001) 'Comment', in Benanke and Guskaunak (2009).

Rose, Sir John (2007) The Dennis Gabor Lecture 'Why Manufacturing Matters' by Sir John Rose, Imperial College, 15 November 2007.

Rowthorn, R.E. (1977) 'Conflict, Inflation and Money', *Cambridge Journal of Economics*, 1, 215–239.

Rowthorn, R.E. (1995) 'Capital formation and unemployment', *Oxford Review of Economic Policy*, 1, 26–39.

Rowthorn, R.E. (1999a) 'Unemployment, wage bargaining and capital-labour substitution', *Cambridge Journal of Economics*, 23(4), 413–25.

Rowthorn, R.E. (1999b) 'Unemployment, capital-labour substitution and economic growth', International Monetary Fund, WP 99/43.

Rowthorn, R.E. (2000), 'Kalecki Centenary Lecture: The political economy of full employment in modern Britain', *Oxford Bulletin of Economics and Statistics*, 62 (2), 139–173.

Rowthorn, R. (2009) 'Manufacturing and the balance of payments', in R. Lea (ed.) *Nations Choose Prosperity: Why Britain Needs an Industrial Policy*, CIVITAS.

Rowthorn, R.E. and R. Ramaswamy (1997), 'Deindustrialisation: Causes and Implications', IMF Working Paper WP/97/42.

Sargent, J.R. (1995). 'Roads to full employment', *National Institute Economics and Social Review*, February, 74–89.

Sbordone, A.M. (1997) 'Interpreting the procyclical productivity effect of manufacturing sectors: External effects or labour hoarding', *Journal of Money Credit and Banking*, 29, 26–45.

Schettkat, R. (2003) 'Are institutional rigidities at the root of European unemployment?', *Cambridge Journal of Economics* 27, 771–787.

Schmidt, M. (2003) 'Savings and investment in Australia', *Applied Economics*, 35(1), 99–107.

Schularick, M. (2006) 'A tale of two 'globalizations: Capital flows from rich to poor in two eras of global finance', *International Journal of Finance and Economics*, 11, 339–354.

Smithers, A. and S. Wright (2000) *Valuing Wall Street: Protecting Wealth in Turbulent Markets* (New York: McGraw Hill).

Stein, J. (2003) 'Agency, information and corporate governance', in G.M. Constantinides, M. Harris and R. Stulz, *Handbook of the Economics of Finance* (Amsterdam: Elsevier) pp. 113–126.

Stiglitz, J. (1974) 'Risk Sharing and Incentives in Sharecropping', *Review of Economic Studies*, 41, 219–256.

Stiglitz, J. (1994) *Whither Socialism?* (Cambridge (MA): MIT Press).

Stiroh, K.J. (2000) 'Investment and productivity growth: A survey from neoclassical and new growth perspectives' Industry Canada Research Publications Programme Occasional Paper No. 24.

Stockhammer, E. (2005/2006) 'Shareholder value-orientation and the investment-profit puzzle', *Journal of Post Keynesian Economics* 28, 2, 193–216.

Stockhammer, E. (2008) 'Is the Nairu theory a Monetarist, New Keynesian, Post Keynesian or a Marxist theory?,' *Metroeconomica*, 59(3), 479–510.

Stockhammer, E. (2010) 'Financialisation and the Global Economy', WP#240 Political Economy Research Institute.

Stockhammer, E. and E. Klar (2011) 'Capital accumulation, labour market institutions and unemployment in the medium run', *Cambridge Journal of Economics*, 35(2), 437–457.

Stout, D.K. (1979) 'Deindustrialisation and industrial policy', in F. Blackaby (ed.) *De-industrialisation* (London: NIESR), 171–195.

Stout, L. and M. Blair (2001) 'Trust, trustworthiness, and the behavioural foundations of corporate law', 149 *University of Pennsylvania Law Review*, 1735–1810.

Stout, L. (2005) 'New thinking on "shareholder primacy"', <http://cdn.law.ucla.edu/SiteCollectionDocuments/ucla-sloan%20foundation%20conference/new%20thinking%20on%20shareholder%20primacy.pdf> accessed 13 April 2012.

Stulz, R. (1999) 'What's wrong with modern capital budgeting?', Address delivered at the Eastern Finance Association meeting in Miami Beach, April 1999.

Sumner, M.H. (1999) 'Long run effects of investment incentives' in C. Driver and P. Temple (eds.) *Investment Growth and Employment: Perspectives for Policy* (London: Routledge) pp. 292–300.

Swann, G.M.P. (1998) 'Quality and competitiveness', in T. Buxton, P. Chapman and P. Temple (eds.) *Britain's Economic Performance*, 2nd edition (London: Routledge).

Swann, G.M.P, P. Temple and M. Shurmer (1996) 'Standards and trade performance: The UK experience', *Economic Journal*, 106.

Taylor, M.Z. (2004) 'Empirical evidence against varieties of capitalism's theory of technological innovation', *International Organization*, 58, 601–631.

Taylor, R. (2003) 'Skills and Innovation in Modern Workplaces' available at: <http://www.leeds.ac.uk/esrcfutureofwork> accessed 13 April 2012.

Temple, P. and G. Urga (1997) 'The competitiveness of UK manufacturing: Evidence from imports', *Oxford Economic Papers*, 49(2), 207–227.

Temple, P., G. Urga and C. Driver (2001) 'The influence of uncertainty on investment in the UK: A macro or micro phenomenon?', *Scottish Journal of Political Economy, Scottish Economic Society*, 48(4), 361–82.

Thirlwall, A.P. (1979) 'The balance of payments constraint as an explanation of international growth rate differences', *Banca Nazionale del Lavoro Quarterly Review*, 34(139), 45–53.

Thompson, S. and M. Wright (1995) 'Corporate governance: The role of restructuring transactions', *The Economic Journal*, 105(430), 690–703.

Tirole, J. (2001) 'Corporate governance', *Econometrica*, 69(1), 1–35.

Tirole, J. (2006) *The Theory of Corporate Finance* (Princeton (NJ): Princeton University Press).

Tobin, J. (1997) 'Supply constraints on employment and output', Cowles Foundation Discussion Paper 1150 New Haven, Connecticut.

Tomorrow's Company (2011) 'Tomorrow's Stewardship: Why stewardship matters', London.

Toynbee, P. and D. Walker (2011) *The Verdict: Did Labour Change Britain?* (London: Granta Publications).

Tucker, P. Executive director of the Monetary Policy Committee of the Bank of England at the Leeds Financial Services Initiative – 'Credit Conditions and Monetary Policy' 28 August 2003: <http://www.bankofengland.co.uk/publications/speeches/2003/speech201.pdf> accessed 13 April 2012.

Tylecote, A. (2007) 'The role of finance and corporate governance in national systems of innovation', *Organization Studies*, 28(10), 1461–1481.

Tylecote, A. and P. Ramirez (2006) 'Corporate governance: The UK compared with the US and "insider" economies', *Research Policy*, 35(1), 160–180.

Tylecote, A., P. Ramirez, J. Solomon and A. Solomon (2002) 'UK corporate governance and innovation' Paper submitted to European Commission (DG XII) under the Fourth Framework Programme.

Tylecote, A. and F. Visintin (2008) *Corporate Governance, Finance and the Technological Advantage of Nations* (Abingdon: Routledge).

Usher, K. (2011) 'Labour's record on the economy' in P. Diamond and M. Kenny (eds.) *Reassessing New Labour: Market, State and Society under Blair and Brown* Special issue of Political Quarterly (Oxford: Wiley-Blackwell) pp. S108–122.

Van Ark, B., M. O'Mahony and M.P. Timmer (2008) 'The productivity gap between Europe and the United States', *The Journal of Economic Perspectives*, 22(1), 25–44.

Vickrey, W. (1993) 'Today's tasks for economists', *American Economic Review*, 83(1), 1–11.

Wadhwani, S. (2001) 'The new economy: Myths and realities', *Bank of England Quarterly Bulletin*, Summer, 233–247.

Wall, H.J. and G. Zoega (2002) 'The British Beveridge curve: A tale of ten regions', *Oxford Bulletin of Economics and Statistics*, 64, 3.

Wardlow, A. (1994) 'Investment appraisal criteria and the impact of low inflation', *Bank of England Quarterly Bulletin*, August 250–254.

Webster, D. (2000) 'The geographical concentration of labour-market disadvantage', *Oxford Review of Economic Policy*, 16:1, 114–128.

Wen, S. and J. Zhao (2011) 'Exploring the rationale of enlightened shareholder value in the realm of UK company law – the path dependence perspective', *International Trade and Business Law Review*, (14), 153–178

Westaway, P. (1997) 'What determines the natural rate of unemployment and what does not?', European University Institute, RSC 97/43.

Wilkinson, F. (2000) 'Inflation and employment: Is there a third way?', *Cambridge Journal of Economics*, 24, 643–670.

Williamson, O.E. (2002) 'The theory of the firm as governance structure: From choice to contract', *Journal of Economic Perspectives*, 16(3), 171–195.

Wolfe, E. (1991) 'Capital formation and productivity convergence over the long term', *American Economic Review*, 81(3), 565–7.

Wood, A.J.B. (1994) *North-South Trade, Employment, and Inequality* (Oxford: Oxford University Press).

Wren, C. (2001) 'The Industrial Policy of Competitiveness: A review of recent developments in the UK', *Regional Studies*, 35 (9), 847–60.

Wright, M., S. Thompson and K. Robbie (1992) 'Venture capital and management-led leveraged buy-outs: A European perspective', *Journal of Business Venturing*, 7, 47–71.

Wulf, J. (2002) MIT Sloan management review summer, 'the flattening corporation' interview with Caroline Ellis p.5.

Yokoyama, H. (2007) 'Business Diversification Strategies in U.S. and Japanese Electric Utilities' USJP Occasional Paper 07–16.

Yong, G. (2002) 'Lessons learnt from the National Enterprise Board: The do's and don'ts of equity investments', Imperial College MBA Thesis.

Zingales, L. (2000a) 'In search of new foundations', *The Journal of Finance*, 55(4), 1623–1653.

Zingales, L. (2000b) 'Corporate Governance and the Theory of the Firm', villa Borsig Workshop Series 2000 – the institutional foundations of a market economy revised version of 'Corporate Governance', in *New Palgrave Dictionary of Economics and the Law* (Basingstoke: Macmillan 1998), 497–503, <http://www.inwent.org/ef-texte/instn/zingales.htm> accessed 13 April 2012.

Index

Lightning Source UK Ltd.
Milton Keynes UK
UKOW07f0646281114

242329UK00006B/72/P